# Settlement Archaeology in a Fjordland Archipelago

Network Analysis, Social Practice and the Built
Environment of Western Vancouver Island,
British Columbia, Canada since 2,000 BP

## Quentin Mackie

BAR International Series 926
2001

Published in 2019 by
BAR Publishing, Oxford

BAR International Series 926

*Settlement Archaeology in a Fjordland Archipelago*

© Quentin Mackie and the Publisher 2001

ISBN  9781841711713  paperback
ISBN  9781407352725  e-book

DOI  https://doi.org/10.30861/9781841711713

A catalogue record for this book is available from the British Library

This book is available at www.barpublishing.com


BAR Publishing is the trading name of British Archaeological Reports (Oxford) Ltd.
British Archaeological Reports was first incorporated in 1974 to publish the BAR
Series, International and British. In 1992 Hadrian Books Ltd became part of the BAR
group. This volume was originally published by John and Erica Hedges in conjunction
with British Archaeological Reports (Oxford) Ltd / Hadrian Books Ltd, the Series
principal publisher, in 2001. This present volume is published by BAR Publishing,
2019.

# BAR
PUBLISHING

BAR titles are available from:

BAR Publishing
122 Banbury Rd, Oxford, OX2 7BP, UK
EMAIL    info@barpublishing.com
PHONE  +44 (0)1865 310431
FAX    +44 (0)1865 316916
www.barpublishing.com

# ABSTRACT

Investigation of the archaeological record of people who live by hunting, gathering and fishing has frequently been concerned with the origins of social complexity. Yet, "social complexity" is not a straightforward variable, and the category "complex hunter-gatherer" may create more problems than it solves. Rejection of the category does not, however, eliminate nor account for real variation in the social organisation and archaeological signatures of hunter-gatherers. Archaeological analyses of hunter-gatherer economies have frequently considered time-budgeting constraints associated with the production, storage, and redistribution of surpluses to be central. However, examination of these time constraints show that they are not necessarily a constraint upon the development of social complexity, but are an expression of the relationship between individual humans and their environment. Spatial and temporal constraints are manifested through the individual's body, and are expressed through technology, settlement pattern, and mobility practice. Some spatial approaches in archaeology, such as locational analysis, have focused on the individual monad but few have done so in a manner that adequately expresses the possibilities and constraints of the individual and individual agency. Instead, most analyses have cast the individual as either a simple optimising "Homo economicus" making rational decisions within a neutral environment, or as subject to a highly normative culture, or both. It is argued in this thesis that re-conceptualising the individual as living within a "habitus" may be conducive to understanding some aspects of the archaeological record. In particular, conceiving of the individual -- environment relationship as one of non-Cartesian mutualism leads to an appreciation of the paired importance of the mobile individual in a built environment. From this perspective, a case study from Vancouver Island on the Northwest Coast of North America is introduced. The $p$-median model in a Location-Allocation analysis is applied to a network formed by transportation linkages between 238 habitation zones, created by clustering 576 archaeological sites. It is shown that centrality of place within a network matters, as the more central places are also larger sites, but this pattern only occurs at a spatial scale difficult to reconcile with deliberate optimising behaviour. It is therefore concluded that this descriptive spatial geometry is irreconcilable with any plausible underlying generative social geometry based on either normative cultural rules or deliberate optimisation. Recognition that the built environment is an interrupted process rather than a planned, finished product, allows one to avoid imposing the "fallacy of the rule:" in this case ascribing to the inhabitants of the study area a totalised decision-set for site location and intensity of use based on the location-allocation solution sets. Instead, it is argued that the observed spatial patterning in the case study is better seen as the archaeological signature of long-term, wide-scale, practical activity of individuals within a landscape of habit. The result is the discovery of an important threshold in the spatial scale of the culturally-perceived environment. Discussion follows of the implications of this thesis for the interpretation of social complexity, for the predictive modelling of site location, for the establishment of relevant spatial units of analysis, and for such familiar spatial ecological variables as "population density," on the Northwest Coast and elsewhere.

# TABLE OF CONTENTS

CHAPTER 5. MOBILITY, BUILDING, AND SOCIAL PRACTICE ON THE NORTHWEST COAST

CHAPTER 6. INTRODUCTION TO THE CASE STUDY

CHAPTER 7. RESULTS AND DISCUSSION

CHAPTER 8. CONCLUSIONS

# LIST OF FIGURES

# LIST OF TABLES

# ACKNOWLEDGMENTS

This volume is a somewhat revised version of my 1998 Ph.D. thesis from the University of Southampton, U.K. I arrived in Southampton with a research topic on the "typology of fishtraps." I shall remain grateful to my supervisor, Clive Gamble, for allowing me to escape that net and swim freely into a much bigger pond. Clive gave generously of his time, insight, encouragement and patience throughout this project. Near the beginning of this project someone said to me on learning that Clive was my supervisor that, "I didn't know how lucky I was." I know now. I am also grateful to Stephen Shennan for timely insight, and to James Steele for many stimulating discussions. Dave Wheatley gave considerable help with GIS and with UNIX computing and also, through his own research, showed the way into how GIS can be used outside of the narrow frame of site management. Tim Sly also provided help with the computing side of this thesis. Yvonne Marshall gave me regular Northwest Coast reality checks, and was a friendly inspiration through some of the dog days. Mary Stubbington was a constant help with the logistics of being an overseas student. Help from the Archaeology Branch of the Province of British Columbia was essential: I thank Pradeep Singh, Heather Moon, Jack Foster and Alexander Mackie. Steve Lipscomb of Timberline Resources (and kindergarten) helped with some Arc/Info scripts and know-how. Rosaline Canessa, aided by Amy Dean, prepared the final copies of many of the maps in this thesis. Margot Wilson-Moore and George Mackie helped proof-read the final drafts. Ben Alberti and Yoelle Carter Martinez kindly helped me submit this thesis long-distance from Canada. Cynthia Lake was indispensable in helping prepare this version for publication, and Gordon Frazer gave me use of some of his publishing software.

I am fortunate to have made so many good friends while in England, and I thank them for their warm welcome and intellectual stimulation: Katharina Hall (and Jack!), Cressida Fforde, Siân Jones, Ben Alberti, Steve Dorney, Rose Lindsey, Gil Marshall, Rob Hosfield, James Steele, Yvonne Marshall, Andrew Crosby, Stephanie Moser, Tony Firth, Dave O'Regan, Claire Jowitt, Francis Wenban-Smith, Stephanie Moser, Vanessa Balloqui, Ingereth Macfarlane, Maggie Ronayne, Pippa Smith, Dale Serjeantson and the denizens of FRU. Jane Hubert and Peter Ucko provided red wine, carrots, sticks and crutches in equal measure. The members of the department at the University of Southampton created a friendly and welcoming intellectual environment: in addition to those named above I thank Tim Champion, Sara Champion, Nick Bradford, Julian Thomas, Simon Keay and Brian Sparkes for their many small acts of kindness. The *chicos* and *chicas* in Argentina helped me keep my head screwed on, in particular, Gustavo Martinez, Gustavo Politis, Dolores Elkin and Maria Gutierrez. In Victoria, Jennifer Hopkinson, Lisa McGuinness, Pamela Smith, Susan Crockford, Becky Wigen, Heather Moon, Sandra Peacock, Alastair Murray, Steve Lipscomb, and the crew of the Flattery all helped me through the writing up. The support of my family was, as ever, essential. Friendship combined with childminding was given by Beth McMillin, Kjerstin Mackie, Gillian Mackie and Angela Murphy. I also thank Anne Hellman, Claudia von Kreuzig-Grinnell, Tracy Zollinger Turner and Melinda Montbriand.

Both the Social Science and Humanities Research Council of Canada and the Association of Commonwealth Universities (U.K. Division) provided generous financial support. The British Council administered the Commonwealth Scholarship very efficiently, and also funded my stimulating research trip to Argentina during which I developed many of the ideas found in this thesis.

This volume is dedicated to Charlotte Elizabeth Mackie.

# CHAPTER 1—INTRODUCTION

## 1.1 Introduction

The archaeology of the Northwest Coast of North America has been described as "fundamentally atheoretical" (Maschner and Fagan 1991:921). Typical studies focus on subsistence and ecology, drawing on highly detailed portraits of one or several key sites, using uncritical applications of the direct historic approach (Maschner and Fagan 1991; Fladmark 1982:101).

Such attention to detail places Northwest Coast archaeology firmly within the holistic, historical particularism of Boasian anthropology. Franz Boas, whose ethnography dominates the region, was German by birth and by training in geography and physics (Stocking 1966). Both Stocking (1966:871) and Gruber (1986:176) have noted that Boas' concept of culture was rooted in a European tradition. Gruber characterises this as,

> a product of an earlier, persistent, and essentially German theme borne of German Romanticism in which a human group, the Volk, possessed a historical unity and particularity expressed in the total range of everyday behaviour. (Gruber 1986:176)

Interpreting prehistoric "cultures" in this manner necessitates a holistic approach which can only be realised archaeologically through massive and direct use of ethnographic analogy. Ethnohistoric and ethno-archaeological studies, largely performed by archaeologists, have built on the strengths of the minutely-detailed Boasian corpus with the aim of ever-improved application of the direct-historical approach. Such a research programme has probably seemed feasible because most excavations have been in shell middens which, being characterised by good preservation of faunal remains and perishable artifacts, offer alluring detail on this total range of everyday behaviour. Prehistory on the Northwest Coast thus frequently consists of a simple stacking of ecological snapshots. Yet, for the First Nations, the anthropological archaeologist's search for internally consistent, holistic, cultural behaviour has required a "remembered past transformed into an ethnographic present (Gruber 1986:177)." Only rarely (e.g., Ames 1991b; Marshall 1993) are the processes of continuity and change given equal prominence.

In its dual allegiances to ecological reconstruction and the ethnographic record, the prevailing approach to the regional archaeological record has been exceptionally data-driven. The challenge on the Northwest Coast is to escape simplistic analogies from the constructed ethnographic present without falling into either timeless, ecological generalisations lacking historical context or into historical generalisations that amount to little more than teleologies. I suggest the time is now right to heed Ingold's call to move beyond the division between "the 'scientific' study of an atemporalized nature, and the 'humanistic' study of a dematerialized history," which will only be accomplished by a subtle understanding of the "temporality" of the landscape (Ingold 1993:172).

## 1.2 Social complexity and fjordland archaeology

Indigenous societies of the Northwest Coast have long stood as the ethnographic archetype of the "complex hunter-gatherer." These societies have been used as exceptions to prove the rules about "simple" hunter-gatherer societies, and/or have been de-historicised into an exemplary stage on the continuum of "complexity," further "advancement" along which they did not reach because they never developed agriculture. Thus, archaeological interest in these supposed cases of arrested development has centred on when and how they, amongst the world's stratified, sedentary societies, managed to achieve the "most with the least." This research orientation ignored the underlying evolutionary assumptions and operational problems behind the variable "complexity," and its unholy partner, "the complex hunter-gatherer." While the constituents of "complexity" are important and of real archaeological interest, it is unhelpful to bundle them together in an omnibus variable without a better grasp of their complex mutual relationships. To gain such an understanding a different approach is needed, one which centralises the temporal and spatial dimensions underlying many of the constituents of the complexity "black-box."

Fjordland archipelagos, such as those of coastal British Columbia, are highly directional environments in which many important resources, such as salmon are both spatially and temporally circumscribed. This geographic aspect has knowable implications when considered together with the inherent constraints and opportunities of human materiality and the technological and available social means of circumventing such constraints. Technological "solutions" include transportation, mass harvesting, and storage technologies, while social "solutions" may include aspects of community size, social stratification, and the division of labour. However, it is important not to separate these solutions from each other, nor either from the environment itself. Storage, for example, is closely bound to mobility, property, ownership, sharing, and so forth. Transportation can alter the perception (and thus possibilities) of the environment, while the use of watercraft reverses the inherent directionality of fjordland archipelagos. By changing the paths people take through the environment, it changes their very perception of that environment (Gibson 1979). Indeed, following Ingold (1986, 1992, 1993), it will be suggested that Gibsonian ecological psychology may provide insight into important general constructs such as "nature," "the environment,"

1

"the archaeology of place," "empty spaces," "territoriality," and "social networks." Nevertheless, as will be shown, ecological psychology alone is not particularly useful in archaeology. In this thesis, it will be made useful by being allied to both social theory and to quantitative spatial-analytic tools.

Taken altogether, this allows a humanistic human ecology, of which the main four elements are:

- An understanding of the environment rooted in Gibsonian ecological psychology which stresses the mutualism between observer and environment,
- an emphasis on places and routes rather than sites and the spaces between them,
- an action-oriented social theory rooted in time and space, such as that of Pierre Bourdieu,
- a suitable method of quantitative analysis which allows the determination of real spatial patterns without predetermining their explanations.

### 1.3 Hunter-gatherers and the built environment

Most archaeological studies of mobility start with a known set of sites and infer the likely routes that would have been followed in order to fulfil subsistence needs. These routes are determined by material culture and other remains from archaeological sites. If, however, the routes are known (as I argue they are in fjordland archipelagos), then the starting point can be quite different. Attempts to understand these routes can precede discussion of the archaeological evidence, which can then be introduced later to assess any conclusions gained from studying the routes.

The above suggests that the spatial dimension in archaeology can be conceptualised in relation to the mobility profile of people. Indeed, movement creates a sense of spatiality, which does not occur in an empty, three-dimensional Cartesian space. Such a focus on movement also implies the adoption of a social time frame (Gosden 1994). Without wanting to reduce time to space, or vice versa, the two dimensions are surely linked in everyday life, as exemplified by the Swedish school of time geography (e.g., Carlstein 1982). Chronological and linear conceptions of time are considered to have little bearing on everyday life, particularly in non-industrial societies. Social time is equivalent to a time of "practice" (Bourdieu 1977), and is relevant for the interpretation of archaeological material. In particular, a social-time perspective replaces the inevitability of the "future in the past" with a better understanding of the many possible futures, the "temporal maps" (Chapter 4; and Gell 1992), that were possible at any given time in the past. The constitutive acts of being in the world are "practical tasks," which cumulatively define a "taskscape," the measure of which is social time (Ingold 1993:158).

The environment is simply defined as the surroundings of animate beings (Gibson 1979). It is neither a Nature of neutral objects, nor a container that can be filled with meaning. Rather, it exists only in relation to observers, and is filled with affordances for those observers. These affordances are situational, according to the needs of the observer. A key point about animate observers is that they are mobile, and their perception and knowledge of, and relationship with the environment is experienced through movement. Some vectors of movement are more favoured (for social or environmental reasons), and so individuals' routes become bundles of collective mobility, which afford interaction, and help delimit public knowledge. These routes both structure, and are structured by, the built environment.

### 1.4 Modelling the built environment

A broad definition of "building" is used in this thesis. A building is, "any durable structure in the landscape whose form arises and is sustained within the current of human activity" (Ingold 1993:169). The archaeological record is therefore a record of the built environment, though not necessarily a complete one, given the vagaries of preservation, site formation processes, etc. In Chapter 5, it is suggested that shell midden sites on the Northwest Coast despite whatever specific functions they may have served, are a durable record of general activity. Individually they meet Ingold's definition of a building and collectively they can be considered as part of a built environment. The size of the shell midden has been used as an indicator of intensity of use (Maschner and Stein 1995), and is so used here. Other archaeological site types, such as rock art, fishtraps, burials, etc., do not necessarily record *general* activity, and while they are part of the built environment, they are not easily comparable to the sorts of general activity mapped by shell middens.

Taking the known distribution of shell middens as a starting point, the almost 600 such sites within the study area are clustered into some 238 "Midden Zones," conceived of as nodes or concentrations of general activity in the environment. The study area and clustering procedure are discussed in Chapter 6. Having a set of locations ("buildings") and knowing the likely transportation routes between them (Chapter 3), it is possible to perform network analysis to understand their spatial inter-relationships. In particular, interdependent centrality is calculated using the *p*-median Location-allocation model, and such centrality is found to correspond (at some scales) to intensity of site use.

### 1.5 Avoiding the "fallacy of the rule" in archaeological explanations

Having modelled aspects of the built environment of the Northwest Coast, with its implication for mobility and for long term habitual action, it becomes important not to make the easy mistake of confusing a descriptive geometry of space with a generative grammar of intentional social behaviour. It is argued that the patterns of optimal behaviour which are demonstrated in this study are the result of *unintentional* optimisation across a broad-scale landscape of habit. This sort of behaviour might be termed "unintentional harmonic action," the proximal means of which is analogised to stigmergenic communication. Such patterns are best explained as the result of non-teleological action performed in a *habitus* (Bourdieu 1977) rather than as expressions of calculated optimal foraging or centralised planning. It is concluded

that the archaeological signature of mobility and general activity can include patterns which might be interpreted as indicating social complexity, but which are merely emergent scalar properties of the individual:environment relationship.

## 1.6 Summary

Any thesis records work that takes place over time and reflects changing ideas. Challenging the unitary variable "social complexity" led to a reconsideration of time and space and the way that these are differently constructed by archaeologists than by the people who produced the archaeological patterns which are being studied. The advantages of a more subtle, humanistic conception of time and space were clear, yet needed to be weighed against more formal models which define real spatial patterns. In this thesis, mobility, the built environment, and *habitus* are used to bridge the gap between austere, formal (but replicable) models of space and subtle, humanistic (but difficult to apply) social theories of time and space.

## CHAPTER 2—COMPLEXITY IN HUNTER-GATHERER SOCIETY

### 2.1 Introduction

Archaeologists and anthropologists have used the term "complexity" to summarise a variety of different socio-cultural traits and processes, yet there is widespread disagreement over both its definition and application. Some favour a formal definition of complexity in the abstract, as an element or derivative of social theory (e.g., Bender 1989, Brumfiel 1989, Marquardt 1985). Others prefer to compile trait lists of ideological, social or material variables that cumulatively indicate, or correlate with, an otherwise vague notion of complexity (e.g., Arnold 1993, Cohen 1985, Hayden 1992, Price and Brown 1985, Rowley-Conwy 1983). Wason reviews a number of these sources in a lengthy commentary on the inferential nature of archaeological approaches to social complexity, concluding that the use of multiple lines of evidence "especially those that at first seem incompatible" is the best way to proceed (Wason 1994:35). Nevertheless, others argue against the very use of complexity as a unitary variable, preferring, for diverse reasons, to either dismantle it into more useful abstract components and/or to abandon it altogether (e.g., Binford 1990, Gamble 1993, McGuire 1983, Rowlands 1989).

Both of these general approaches have weaknesses. Abstract definitions developed from ethnography (via ethnology or social theory) must be related to material culture or visible patterning of other remains before they can be applied archaeologically. Conversely, trait list definitions are static, and so require direct and defensible relation to a cultural process or dynamic. Indeed, they probably derive originally from some such processes, introducing the possibility of circularity of argument. Efforts to unpack "complexity" risk merely shifting the problem of definition to a different level or scale, while arguments for abandonment of the term must offer a viable replacement or replacements as there surely are real-enough social phenomena which the omnibus construct of "complexity" inadequately addresses.

Apart from utility, definition, and application, there are at least three other, general problems in the use of complexity as a unitary variable. The first is its close association with outdated schemes of unilineal evolution: band-tribe-chiefdom-state can too easily be interpreted as a quartile, ordinal typology of progressive complexity (Claessan 1981). The second problem is the close positive association that is often made between complexity and social inequality. "Egalitarianism" is defined by default as "lack of complexity," with the consequence that social equality is naturalised and not seen to need explanation in its own right (Flanagan 1989). The third is the contrast between "complexity" and the general disciplinary movement away from categorical thinking towards explanations which focus on multi-causal or contextual social process. In such accounts, complexity is redefined while being made obsolete as a unitary variable (e.g., Upham 1990a, 1990b, or, more critically, Rowlands 1989).

Further questions about the inherent utility of the concept are raised when it is coupled to the economic category "hunter and gatherer." By default this creates a dichotomous variable with the states "simple" and "complex," leaving little room for intermediate positions. The origins or characteristics of this false dichotomy may then become a subject of inquiry in its own right (e.g., Hayden 1994, Keeley 1988).

In this chapter the troublesome nature of the construct "social-cultural complexity" will be critically examined. Attention will focus mainly on whether it is appropriate to use the recently popular analytical category "complex hunter-gatherer"; less attention will be paid to issues of complexity in relation to agriculturists. First, a brief review of hunter-gatherer studies is given.

### 2.2 Complexity and "complex hunter-gatherers"

Anthropological perceptions of hunter-gatherers underwent a fundamental re-evaluation coincident with the publication of the conference proceedings *Man the Hunter* (Lee and DeVore 1968). Within this volume, Marshall Sahlins summarises the foregoing stereotype:

> Our textbooks compete to convey a sense of impending doom, leaving the student to wonder not only how hunters managed to make a living, but whether, after all, this was living? The spectre of starvation stalks the stalker in these pages. His technical incompetence is said to enjoin continuous work just to survive, leaving him without respite from the food quest and without the leisure to "build culture." . . . he is condemned to play the role of bad example, the "subsistence economy." (Sahlins 1968:85)

This Hobbesian view was replaced by one which characterised hunter-gatherers as existing in a state of "Zen affluence," with their limited wants and limited needs being satisfactorily filled (Sahlins 1968). Thus, the notion of an "original affluent society" became anthropological received wisdom, a development that can probably be closely tied to a 1960s political *Zeitgeist* of ecological awareness and alternative lifestyles. Behavioural models and data drawn from ethnographies of mobile hunter-gatherers inhabiting marginal environments, such as the !Kung and Hadza, were then used as analogues in a wide variety of archaeological applications.[1]

Effectively, however, one stereotype of hunter-gatherer behaviour was exchanged for another. Groups such as the !Kung San of the Kalahari have since had their history restored, and are now better understood as marginalised peoples situated within a wider cultural environment or world system. San agricultural pursuits, enslavement by neighbouring groups, and even their conscription into the South African army were passed over by both ethnographers and archaeologists, perhaps because they did not fit the existing fixed ideas.[2] Realisation that the ethnographic material was being oversimplified played a role in puncturing the easily affluent stereotype of hunters and gatherers.

Concurrent with this revisionist ethnological programme has been an increased archaeological interest in various well-known exceptions to the mobile, small group, limited-needs stereotype, namely, relatively sedentary hunter-gatherers, living in large groups, with social inequality and vociferous inter- and intra-group competition. Discussion of "complex hunter-gatherers" was included in the *Man the Hunter* volume, such as those of northwestern North America (Suttles 1968) and the Ainu of northern Japan (Watanabe 1968). However, only in more recent years have they ceased being seen as anomalous cases (e.g., Koyama and Thomas 1981, Price and Brown (eds.) 1985). Archaeological interest has been accompanied by more ethnological attention to "mid-range" (Upham 1987) societies: those which are classically—and uneasily—known as tribes and, especially, as chiefdoms, both of which categories include hunter-gatherer societies (e.g., Drennan and Uribe 1987; Earle 1987b, 1991; Gregg (ed.) 1991). Increased focus on these mid-range societies included interest in the genesis, rather than the generalised evolutionary or historical trajectories, of social-cultural complexity. Material from hunter-gatherer archaeology and ethnography had a role to play in this new field of research, and the result was the creation of the category "complex hunters and gatherers," a term which in the 1960s and 1970s would have bordered on the oxymoronic. The term was formed by the unholy alliance of a long-established economic category, "hunter-gatherer," with an existing social construct, "complexity," which was developed mainly with reference to larger-scale societies

and, ultimately, with reference to states.[3] Before discussing the implications of this new category, various ways of defining complexity will be reviewed.

## 2.3 Defining complexity

There are two related ways of defining complexity: either an abstract social-theoretical definition is formulated, or traits are listed which are asserted (in some combination) to be correlated with (or to cumulatively define) the social category. The former can be seen as a first-order definition, in that it is derived directly from social or anthropological theory. The latter can be seen as a second-order definition, in that the trait list cannot be arbitrary, but must in some way relate to an abstract definition or preconception of what is meant by "complexity." Despite this inter-dependence, at this point they will be discussed separately.

### 2.3.1 Trait list definitions of complexity
Trait lists are a popular way of defining complexity amongst hunter-gatherers. These lists can be both long and redundant. For example, Keeley (1988:373-74) lists ten traits, Price and Brown (1985:5) list eleven,[4] while Cohen (1985:105) compiles twelve. The itemised traits of a complex hunter-gatherer way of life are said to include, relative to simple/generalised hunter gatherers, the following (compiled from the above sources and Hayden 1992):

1. a more complex technology
2. an intensified subsistence economy
3. greater sedentism
4. larger, more internally differentiated settlements
5. some occupational specialisation at individual, familial or settlement level
6. greater territoriality
7. a substantial dependence on stored foods
8. larger and wider amounts of trade
9. the use of some sorts of standard mediums of exchange
10. non-egalitarian allocation of wealth, and hence the existence of ranks, classes or incipient stratifications
11. differences in mortuary practice beyond age-sex grades.

At the opposite extreme, Earle (1987a:64) limits himself to a single, quite narrow, trait: "[craft] specialization is the economic essence of complex society."

The benefit of such lists is their suitability for correlation with the archaeological record as most of the traits (but not

---

[1]. Yoffee (1993) rather sardonically suggests this is because archaeologists wanted to unite with ethnologists in "one big happy family of anthropologists." It would be ironic if the promotion of unilineal evolutionist thought were an institutional by-product of the anti-evolutionist Boas' four sub-disciplinary conception of holistic anthropology.

[2]. See Miracle *et al* (1991) and Headland (1997) for general discussions of revisionist hunter-gatherer studies; for the San case see Kuper (1993), Lee and Guenther (1993) Wilmsen (1989), among many other published discussions.

[3]. For example, Gilman (1991:146) can write "chiefdoms are societies at the threshold of social complexity," implicitly reserving "complexity" for states and states alone. This illustrates a general problem with complexity: defining where and when it starts. As a counter-example, Smith (1993:17) explicitly accepts the "evolutionary scale" and deplores reference to complexity below *chiefdom* level "even to include hunters and gatherers," thus conflating complexity, political organisation and subsistence, despite his call for greater rigour and better problem orientation.

[4]. Writing alone, Brown (1985:201-202) only lists seven such traits.

all, especially burials, storage, and subsistence intensity) have relatively direct and unproblematic material expression. Indeed, it is archaeologists who seem most interested in this sort of definition. For the most part, social anthropologists are more aware of cross-cultural idiosyncrasies and less interested in general processes of cultural evolution. Difficulties in the archaeological use of the trait list approach are numerous.

First, there is the above-noted disagreement about how many traits are needed to define complexity as an anthropological construct. Partly, this is a problem of the splitting and lumping of more generalised social features. For example, in the list given above, Trait 4 (site size and differentiation) and Trait 11 (mortuary differentiation) could be subsumed as natural correlates of Trait 10 (social inequality). Hence, a trait list with many of these redundancies might actually measure an unknown or unacknowledged number of dimensions of social structure. This is well illustrated in Williams' trait list:[5]

> Complex hunter gatherers can be described as those groups who: are sedentary or semi-sedentary; live in sizeable settlements which are often termed 'villages'; construct large, durable structures and manipulate the environment in ways that alter the availability or abundance of resources. Some groups also store food on a large scale. (Williams 1987:310-11)

Apart from the inherent ambiguity in such terms as "semi-sedentary" and "large scale," the first three items on this list redundantly focus on multiple correlates of a single underlying variable: sedentism. In effect, Williams is using "sedentary" as a near-synonym for "complex," which determines her emphasis on mound features as indicators of "a more sedentary occupation of sites (Williams 1987:317)," and hence, greater complexity.

Further, there is also the related problem of how many, and to what extent, traits from a given list must be present in the archaeological record before a valid inference of complexity can be made. Referring back to the composite list cited above, the various traits include both intra-site and inter-site data, and other data only available from special contexts such as burials. Arnold (1993:77), for example, explicitly avoids referring to "specific socio-economic conditions or features such as storage, slavery, craft specialisation, sedentism, number of levels of authority, community size, regional population size, domestication, and the like" when compiling her trait list, which focuses

on hierarchy and the domination of elites. Nevertheless, when used in her case study (Arnold 1992; Arnold 1993:102-107), complexity is tracked by such features as craft specialisation, mortuary practice, and the presence of exotic durables. It would seem to be a matter of investigator preference whether these traits are considered directly indicative of complexity, or whether they are subsumed into higher-order social-analytic categories, as Arnold does. In either case, both the length and composition of the trait list itself will be influenced by the preconceptions about social structure which govern its creation. This is the very reason given by Arnold (1993:77) for abandoning most direct material correlates of complexity, as discussed above. And, indeed, not all trait-list definitions are so seemingly precise, as Renouf illustrates:

> The term complexity is inexact because there is a tendency to use it in different ways. I use the term to mean social heterogeneity, for example task specialisation, and wealth or power differences, or both. I also use the term to refer to economic elaboration, such as organised communal hunts, high input of labour for delayed returns (which usually involves storage), and increased production (sometimes called intensification). (Renouf 1991:101)

Binford (1990) criticises trait-list definitions, arguing that complexity is not in any scientific way a variable, and hence it cannot have a single instrument (i.e., a trait list) for its measurement. Instead, it is a multidimensional variable (cf. Schalk 1981), the perception of which will vary according to the researcher's questions. However, there may well be, according to Binford (1990), reliable ways, mainly through middle range theory, to set up situational measurements of the components of "complexity." In such a procedure, Renouf would presumably have to outline precisely the circumstances under which she would choose between the various options she lists (cf. Zeidler 1987:235). On the other hand, at least Renouf's scheme (intentionally or otherwise) acknowledges the operational imprecision of the construct "complexity."

The second major problem with trait list definitions of complexity is that they may incorporate circular reasoning. If the measure for complexity includes a variable such as population size, it would be circular to use that measure to test for the correlation of population size and complexity (McGuire 1983:96). Yet, if the measure is dropped then a potentially valuable analytic tool is lost (Upham 1990b:90). In essence, the traits determine the presence or absence of complexity, which is a social phenomenon they

---

[5]. This trait list is referenced to Rowley-Conwy (1983:11-12) but there is little correspondence to that work. Rowley-Conwy includes complex technology, increased territoriality and resource ownership, while assigning sedentism a causative role.

cumulatively hope to define.[6] This illustrates the need for a tight connection between the social theory and its practical application through the identification of knowable correlates, and introduces the second way of defining complexity: abstract definitions rooted in social theory.

### 2.3.2 Abstract definitions of complexity

Most abstract definitions of complexity focus on the amount of internal differentiation within a society without actually specifying which social structures are alike or different, or in what way. For example, Brumfiel (1989:127) writes "social complexity is conventionally defined in terms of the number of *unlike* parts in an integrated whole." Similarly, Paynter suggests (1989:369) "the concept of complexity concerns the degree of internal differentiation and the intricacy of relations within a system," while Marquardt contends that:

> *Complexity* usually refers to a condition or quality of being composed of many elaborately interrelated or interconnected parts . . . . Thus complexity includes aspects of *multiplicity* and *integration*. A number of anthropologists also add *differentiation* to the concept. (Marquardt 1985:71) [emphasis in original]

The main problem with abstract definitions of complexity is that in order for them to be *archaeologically* investigated, material correlates will have to be recognised and defined, bringing the process back to a trait list approach. Ideally, a tight connection between the social theory and the derived correlates would produce a more unified and coherent set of traits. Yet, while the trait lists may be somewhat arbitrary but comprehensive, the correlates of the abstract model may be highly selective and biased towards a narrow range of the social theory from which they are derived. Marquardt (1985), for example, after proposing an abstract definition, and after a general discussion of "complexity," selects just three material correlates which he claims are relevant to his western Kentucky case study. A similar point is discussed by Zeidler (1987:326-27) who notes that empirical studies necessarily decompose society into *visible*, functioning traits. Ideal types are then reconstituted from these abstract concepts, themselves mere descriptive resumes of traits abstracted from the whole to which they belong. The issue thus becomes the relational specificity between the correlates and the dynamics of the social system that they address: namely, is there a direct relationship? It is this gap which middle-range theory is supposed to bridge.

---

[6]. The recent review article by Smith (1993) exemplifies the difficulty or unwillingness to make this tight connection. Despite explicitly basing his approach on McGuire (1983), Smith's material correlates of complexity (which structure his review) are nowhere supported except by empirical generalisation, vague assertion, or appeal to peer consensus.

In summary, trait list and abstract definitions of complexity exist together in an uneasy state of mutual interdependence. Without support from social theory, trait lists can be no more than empirical generalisations from cross-cultural or archaeological evidence. Social theories which do not spin off archaeologically identifiable correlates can never be properly evaluated. In both cases, bridging arguments are often little more than empirical generalisations.

## 2.4 Critiquing complexity

Regardless of the manner in which social-cultural complexity is defined, it remains a problematic construct to actually apply. This section examines some specific criticisms that have been made.

Perhaps the most specific criticism is that complexity is generally used as a multidimensional variable, which may lump together aspects of social organisation or social structure best analysed separately. The important paper by Randall McGuire *Breaking Down Cultural Complexity: Inequality and Heterogeneity* (1983) exemplifies this critical viewpoint. As the title suggests, McGuire believes that the "black box" of complexity needs to be decomposed into two constituent parts so that its workings might be identified (1983:92). The problem with complexity, McGuire notes, is that it includes *too much*, such that its usage as a unitary variable measuring evolutionary change—while simultaneously providing a direction for that change—obscures a number of potentially independent variables, most notably heterogeneity and inequality.

McGuire defines heterogeneity and inequality with reference to the multiple social personae which individuals hold, and which cumulatively define the social structure. Overlapping social parameters, such as gender, age, wealth and religion, define the social personae, and a society is "more complex" if it contains a larger number of distinct social personae (McGuire 1983:101). Social structure is thus defined by the relative distribution of the population across social roles. Cultural evolution, according to McGuire (1983:110), is not a simple process of lock-step increases in heterogeneity and inequality. In a similar vein, Paynter (1989) argues that the relationship between complexity and inequality has been badly misrepresented in that a strong positive correlation is often assumed, rather than demonstrated. Accepting this, it follows that studies that have assumed that social hierarchies or ranking are an integral part of social complexity may be mistaken. For example, Nash (1983:vii) introduces the concept with the words, "social complexity, i.e., the specialised or hierarchical arrangements of stratification and ranking." Bender (1989:83) writes that "complexity involves a degree of institutionalised social inequality," while Kelly (1991) uses socio-political inequality as a virtual synonym for complexity.

Two important points arise from McGuire's and Paynter's papers. First, "complexity" is hopelessly linked to a unilineal, typological approach to cultural evolution, as will be discussed in a further section of this chapter. Second, by unpacking "complexity" into its constituent parts, not only are inherent contradictions within the concept exposed, but also archaeological correlates of the disassembled components are more easily identified and investigated.

A more political criticism of complexity is given by Lee (1990:226) who suggests that the very indices used by archaeologists to determine social complexity are in fact indices of social inequality. The invariant linking of inequality to complexity has the effect of naturalising equality within "simple" societies, a category created by the unreasonable dichotomization of hunters and gatherers into two groups: simple and complex. Categorical or definitional thinking is imposed by this division (Gamble 1993). It then becomes all too easy to relate this artificial dichotomy to other variables, especially ecological ones such as climate or continentality (e.g., Keeley 1988). Furthermore, Flanagan (1989) argues that "simple" societies act as a "pre-political" starting point for evolutionary studies, and hence become naturalised by being placed in opposition to "complex" societies. This distinction is misleading and is "tied to an outmoded progressivism which promises much more than it delivers (Flanagan 1989:248)." Kelly elaborates this point when summarising his problems in using complexity:

> Use of the term *complex hunter-gatherers* implies that there is more going on—a greater number of interrelationships between variables—in some societies than in others and that mobile hunter gatherers can be understood in simple terms, different from those of "complex" ones. I disagree with such an implication for a variety of reasons, including, as I point out in the text, the fact that "complex" hunter gatherers probably have fewer intergroup relations than "simple" hunter-gatherers. (Kelly 1991:153)

However, as noted above, Kelly himself employs complexity as a descriptive term roughly synonymous with socio-political inequality. In any case, the point is that maintaining and reproducing so-called simple or egalitarian societies requires as much (or more) effort and regulation as maintaining complex or hierarchical societies (Rayner 1988; Flanagan 1989). Complexity is typically seen as a problem solver, not a problem creator, with the implication that "simple" societies are "problem free" (Paynter 1989:374). Paynter challenges this view by citing a variety of examples which show that (a) "complexity" creates as many problems at it solves, and (b) complexity is not,

contrary to the neo-evolutionary view, associated with stability. That is, complex systems, whether social or ecological, are not inherently more stable than "simple" ones. Paynter thereby deprives the evolutionary framework of both its starting point and its teleological target, and encourages more idiothetic explanations for the historical development of any given archaeological case study.

The most sweeping criticism of complexity is given by Rowlands who sees the presumed progression from simple to complex as an interdisciplinary "meta-narrative of western thought," a master discourse of the ethos of Western modernisation which can be traced back to the Book of Genesis (Rowlands 1989:31,36). More concretely, Flanagan (1989:260-61) suggests that the predominantly progressivist mode of anthropological theorising since the 19th century has had two unintended consequences:

(a) Egalitarian forms of organisation are first idealised, then naturalised, and consequently ignored. It is possible this process can be identified in the recent history of hunter-gatherer studies outlined above: the original affluent society is an idealised construct that quickly became emblematic of a natural (i.e., ecologically harmonious) existence. However, following the revisionist critique, these groups have lost their status as living fossils and thus become increasingly irrelevant to archaeological studies. Meanwhile, anthropologists have switched their focus to the historical processes in the surrounding cultural environment and world system.

(b) The naturalisation of equality was an equality of men, masking inherent internal conflicts within egalitarian societies, and allowing the equation of biological sex with social gender (Flanagan 1989).

This contrast between the ideology and social reality of *equality* has long been noted. For example, the Bolshevik Lenin implied that strict equality could not exist when he described it as the "unworkable condition in which everyone does everything, and nothing gets done (Lenin in Rayner 1988:20)."

## 2.5 Various trajectories towards social "complexity"

Given that there is disagreement even in the definition of social complexity, it is not surprising that there should be disagreement over how it arises and is maintained. Arguments concerning the genesis of social complexity fall into two main categories: those which invoke external factors into a basically systemic model of society, and those which focus mainly on the internal dynamics, conflicts, and contradictions within societies. Brown and Price (1985:439-40) note other oppositional labels, such as: societal:individual, exogenous:endogenous (cf. Arnold 1993), long-term:short-term, and ecological:structural, nevertheless the internal:external difference seems most central and will be followed here.[7]

## 2.5.1 Explanations invoking external causation

The external approach is closely allied with the neo-evolutionary school of thought, and is traceable back to Leslie White (1949), if not further.[8] The evolution of living things can be broadly seen as a sequence of increasing complexity: from single-celled to multi-celled to multi-organed involves increasing the number, the heterogeneity, and the control hierarchy of a system. It is but a small step to impose this onto cultures as well:

> The second law of thermodynamics tells us that the cosmos as a whole is breaking down structurally and running down dynamically . . . But in a tiny corner of the cosmos, namely in living material systems the direction of the cosmic process is reversed: matter becomes more highly organized and energy more concentrated. (White 1949:367)

White's work paved the way for neo-evolutionist studies of complexity, particularly the typologies of band-tribe-chiefdom-state proposed or elaborated by his students, notably Elman Service (1962).[9] This social typology had several disadvantages for the study of cultural evolution. First, by encouraging typological thinking it may have caused researchers to look for sudden jumps or transformations rather than smooth progressions (Price 1981).[10] Second, there are many clear examples, both biological and cultural, where structures become simpler over time, or move through cyclical changes. As Paynter (1989:386) notes "the metaphor of simple to complex is now discredited because it can be empirically disproved in many cases." Nevertheless, in a relatively recent work Gregg (1991:xvii) writes that her edited volume exists within a "construct of social organisation in which the trajectory of development inevitably progresses from simple to complex." Sometimes, the circular argument is joined completely, as in another recent study:

---

[7]. Gould (1985) has labelled these modes of explanation as "adaptationist" and "transformationalist". Brown and Price (1985:439-40) criticise Gould's usage, arguing that the former is macro-evolution, whilst the latter emphasises micro-evolutionary process. In this way, they recast Bender (1985) as a small-group ecologist. I retain the use of "external" and "internal" because it encapsulates the fundamental difference, but I acknowledge that most explanations contain elements of both when actually applied.

[8]. Discussion of evolutionary traditions in anthropology with relevance for the simple:complex debate can be found in Flanagan and Rayner (1988), Claessan (1981), Netting (1990), and Upham (1990).

[9]. Upham (1990b:89) traces the problems of typological thinking in an evolutionary context even further, to Lewis Henry Morgan.

[10]. Arnold (1993) suggests the punctuated-equilibrium model of evolution may help explain certain instances of rapid change in some archaeological sequences. In fact, this is only a difference in the shape of the progressive slope, as it still does not allow for any "backsliding."

> As used here, the term "complex" refers to chiefdom-like in organization, with an emphasis on features associated with the simple chiefdom. (Arnold 1993:77)

In other words, Arnold uses the term "chiefdom" (an interval on a scale of relative social complexity) to define that which it measures. A similar problem with this kind of typological thinking is what Shennan (1993:54) calls the "fallacy of affirming the consequent:" types (tribes and chiefdoms in his example) are preconceived and have archaeological data funnelled into them without autonomous lines of reasoning. For example, in a recent canonical work on Northwest Coast archaeology, complexity is "achieved" when the "developed" Northwest Coast ethnographic pattern becomes archaeologically visible ca. 2,500 years ago (Matson and Coupland 1995:199)

Furthermore, typological thinking may distort the very evolutionary reasoning from which it arises. Paynter (1989:376-80) disputes whether bounded social entities — the situational manifestations of the ideal evolutionary types—are feasible units of interpretation for archaeological study. Their use arose primarily as a reaction to the excesses of diffusionism, yet bounded social entities are the units which, in some sense, compete against each other in an evolutionary model (Paynter 1989). A problem is that use of bounded, integrated social units of analysis discourages considerations of regional social systems, mating, alliance and information networks, analysis of core:periphery relations, not to mention the agency or fitness of individuals. All of these are of potential importance in evolutionary explanations and, indeed, in other explanatory frameworks. More consideration of defining bounded units of analysis will be given in Chapters 4 and 5, while problems in analytical scale are discussed in Chapter 5 and 6. The benefits of abandoning bounded social units can be found in the discussion of the case study: Chapter 7.

## 2.5.2 Explanations invoking internal causation

These sorts of explanation fall into two general types: classic Marxist explanations are based solely on the relations of production and other Marxist or materialist constructs; while hybrid explanations allow for some degree of external influence.

Marxist or historical-materialist explanations are defined as those in which the contradictions and conflicts between people bearing different relations to the means of production are granted precedence (Perusek 1994). Class-based explanations may seem to have little relevance to hunting and gathering societies in which production or extraction may be based on household or kinship lines. Attempts to discuss classical Marxist concepts usually are forced onto a small enough scale that more vitalistic forces take over. Arnold (1993, cf. Hayden 1994), for example, has attempted to synthesise various explanations for "complexity" into a discussion of emerging elite control over labour under certain demographic and environmental conditions. This interest in the *emergence* of complexity is clearly tied to the notion of most hunters and gatherers as the zero point on the complexity scale, as discussed above, and results in Arnold relying on relatively vitalistic assertions about human nature. This is probably a common problem to most classic Marxist approaches to small-scale societies, approaches that were, after all, proposed in the context of state capitalism. Thus, these explanations refer to non class-based conflict between interest groups or ascribed categories.

In these explanations it is usually asserted that superstructural change is operating independently of, or precedes, the historical development of the forces of production. Arnold (1992, 1993), as noted, moves from a synthetic analysis of the relations of production to one that incorporates human intentionality. Maschner (1991:931) is more direct, invoking the "hierarchic strivings" of the "higher primates" to explain emergent complexity amongst the Tlingit. Similarly, Coupland (1988) ascribes emergent complexity amongst the Tsimshian to individuals' attempts to consolidate their chiefly leadership.

A focus on individual action is both the strength and weakness of these arguments. The processes, which can loosely be labelled under headings such as domination and resistance, or factionalisation, and which can also include those which emphasise gender and age relations, lie outside sanctioned socio-political structures. They can be, and are, found at societies of all scales,[11] and so are not fatally tied to notions of progressive unilineal complexity. For example, factional activity in chiefdoms can sow the seeds of repeated organisational collapse (Yoffee 1993:63), which is not compatible with unilineal progressive evolution. Assertions about the role of factionalisation can be quite ambitious:

> The often-cited factors of population growth/urbanism, hereditary leader-ship/stratification and ecological symbiosis/trade emerge as conse-quences of factionalisation (Fox 1994:205).

On the other hand, such statements may fall into easy assertions of vitalism or naïve voluntarism (Bender 1990:257). In an early exploration of this theme of dynamic egalitarian societies, Wolf summarises:

> In contrast to others, therefore, who tend to see societies built up in the kin-ordered mode as egalitarian, I argue instead that they are replete with real inequalities and plagued by resulting tensions. They attempt to cope with conflicts by atomising them, by generalising and displacing them onto the supernatural, or by break-up and fission. Unlike societies built up on the tributary or capitalist mode, they lack the ability to aggregate and marshal social labour apart from particularate relationships, and therefore they also lack the means of holding society together, internally or externally, by internal and external violence that ensures the continuity of class domination and contradiction. (Wolf 1981:55)

Wolf sees inequality as a by-product of the mode of production. In the kin-ordered mode, inequality stems from factionalisation (including gender and age interest) and individual intentionality. The mechanisms for this can be subtle, and require subtle understanding of (often too rigid) anthropological constructs such as ethnicity and kinship. For example, Fox (1994:200-01) discusses the deliberate factional manipulation of malleable ethnicities and mythological identities in the context of the post-Classic Maya. It seems clear that any attempt to develop these lines of argument about interest-group conflict and structured inequalities into useful archaeological applications will have to abandon over-reliance on borrowed ethnological typologies or constructs, and that this abandonment leads directly to a more historicising mode of explanation.

## 2.6 Conclusions: salvaging complexity?

Complexity is a problematic construct not only because it is poorly and variously defined, but because of its close association with unilineal evolutionist typologies. When used in conjunction with the economic category "hunter-gatherer," a two-state ordinal typology of simple and complex hunter-gatherers has resulted. This is a spurious categorisation that has been invoked to explain prehistoric social change, and, worse, has occasionally become an object of investigation in its own right. A variety of solutions to the widely recognised problems with using complexity as a social variable have been suggested, ranging from abstract redefinitions of its constituent dimensions, to suggestions that it be abandoned altogether.

Complexity may be meaningless, or at least undefinable, when used as a unitary measurement for a generalised progression or social evolution. However, it is arguably worthwhile to "unpack" complexity into its constituent

---

[11]. A cogent example is Rayner's (1988) discussion of the ironies of factionalisation in the Trotskyist International Marxist Group.

components, which might singly or in combination be worthy of further study. For example, three sub-components of some importance are mobility/sedentism, the production of surplus, and the processing/storage of the surplus. However, when arguments are made using these traits, different causal sequences have been invoked. For example, Bender (1990:253) states that "sedentism permits storage and facilitates the ironing out of seasonal and annual fluctuations in supplies" while conversely, Testart (1982:524) claims that "the accumulation of stocks urges people to adopt a settled way of life." Croes and Hackenberger (1988:27) suggest "intensified resource use and increased storage permitted higher human carrying capacities and increased the sedentism of social groupings," contradicting Keeley (1988:404) who claims that storage dependence is a consequence rather than a cause of population pressure.

Whether in a case study or a generalising mode of explanation, there will evidently be a need to choose between these contradictory, and cumulatively circular, arguments. The components of "complexity," such as storage, sedentism, stratification, and so forth, are surely real enough and widespread. For further archaeological investigation to be productive they must be removed from the limits of categorical thinking imposed by constraining them as sub-components of "complexity." The following chapter commences the creation of a method to unpack the "portmanteau complexity" (Upham 1990a) and hence rehabilitate discussion of the varied social processes contained therein.

## CHAPTER 3—SPATIAL AND TEMPORAL ASPECTS OF LIVING IN FJORDLAND ARCHIPELAGOS

### 3.1 Introduction

The previous chapter concluded that the category "complex hunter-gatherer" would remain at best meaningless and at worst misleading unless there was greater understanding of how its diverse "contents" relate to one another. This chapter starts that process of "unpacking complexity" by examining the spatial and temporal dimensions of some of its core constituents. In particular, it was previously suggested that the triad of surplus, storage and sedentism was central to many discussions of complexity amongst hunter-gatherers and might be an entry point to the debate. Generalising statements about the inter-relationships of these may depend on the researchers theoretical stance (e.g., Bender 1990; Keeley 1988; Testart 1982), in which the relations between surplus-related or relative mobility factors are fitted into preconceived ideologies or existing models, with one or another blessed as the "prime mover." This means that one could adopt a new *a priori* prime mover, make a contribution to the debate, and hope that at some point a consensus will emerge. But such an approach may easily result in circular arguments, if not within any given contribution, certainly when different researchers' lines of reasoning are overlapped. At issue is not that different investigators reach different conclusions, which is to be expected, but that their conclusions are often mutually exclusive, contradictory, or cumulatively circular. The linkages of these circular arguments must be identified and, if possible, cut. At the least, some commonalties are needed which can be used to create a "language" to facilitate discussion of the problem. While this approach implies a lowest common denominator and hence may not be terribly profound, it does depart from the irrational fractionation of previous studies.

One appropriate common denominator is the temporal and spatial structure of the physical and cultural environment. This approach is useful because the "social complexity bundle" contains many features that can be expressed or analysed with the common language of time and space. Storage, for example can parsimoniously be defined as "behaviour or technology which acts to introduce an artificial time delay between production and consumption." Transportation technology can be defined as "technology which aids or increases interaction between two points in space." Untended mass-capture facilities can be defined as "technology which stores labour time and releases it as needed." All these technologies are thus solutions to time-budgeting problems set by the natural or cultural world. It is hoped that this approach will at least bring a subtler understanding of these constraints and provide a coherent way to discuss any closely related technological and social conditions. Later sections discuss more philosophical aspects of time and space, while the following chapter is largely devoted to the theme of humanistic environments, paths, and places, according to the theories of the ecological psychologist James Gibson. However, conventional notions of "time" and "space" are used in the following sections, which discuss a certain kind of environment, the fjordland archipelago, and aspects of the subsistence of two groups of people who inhabit them: the Tlingit of South East Alaska and the Yamana of Tierra del Fuego.

### 3.2 "Time stress" and the environment

Robin Torrence (1983) introduces the concept of "time stress" as a key factor in describing an environment and analysing the behaviour of the people who lived in it. Yesner (1994:153) notes that stress results when there is a "time lag between the onset of the [environmental] stressor and the ameliorative [cultural] response." It might be preferable to discuss the temporal unevenness of the environment as consisting of constraints[12] and opportunities, some of which may have an effect on social organisation or subsistence through the proximate cause of "time stress." Thus, I will speak of environmental constraint and social stress, in effect separating "aetiology" from "symptom." The kind and quantity of behaviour influenced by environmental constraint is said by Torrence (1983:11-14) to have direct correlates in the material culture and hence is reflected in the archaeological record. Torrence's analysis of time budgeting has the character of a "general theory" which can be demonstrated with reference to ethnographically-described material culture, but she suggests (1983:21) that to be applicable to the archaeological record there is a need for bridging arguments. Of particular interest to archaeologists are spatial and temporal constraints, discussed below. Further below, the more prosaic constraints of the human body in the material world are discussed in relation to the field of Time Geography.

#### 3.2.1 Spatial constraint
Spatial constraints include both the physical nature/shape of the landform and the distribution of resources across that landform, as discussed below.

*The Landform as a "Push Factor."*
The key component of the landform is what I will term "directionality." Some landforms, such as plains, may have very low inherent directionality since, all else being equal, access to any set of points of equal distance from a starting point is similar. On the other hand, a mountainous region may favour movement along valley floors, resulting in an in-built directionality with unavoidable repercussions for mobility. I use the term "inherent" directionality because transportation technology can alter this aspect of the

---

[12]. Constraints can also be opportunities, of course. For example, temporal or spatial circumscription may, depending on one's perspective, either require or allow mass harvesting of certain resources.

environment. For example, coastal Tierra del Fuego, British Columbia and Norway are flooded mountain ranges. In the presence of watercraft, this heightens the directionality because the contrast between the marine and terrestrial aspects means that some mobility vectors are highly favoured. In the absence of watercraft, the former valley floors (the fjords) become the barriers, and the former terrestrial barriers (the slopes) become the only possible routes for mobility. Hence, the inherent directional relation between an unflooded mountain range and a flooded one is roughly inverse (provided the land and water are roughly mirror images). The *actual* directionality is a function of the transport technology. Another example is transportation corridors across deserts, in which a planar environment, punctuated by water holes, is given direction by the drinking needs of camels, or for that matter, the refuelling needs of automobiles. However, this differs from the marine case in that the directionality is not necessarily inverted: the camel and road routes may also be the appropriate foot routes. The difference probably lies in whether the technology can afford support in new parts of the media[13] (Gibson 1979, and see Chapter 4): watercraft and aircraft give otherwise unavailable access through air and water, which previously did not support mobility.

It may be useful to conceive of low direction environments as approaching an even plane, while highly directional environments (e.g., major river corridors) approach complete linearity. In this sense, increasing linearity is a reduction in the number of possible or attractive movement vectors, rather than a "straightening" of existing vectors.

*Resources as "Pull Factors."*
The second main component of environmental constraint is the inherent spatial distribution of resources across the landform, expressed as relative homogeneity and heterogeneity. Resources are here defined simply as things people both know about and want. "Patches" of resources can be separated by "empty space"[14] or by other sorts of patches, and they can be of any size and shape. It is these resource nodes which attract people to certain places. If the directionality of the environment is incongruent with respect to these nodes, then a transportation or scheduling solution is required.

The inherent nature of the landform can directly influence the distribution of resources. A good example of a planar but punctuated landform is certain areas of the Canadian Shield, where a basically planar environment is riddled with small lakes. Assuming travel is by foot only, any point can be reached with approximately equal cost, but there are "holes" (lakes) in the physical fabric that could only be filled in with technology such as watercraft.

Another such example is the Aegean-type archipelago, where, given boats, any destinations of similar distances can be reached with similar costs (i.e., large distances between small islands means it is largely irrelevant which side of the island you travel to), but some destinations are coastlines and others are open water. An example of a linear, punctuated environment is the Aleutian archipelago, in which a 1,600 kilometre linearity is broken into short (about 15 kilometre) segments. In other words, to describe the physical environment is to partially describe the distribution of terrestrial resources.

But unequal spatial distribution of resources reflects many other environmental features and is somewhat independent of the gross landform. As a basic concept in cultural ecology it is not necessary to discuss biological distributions and their underlying causes in detail; it is enough to note that for whatever reason, the living inhabitants of the earth are not evenly distributed over its surface. Of interest in the study of coastlines is the distribution of marine resources, frequently hidden, which must pose special problems in both perception (see Chapter 4, Section 4.3) and in creating a "mental map" (e.g., Gell 1985).

### 3.2.2 Temporal constraint
Overlaying the patchiness of the environment on the directionality of the landform is a good start towards developing a realistic picture of the push and pull factors which may influence foraging behaviour. But a second overlay[15] is needed. The change over time (whether cyclical or not) in the resources, and to a lesser extent, the change in the physical environment must also be considered. In other words, the temporal patchiness of the environment means people not only want to be in a certain place to get resources, they want to be there at a certain time. Good timing depends on knowledge of temporal variation in both the physical and biological worlds, which together transcend simple seasonality. Both kinds of variation can best be seen at four scales, which work together to create a complex, but not wholly unpredictable, pattern of variation.

- Hourly variation in light, temperature, and tides is fundamental to the structure of the day, and to human activity. It is so fundamental that it cannot be ignored, even at the risk of appearing banal.
- Daily variations include the phases of the moon (and their influence on tides and nocturnal activities), day to day weather, the intersection of daylight and tides, and the related behaviour of plants and animals.
- Annual variations include the seasonality of weather and solar cycles, and obvious related changes in plants

---

[13]. Gibson (1979:16-19) defines media as substances through which detached objects can move with relatively little resistance, such as air or water.
[14]. Discussion of the fallacy of empty spaces within an environment is found in Chapter 4.

[15]. Use of the term "overlay" has been criticised by Ingold (1993:171-72), since it implies a neutral environment or nature that is overlain with human meaning, insulating human ecology from the existence of the people who actually dwell in those environments. Its use in this Chapter echoes its technical use in GIS (Chapter 6).

and animals, such as reproduction, mortality, migration, hibernation, and so forth.

- Inter-annual variation includes changes in the degree and proportion of all the above physical and biological components, which arrive in a different mixture each year. Sometimes this change is predictable, as in some game or fish cycles, but often it is not. This category also includes singular events such as tsunamis and landslides.

These variations partially set constraint problems resulting in such time stresses as the desire to do two things at once, and the desire to be in two places at once. It is apparent that "time budgeting" includes a spatial component. Indeed, as Gell (1992:198) notes, any division of labour — whether one's personal labour budgeting or more co-operative efforts — are in the most basic sense geometric problems requiring proximate geometric (not to mention ultimate social) solutions (cf. Gosden 1994:184).

### 3.2.3 Additional environmental constraints

This framework for analysing the spatial and temporal nature of the physical and biological environment does not stand alone; it must not be forgotten that the cultural environment is also important. Minimally, this can be taken as a caution that the principle of least effort and "optimality seeking" may not be useful (or at least must be demonstrated), because purely cultural pushing (aggressive neighbours) and pulling (trade for exotica) will act to further warp and wrinkle the temporal-spatial landscape.[16]

In summary, environmental constraint occurs along spatial and temporal dimensions as they are perceived and mitigated by cultural behaviour. The degree of time stress experienced bears no inherent relation to the productivity of the resources. It is merely a way of describing where and when resources are available and how people might arrange their behaviour to be able to exploit these resources to their perceived advantage.

### 3.3 Time Budgeting Behaviour and Technology.

Having defined this lumpiness in time and space, it is necessary to look at the ways in which people might act to smooth out the wrinkles or fill in the holes. As Torrence puts it:

> Given the basic assumption that time budgeting is crucial to hunter-gatherer behaviour, the technology used by these groups can be expected to vary according to both the severity and the character of time stress. (Torrence 1983:12)

In the first case, the shorter time available to perform a task will favour more efficient technology to increase the speed at which the task is done. In the second case, there might be plenty of time overall, but different activities will be competing for this time and so tasks will be juggled. One method of juggling time is scheduling, another is embedding.

Embedding has become a commonplace concept in archaeology since Binford (1978) suggested "embedded procurement" was used as a means of alleviating subsistence and procurement scheduling difficulties amongst the Nunamiut. However, as a more general time budgeting solution it has not been widely or explicitly analysed. For example, such activities as childcare and tool manufacture are frequently embedded in other tasks. Embedding can be seen as an indicator of time-budgeting "opportunity costs," i.e., the reciprocal of time-budgeting: how to budget what cannot be done, delayed or embedded. The following discussion, however, centres on material culture rather than the behavioural organisation of time management.

### 3.4 A comparison of some time budgeting behaviour and technology between the Tlingit and the Yamana

The following sections outline some of the ways in which ethnographic material help thinking about the archaeology of archipelagos. Comparative ethnographic material describing the Tlingit and the Yamana, who traditionally inhabited fjordland archipelagos, is introduced.

### 3.4.1 Environmental and ethnographic profiles of the Yamana and the Tlingit

Tlingit and Yamana traditional territories stand out because of gross similarity in the underlying landforms, latitudes, precipitation regimes, and marine orientation, while the ethnographies show differences in many areas of social organisation. Notably, the Tlingit stand as an archetype of a "complex" hunter-gatherer group, with the Yamana as their "simple" counterpart (discussion of these terms found in Chapter 2). This enables discussion of their environments which precludes a simplistic conclusion of environmental determinism for the differences in ethnographic profile.

*Physical Geographic Profile.*
Both territories encompass fjordland archipelagos, characterised by a myriad of large and small, mainly mountainous islands separated by narrow channels of water up to 300 fathoms deep. The mainland coasts are volcanic and mountainous with similar degrees of relief, and extensive glaciers that occasionally reach the water. Both territories include stretches of straight, non-involuted coastline, some exposed to the open ocean, but more typified by a mixture of broken coastline with both exposed outer coast and relatively sheltered "inside" coast and

---

[16]. In Chapter 4 it will be argued that the environment necessarily includes these cultural factors, and, indeed, the concept of a neutral nature as a backdrop to human behaviour is itself a cultural construction that bears little relation to how people perceive and dwell in the environment.

waterways. Winter (June/January) mean temperatures are 2 degrees in Yamana territory and 5 degrees in Tlingit territory. Summer means are about 12 and 15 degrees respectively, while precipitation is over 2,000 mm annually in both areas, with over 200 days of rain or snow a year. Yamana territory lies between south latitudes 54 and 56, while Tlingit territory lies between north latitudes 55 and 60. Both include frontage on some of the roughest ocean water in the world. While Tierra del Fuego is cooled by Antarctic winds, the Alaskan coast is subject to periodic cold fronts which escape their continental confines. The overall climate and degree of "continentality" is reasonably similar.

Within the set of coastal environments, tightly packed archipelagos have some special features. The most obvious is the increase in linear coastline that is gained for a given area. For example, Tlingit territory can be encompassed within a polygon measuring 800 by 200 km. A perfectly straight coastline longitudinally bisecting this box would be 800 km long. However, the actual length of coastline within Tlingit territory is about 3,800 km. This gives an "involution index" (actual coastline divided by expected) of 4.75:1. Yamana territory would fit within a polygon 375 km by 125 km. The actual length of coastline is about 2,000 km (Jackson and Popper [1980:41] estimate 970 kilometres but I use a higher figure to maintain comparability with my Tlingit estimate; these estimates are also subject to scalar measurement problems), giving an index of 5.33:1. It is possible in this way to compare the involution of different archipelagos.[17]

This emphasis on the coastal zone has implications for indices such as population density. For example, a measure of "persons per coastal kilometre" is more realistic for predominantly marine adaptations than "persons per square kilometre." The figures obtained using contact population estimates are: Yamana—1.5 per coastal kilometre (ckm) (3,000 people, 2,000 ckm), and Tlingit—2.63/ckm (10,000 people, 3,800 ckm). These figures, while preliminary, are more similar to one another than might be expected based on the very different levels of "complexity." They are certainly more similar than the population densities usually cited indicate: about 0.1-0.26 per km² for the Yamana and 2.6 per km² for the Tlingit (given in Keeley 1988). This raises an interesting question. Was (prehistoric) Yamana subsistence really less intensive than that of the Tlingit, or only apparently so because that subsistence was differently organised? This sort of analysis leads directly to scheduling issues and complements the archaeological data from Tierra del Fuego, which seem to point in a similar

direction, to a proto-historic decline in apparent "complexity" amongst the Yamana (Yesner 1990).

*Ethnographic Profile.*

There is no room at this point for a detailed recapitulation of Tlingit and Yamana social organisation. It is sufficient to remind the reader that the Tlingit were sedentary for at least four months of the year, lived in large, permanent houses organised into villages of several hundred individuals, kept large numbers of slaves, had a hereditary, ranked aristocracy, were organised into well-defined nested kin groups culminating in exogamous moieties, and had developed notions of private property, extending to ownership of resources and monopolisation of ceremonial knowledge. Their political organisation is usually referred to as being at "chiefdom" level, which is a very nebulous term. Authority was actually quite decentralised, and mainly kin-specific. Among their neighbours were peer "complex" groups (e.g., the Haida and the Tsimshian), as well as "Tlingitised" Inuit groups (e.g., the Eyak) and "simple" boreal-forest hunters and gatherers (e.g., the Tahltan). Tlingit subsistence was largely centred on fish, shellfish, and marine mammals, with a relatively minor plant, land mammal, and bird component (after de Laguna 1990, Oberg 1973, Krause 1956). The archaeology of the Tlingit area shows at least 9,000 years of continuous occupation, with a heavy maritime focus during at least the most recent 5,000 years (Davis 1990).

The Yamana, on the other hand, were relatively mobile throughout the year, rarely aggregating, lived in expedient shelters, were roughly "egalitarian," had little notion of private property, and were at the tapering extremity of a continent with similarly adapted hunter-gatherers for at least several hundred miles northwards. Their subsistence was based on marine mammals, shellfish, and birds, with minor contribution from fish and plant species. They are stereotyped as a typical "band-level" society from the "uttermost ends of the earth (Gamble 1992)."[18] Yesner (1990) gives a concise assessment of the Fuegian ethnographic record, arguing that historical changes leading to the "ethnographic present" produced a highly misleading picture of Yamana culture, which had developed over a 7,000 year span into a sophisticated sea mammal hunting adaptation.

*History Since European Contact.*

The best estimates of Tlingit population indicate a decline from prehistoric levels of about 10,000, to 4,500 in 1890, rebounding to about 14,000 in 1986 (de Laguna 1990:205, Boyd 1990:136). This depopulation took place in seven distinct episodes over the first 100 years (Boyd 1990:147). All writers on the Yamana refer to massive depopulation,

---

[17]. Or, more speculatively the more packed an area is with islands, the more multi-directional it becomes, ultimately approaching a form of "planarity," and the less problematic it becomes to exchange information and maintain social ties across the full extent of the social network. Thus, a coastal archipelago might act as a bridgehead for fully marine-oriented maritime cultures, as they may avoid the costs of linearity outlined by Wobst (1976).

---

[18]. The Tlingit are actually more geographically marginal relative to Europe, if one considers both that they aren't on the way to anywhere in particular, and were contacted several centuries later; but then "uttermost-ness" is a state of the Western mental map.

from perhaps 3,000 individuals to several hundred. Cooper (1946:83) suggests that the population declined by 80%, to 400 individuals, in the period 1881-1886 alone, mainly due to measles and respiratory diseases, coincident with increasing contact with Europeans and routine or permanent settlement in large groups around missions. The Yamana became extinct in the mid-twentieth century (Jackson and Popper 1980:41).

Quite apart from the horrifying consequences for individual and social morale, in ecological terms these depopulations acted to reduce population to well below "carrying capacity," assuming the pre-contact population approached this density. This alone could help account for the apparent low-intensity subsistence of the ethnographic Yamana and their peripheral place in the colonial economic system. Another possible contributing factor is that they may have been practising a mobility strategy that deliberately avoided Europeans, a form of resistance to domination that has been suggested for the neighbouring Selk'nam (Ona) by Borrero (1994:256-259).[19] On the other hand, the recent history of the Tlingit suggests a few key differences. Whereas the Yamana had little to offer colonists and explorers and their physical presence impeded the spread of European exploitation, the Tlingit had much to offer and their participation in the historic exploitation of the resources of the Northwest Coast was indispensable. The Tlingit were important players in both the maritime and terrestrial fur trades, which dominate the early historical economy of the Northwest Coast. Traders could depend on this pool of local labour to gather the furs (which are dispersed inconveniently across the landscape), to sell them relatively cheaply and to act as middlemen and organise transportation to the continental interior. Thus, there was little need to haul labour across the Pacific or around the Horn, and the ensuing financial advantages were tremendous. In contrast, the main commercial resources of Tierra del Fuego were whaling and sheep raising, neither of which was easy to integrate into the existing indigenous economic structure. Additionally, the resources of the Northwest Coast were "highly liquid" in the sense that there was a ready market for furs, fish and lumber. Hence, cash payments for goods stimulated both white and native interest in exploitation without the need for much investment in "infrastructure." The net result may be that historical forces caused intensification and exaggeration (and a shift in focus) of an existing Tlingit economy, while the Yamana experienced an opposite effect.

### 3.4.2 Yamana and Tlingit time budgeting
In this section the material culture and social organisation of the Yamana and Tlingit are examined for clues as to the sorts of time-budgeting problems they may have faced.[20] It follows the work of Robin Torrence, who suggests that there is a close relationship between certain spheres of a material culture and the time pressures of the social units, but will expand beyond the relative complexity of material culture to include storage, mass harvesting and mobility.

*The "Structure" of Procurement Technology.*
Torrence (1983:13) suggests that the time stress of an environment has direct correlates in the composition, diversity and complexity of the subsistence assemblage. Her argument is that there is less room for failure in activities that are temporally circumscribed, and this favours use of efficient, special-purpose, often multi-part tools. For example, time can be invested in manufacturing a complex tool with replaceable parts if the payoff is less time spent on tool maintenance during use, when time is more valuable. But if there is no time stress during use, there is no incentive to budget it in this manner. Torrence demonstrates this by examination of ethnographically described food procurement technologies. Her scheme runs into some trouble because, as she recognises, some procurement technologies are inherently more complicated regardless of the temporal structure of the resource. For example, harpoons must serve the dual function of killing and retrieving whereas spears only have to kill. This says nothing about the time stresses involved in hunting seal versus deer. From reading the ethnography it is clear the Yamana have a relatively low technological diversity (the number of different kinds of tools), and the Tlingit relatively high diversity, but both groups have similar levels of technological complexity, expressed as the number of "techno-units" (Oswalt 1976) per tool.

*Storage.*
Storage is defined simply as cultural behaviour that introduces a delay between procurement and consumption. The motivation for storage need not be to save food for a time when it is unavailable, although this is perhaps the most relevant use. The Tlingit prepare stores for two quite different reasons: winter subsistence/feasting and summer feasting/trade. Both motivations result in a form of time budgeting.

Extensive use of storage technology is a well-known characteristic of the Northwest coast culture area, and the Tlingit are no exception. Foods stored include, in approximate descending order of importance (after Oberg 1973), salmon, fish-oil, herring, other fish, berries and roots, seal oil and other meat. As illustrated by Oberg (1973:76), the storage activities of the Tlingit show a clear

---

[19]. Such a form of resistance (see Chapter2) would be archaeologically visible as a change in the mobility strategy, and in the appropriate prehistoric context might be a useful adjunct to understanding larger scale inter-action and "social complexity." It also relates to Yesner's (1990) comments on the archaeological record of Beagle Channel, noted above.

[20]. Systematic information on time allocation is rarely present in ethnography, perhaps because of Wobst's (1978) general comments on ethnographic limitations. Exceptions include the relatively detailed (yet problematic) information in Oberg (1973), and the often-cited study from Arnhem Land (McCarthy and MacCarthur 1961). Time allocation studies are becoming popular in human evolutionary ecology (e.g., Hames 1992).

bimodal annual distribution.[21] The springtime storage flurry is concentrated on fish, shellfish, fish-oil, seaweeds and plants. The late summer/fall flurry is dominated, of course, by the salmon harvest in September, but also by the storage of berries and meat. During the slack summer months there is mainly direct consumption of fresh food, as a lot of stored foods are consumed in huge chiefly feasts, trade or are given away. Mitchell and Donald (1988), working with Oberg's figures, characterise the Tlingit annual round as five months in which subsistence activities (procurement and storage) occupy more than 65% of the available time, and another five where it occupies less than 15% of the time. "Ceremonialism and leisure" occupy greater than 50% of the time for no less than 7 months of the year. However, the winter months are busy times for tool manufacture and maintenance, which may be embedded within so-called leisure time, or vice versa.

Despite the amounts stored, some hunger (but not actual starvation) during the winter was probably not uncommon, based on records of the very early historic period southwards at Nootka on Vancouver Island (Boyd 1990). The stored food itself could also become unpalatable in the late winter (Oberg 1973:73). Mitchell and Donald (1988:320) cite a shelf-life of six months for dried fish on the Northwest Coast and suggest that this explains the emphasis on the fall salmon runs, rather than the equally large or larger summer runs, which would be spoiled come mid-winter. This is possibly even truer for the Tlingit than for people in areas with a longer salmon spawning season and a drier climate.[22] The fall storage flurry amongst the Tlingit must, therefore, be aimed mainly at laying in winter stocks, with the residual spring stores acting as insurance against a poor fall salmon run.

The Yamana, by contrast, did not engage in much planned storage activity. However, they were certainly aware of some principles of storage, and Gusinde refers many times to certain foods that were stored. It is as difficult to assess the dietary role these played as it is for any other subsistence sector. Gusinde's (1961:336) own remark that "in order to preserve food one would have to go through all kinds of complicated preparations" (due to the inclement weather), is slightly undermined by his own observations and by the similar weather in the Tlingit area. A judicious reading between the lines, where one continually picks up hints of more intense subsistence and settlement behaviours also undermines Gusinde. The main items stored by the Yamana were oil and blubber, and fungi. Oil was stored by the creation of intestinal sausages stuffed with oil, blubber, and entrails (Gusinde 1961:320-321). Gusinde later comments,

> They are always intent on providing themselves whenever possible with their favourite blubber sausages because they do not want to be without blubber for long. Gusinde 1961:325)

The blubber from a beached whale would be cut into slabs, transported back to the family's base camp, and stored in a swamp. Gusinde (1961:337) describes canoe-loads of blubber being stored in this manner, which would keep for months or even a year. If one considers his earlier statement that a Yamana canoe can carry a slain sea-lion, then potentially a lot of blubber is being stored. Fungi are dried but are not said to be of any dietary importance. Honourable mention in the storage category must go to the practice of procuring bark for canoes in the spring and keeping it stored in swamps or water in case of need (Gusinde 1961:115). These stores of bark may in fact be more vital to subsistence than the stores of food, if Gusinde's protestations about the near total non-reliance on stored food are to be believed.

In any case, it seems unlikely that there was a predictable time each year when large amounts of food could be procured and stored. Jackson and Popper (1980:45) diagram the annual fluctuations in resource availability for Yamana territory. In their analysis, almost all resources are evenly available year-round. Exceptions include bird eggs, herring, and some migratory waterfowl. Others are more accessible at certain times of the year because of their habits or local migrations, but are nevertheless available year round. These include the more dietarily important fur seal and elephant seal. However, the critical resources of sea-lion, birds, mussels, molluscs, and fish show little variation. Whales are a more difficult case to assess as their availability is serendipitous in any case and recorded exploitation patterns may reflect commercial whaling practices as well as natural migrations. Yamana storage was opportunistic, and this dovetails with the generally transhumant lifestyle emphasised by Gusinde. Seemingly obvious candidates for storage such as molluscs and herring were not exploited.

*Mass Capture.*
Capture of animals using untended or tended facilities is an important way of budgeting time. In effect, these facilities "work on their own" and free labour for other purposes. Untended facilities solve the geometric problem of being in two places or doing two things at once, increase the spatial and temporal "reach," or alleviate limiting temporal constraints such as nocturnal fish runs. Tended facilities perform the work of corralling animals so they can be systematically and efficiently killed. The following only discusses tended facilities aimed at mass capture.

The Tlingit had several mass harvesting techniques. The fishtrap and weir are foremost amongst these. Of various

---

[21]. These figures are not without difficulty: they seldom add up to 100% for example, nor do they include important activities such as the raiding of stores from other groups.
[22]. See Schalk (1977, 1981) for a broad discussion of the structure of anadramous fish resources.

plans and elaborations, used for both eulachon (an oily smelt processed into a butter-like substance) and salmon, these enabled efficient procurement of fish. These fish then required considerable further investment in time to preserve. No specific data are available for the Tlingit but in a similar situation on the Fraser River in southern British Columbia, it is reported that a single fisher (generally male) at a trap or weir, or with a dipnet, could catch upwards of 200 salmon per night, while a single person (generally female) would only be able to process 30-70 fish per day, in favourable conditions (Hayden 1992:532). In other words, there is a productivity imbalance across the sexual division of labour, which itself introduces time scheduling difficulties. The Tlingit also had devices such as untended longlines for halibut, bird nets, and so forth.

The Yamana seldom made use of mass capture technology, and even then a surplus was only occasionally generated. The most frequent technique was the exploitation of densely schooling fish with simple baskets. Gusinde vividly describes the time stress resulting from operating within these constraints:

> No hands can be idle! In less than an hour the occupants of a canoe, if they keep busy, can fill it so full that they must head for shore. Quickly they take the animals [herring or mackerel] to shore and set out again, for they know that the larger the shoal is, the more quickly it will be pushed out again to the open sea. They cannot draw on it uninterrupted for more than a whole day. After the exertion of such great haste they can feast for days on the varied [includes larger fish and mammals caught chasing the school] booty and meanwhile rest up thoroughly. (Gusinde 1961:271)

It is notable that no mention is made of storage of the product, which must have amounted to several hundred or thousand kilos of fish. However, in general, fish seem to have played a minor or supplementary role in Yamana diet (Gusinde 1961:264). Another mass harvesting techniques is described by Gusinde:

> In exceptional cases the men also build weirs. They decide to do this when there are several families assembled and it is impossible to travel, but a shortage of food threatens. Weirs are used very little, because, I was told, they can be erected only amid all kinds of inconvenience and because they do not promise sure success. (Gusinde 1961:273)

This last comment seems reasonable in view of the lack of anadramous or other fish suitable for sure-fire weir capture, but intertidal fishtraps would doubtless be productive in Tierra del Fuego. Other techniques that could generously be considered as mass harvesting include multi-noosed bird snares and multi-hooked fishlines. The important aspect is that the Yamana understood the principles of mass capture even if they did not practice them.

*Transportation.*
Torrence does not discuss transportation technology, presumably because she limits herself to "procurement technology," which is an arguable exclusion: the role of transportation in alleviating environmental constraints must be critical. Indeed, transportation is so closely bound up in the concept of constraint that it alone determines the difference between the inherent and actual directionality of the environment.

*Canoes.*
The Tlingit had a variety of general and special purpose dugout canoe types. These included river canoes, sealing canoes and transport canoes. Large examples of the latter could hold more than 50 people or carry up to 7 tons of freight. Many were made in Tlingit territory, but the best and largest were obtained in trade, mainly from the Haida, but also from as far south as Vancouver Island. Using dollar values from Krause (1956:119,133), it is possible to calculate that a large canoe costing $150 was equivalent in value to about 30 bear skins (although some other furs were more valuable). Manufacture of a canoe was skilled work, which probably took in the order of two weeks. The product was a highly seaworthy watercraft capable of raiding and trading trips as far away as Victoria, 900 miles to the south (Oberg 1973:71). Rugged when waterborne, they required special care and delicate handling when hauled out as they were very likely to crack if knocked or dried out. A good canoe could last several years to a decade (Oberg 1973).

Traditional Yamana canoes were of a single type. They were made of a wooden frame with bark covering but were, nevertheless, seaworthy since voyages to the remote islands *south* of Cape Horn are recorded (Gusinde 1961:128). Gusinde is on the whole highly complimentary about the canoes (despite their leakiness, which must relate to their flexibility), and notes that one could hold 6-10 people or a large sea-lion (1961:128). The latter, if true, would imply a payload of perhaps 400 kilos, which is respectable even if not in the same class as the Tlingit canoes. Canoes were usually propelled by a single woman and progress was always sluggish even if a man helped paddle. The impression given by Gusinde is of a craft built and handled in a way suitable for the meandering lifestyle that is the Yamana stereotype, but equal to more demanding tasks if necessary. To build a canoe "took an industrious man two to three weeks, if he was undisturbed and could find the parts nearby." With careful use it might last a single year (Gusinde 1961:108-128).

*Portages.*

Portages are of particular interest in an analysis of scheduling activities. They act as short cuts across the inherent directionality of the landform, and should be properly considered as a separate class of transportation technology. Gusinde records three definite and three "hearsay" portages in Yamana territory. Each crossed an isthmus or narrow point of an island "in order to avoid a dangerous or circuitous route (Gusinde 1961:379)." They consisted of corduroy roads over which canoes could be dragged. From comparison with a marine chart, the longest of these portages is about 3 nautical miles (5 km). The maximum travel saving is about 35 nautical miles on the water (about 60 km). They represent a considerable amount of labour investment and organisation, seemingly at odds with the general picture of "simplicity" painted by Gusinde. Krause (1956:51) notes that, for the Tlingit, "many portages shorten distances where there is no direct connection from one inlet to another." Doubtless other information is available for the Tlingit and other groups, as portages are a relatively common feature across the Northwest coast.

*Snowshoes, and miscellaneous transportation aids.*

There is no record of the Yamana making or using snowshoes, despite the frequent presence of snow on the ground. Snowshoes are essential in snowy environments such as boreal forests, but the Yamana probably had little need to enter the interior. The Tlingit used snowshoes a great deal on their interior trading trips, mainly obtaining them from their Athapaskan trading partners. The Tlingit also had a variety of specialised boxes, bags, baskets, backpacks and other aids for the transport of goods. The Yamana seem to have had a relatively modest set of containers, but, as they generally did not carry much food from place to place, this is to be expected.

*Summary.*

These four aspects of material culture (procurement technology, storage, mass capture and transportation) are suggested to be closely linked to time-budgeting behaviour. Others could be examined, notably the degree of mutual embedding or inter-penetration of activities (e.g., embedded procurement of lithic resources; childcare embedded in tool manufacture time, etc.). In summary, however, it appears that both the Yamana and Tlingit were acquainted with the full range of Torrence's material responses to time stress, plus they had appropriate transportation technology. The relative presence or absence of any given feature cannot be explained wholly by technological ignorance, raw material deprivation or environmental possibilism, but must include aspects of choice and need in the context of time and

space.[23] To this point, time and space have been taken as culturally non-specific universals. However, it seems appropriate given their centrality in this research, to introduce some theoretical aspects of these dimensions.

## 3.5 Time geography

Time geography is grounded in an

> analysis of 'choreographing' social activities, given the fact that activities have to be carried out in specific times, by specific actors, in conjunction with specific others. (Gell 1992:191)

This is done in an analytical framework explicitly concerned with the constraints of the material world, and thus is an exploration of the *possible* and its ramifications. Hägerstrand (in Carlstein 1982:49) summarises the basic conditions which govern human spatial and temporal activity as:

1. The indivisibility of the human being (and of other beings and entities),
2. The limited length of each human life (and that of other beings and entities),
3. The limited ability of the human being to take part in more than one activity at a time,
4. The fact that every activity has a duration,
5. The fact that movement consumes time,
6. The limited packing ability of space,
7. The limited outer size of terrestrial space,
8. The fact that every situation is rooted in past situations.[24]

The above "facts of life" can be classed into three categories of constraint: *Capability constraints* are the limits to action imposed by the physicality of the actor (Carlstein 1982:25). They include size, age, sex, sensory reach and lifespan, all referring to a human body which is indivisible. The indivisibility of the human body is important because it forces a continual choice of where to put that body, or "place allocation" (Carlstein 1982:26). A succession of these choices, over their temporal and spatial shifts, inscribe a characteristic path (Carlstein 1982:46), which can be graphed in the familiar time geographic manner (e.g., Carlstein 1982:38-51). Each state of the path constrains the following state, hence continuity implies contiguity. *Coupling constraints* are the limits to action imposed by the need to co-ordinate activities with other people in order to perform tasks that an individual cannot or will not perform alone (Carlstein 1982:25-26). This

---

[23]. And, as Wobst (1990:327) notes, it is only the "environmentally active" parts of material culture that should show correspondence with time stress.

[24]. This last condition is particularly interesting in light of social theory which stresses the importance of historically situated, recursive "practice," such as Bourdieu (1977) and Giddens (1984).

coupling can be in the form of co-presence, serial presence, or communication. *Regulatory* or *steering constraints* (Carlstein 1982:48) or *authority* constraints (Gell 1992:192) are the social limits to action, within what Carlstein (1982:45) calls the control area or domain. They include the volitional, normative and institutional channelling of activities.

These three categories are, of course, interpenetrated, and it is unreasonable to consider them in isolation. As Gell (1992:192) notes, the fact that a bank door is locked on a Sunday is a capability constraint to the action of withdrawing cash, the fact that there are no tellers present is a coupling constraint, while the fact that the bank is closed on Sundays is an authority constraint. It is thus true but not terribly profound to say that one cannot withdraw cash because the bank door is locked. However, from an archaeological viewpoint, capability, and to a lesser extent, coupling constraints may be more knowable, as may technology that directly addresses them.

Time geography assumes close relation between time and space, without explicitly or wholly reducing one to the other. It considers an experiential space only in the sense of the possibilities open to the human body, and is limited to a linear incremental time, as indicated by the z-axis of the path-graphs. Time and space must be related in a world in which people move, since movement takes time. A corollary of the time geographic approach, which treats time and space as resources to be budgeted, is the concept of opportunity costs (Becker 1965, Carlstein 1982:321-27, Gell 1992:206-220). An opportunity cost is the cost of activity foregone. To the extent that activities cannot be embedded in one another, or non-adversely delayed, then there is an implicit cost involved in doing any activity, namely the opportunity cost of doing something else.

A sense of the duration and location of social activity is central to time geography:

> Temporality is *central* to the generation and perpetuation of social forms, not incidental to it, and temporality in turn makes no sense without concepts of spatial presence and absence. (Carlstein 1981:43)

The time geographer's economic approach and the formal limits of their graphing technique incorporates a projection of a Cartesian geometric model of space and linear, measured time, both treated as resources. There is little doubt that it is very valuable to show routes, conflicts and constraints. Yet, people do not live in such a rectilinear world or through such linear time. Time geography fails to consider the social process (e.g., people's projects are tracked by their paths through space-time, but where do these projects originate?) or how there is a mutual, rather than determining, relationship with space (Gosden

1994:80). As will be argued in Chapter 4, it is more realistic to think of people living in a spatial environment that surrounds and exists in mutual reciprocity to the observer, such as the sort of environment envisaged by Gibson (1979) and Ingold (1986, 1992, 1993). Furthermore, as discussed below, it may not be appropriate to think of "time" simply as an even, linear progression or chronology, or as a resource that is budgeted like other resources. Whether time-geography can accommodate a more humanistic vision is uncertain. The next section introduces the study of time and space as culturally created categories.

### 3.6 Time and space as culturally created categories

Human behaviour occurs in time and space, or rather *during* times and *at* places. In other words, it is both historical and located. Archaeologists can study the material correlates of this behaviour in a number of different ways, but all will have both spatial and temporal dimensions. Space and time are natural dimensions but are also culturally constructed. The problem for archaeology is recognising and accounting for the structuring effect(s) of ascribing Western industrial-age spatial and temporal concepts to past societies. Modern time is measured, linear chronological, and clock-oriented, while modern space is measured by Cartesian geometry and scaled map projections. Time and space are now joined, both coupled to global standards.[25] There is every reason to believe, however, that time and space are lived in and experienced in quite different ways to those implied by the clock and the map (e.g., Bloch 1989; Gell 1985, 1992; Gosden 1994), and that these experiential times and spaces contribute to the structure of the archaeological record. The necessarily brief discussion which follows address these issues with rather more emphasis on time than on space, as the latter is also dealt with at length in Chapter 4.

*Space.*
The nature (and very existence) of time and space is one of the oldest themes in western philosophy. Inspired by the philosopher Bhaskar, Gosden (1994) argues for a realist (as opposed to either positivist or constructivist) epistemology of time and space. The essence of realism is the acknowledgement that both

> the world exists independently of us
> and we can only attempt to understand
> the nature of the world's existence.
> However, we never apprehend the
> world as objective observers, as
> positivists claim we can, but as beings

---

[25]. Gosden (1994:2,131-133) notes that an effect of world time was to highlight the differences cross-culturally in temporal perception. One could make a similar argument that creation of a world "prehistoric time" through carbon dating has helped subsume the possibilities of prehistoric experiential time, and at what cost?

involved in the world and in social relations. (Gosden 1994:10).

But these positions of interested, engaged observation are not the sole determinants of knowledge. Rather, "knowledge arises from being, and is an element of our action in the world (Gosden 1994:11)." Part of this action produces material culture, which in itself is productive of further action. Furthermore, material culture is to some extent durable, and so social landscapes, buildings, and portable material culture are rendered "the medium through which habits are inculcated (Gosden 1994:11)." Gosden's (1994:17) contention that material things are not "passive brute objects but are engaged in reflexive relationships with the people who create or use them" is a similar position to the Time Geographers' refusal to see inanimate things as non-social, asserting that there exists an "ecology of technology (Carlstein 1982:8-9)."

Experiential space and time are also partial, in the sense that no single person has complete knowledge of their entire domain. Yet, ethnographies frequently collate the cumulative knowledge of multiple informants, thus burying this fractionation of knowledge. Bourdieu (1977:106) suggests that the adoption of this "analytical privilege of totalisation" precludes the asking of "questions of practice." Kinds of totalised information include descriptions of any broad scale spatial or temporal activity, such as resource maps and the organisation of the annual round. The archaeological record itself, with its temporal and spatial scope, could be considered a totalised phenomenon, but it also contains evidence for single or linked events,[26] as lithic re-fitting studies exemplify.

A very different approach to space is outlined by the cognitive anthropologists Pinxten *et al* (1983:183-85) who create a "Universal Frame of Reference" (UFOR), intended to be a field manual or "Munsell book" for the cross-cultural identification of spatial concepts. Developed in an apparently rigorous and culturally-sensitive manner during fieldwork amongst the Navaho, the UFOR is limited to categorising statements of cultural beliefs about the space in which the Navaho live. It does not draw a corresponding synthesis of spatial perception (just as the Munsell book does not give a universal colour), and so, apart from being a source of some well developed spatial vocabulary, it is of little use archaeologically. It stands in clear contrast to the notion of a human-centred *environmental* "place" outlined by Gibson (1979) and others, the implications of which are discussed in the Chapter 4.

*Time.*

Two recent books by Gell (1992) and Gosden (1994) agree that human time is socially constructed: everyday life is dominated by the times of being, of habit, of practice, regardless of calendrical or chronological superimpositions. Both agree that calendrical devices are often rooted in power structures, and bear analysis on these terms. Nevertheless, the works are quite different.

Gosden (1994 126, 131-138) states there are many levels of time, but distinguishes between three categories: the time of habit, public time, and recursive time. The first corresponds to the time of everyday life, of "personal existence bounded by birth and death," and is intimately connected to the body, to being, and to dwelling in the world (Gosden 1994:137). Public time stems from the time of habit. More specifically, it derives from conscious responses when unconscious habit is confounded by out-of-the-ordinary situations (Gosden 1994:125). It is marked by consciously manipulated symbols, meanings, and narratives, which ultimately, through repetition, may become unconsciously subsumed within habitual times. Recursive time pulls the present into the past and creates anticipations for the future. It is solidly represented in material culture, enduring forms of which provide a "feeling of rightness" to habitual time (Gosden 1994:137-38). Gosden makes no particular claims for the actual way in which people experience these sorts of temporalities because he believes that time is created through action, and is not a medium through which action unfolds (1994:165).

Public time is particularly interesting because it is said to be the result of thoughtful action or analysis when habit meets the unexpected (Gosden 1994:184). Multiple possible worlds can unfold from any given moment. The past is crucial in anticipating the future, not just through experience, but through habit and the persistence of material culture.[27] Anticipation of future contingencies can be mapped (Gell 229-60). Thus, "the present" in the past is crucial to an archaeological consideration of social practice, especially in its contingent relationship with the vagaries and regularities of subsistence. The role of technology is exemplified by storage, in which certain of the possible worlds — starvation or survival — are predicated upon the existence and implementation of a certain kind of technology.

Gell asserts that social time (the so-called A-series time) is underpinned by a universal acceptance of linear progression and sequential logic (B-series time). Thus, his main point of departure with Gosden is asserting both an external and

---

[26]. The visual ecological view of the environment (Chapter 4), with its emphasis on the private (partial) environment of individuals and the construction of public knowledge or consensus through co-perception and interaction, could be considered as a non-totalising analytical framework. Because it is based on putatively universal theories of perception and information pickup, it may provide a route to the archaeological analysis of experiential practice over time and space.

[27]. Following Gell (1992:323), this brings the economic approach of opportunity costs closer to a "theory of practice" because it engages the material world with contingent, unrealised future worlds that are anticipated through the recursive past in the present. It is this anticipation of an unknown future that Bourdieu (1977:8-9) claims is a fallacy of projecting linear time backwards: it makes the dynamic negotiations of social practice appear teleological in retrospect.

an internal B-series, with the A-series as the experiential time in the middle, underpinned and overridden by B-series. In effect, Gell claims (1992:291-92) that experiential time is "mapped onto" an underlying series of B-series representations during interpretation. He gives the example of the Umeda lunar calendar. In this method of time reckoning, the moon is believed to grow like a vegetable, sometimes quickly and sometimes slowly. Empirically this is not true, as the progression of lunar phases proceeds regularly. Yet, Gell claims one does not have to accept that social (A-series) time amongst the Umeda is shaped by this perception. Rather, this belief itself is shaped by the belief that the moon is a large vegetable. Hence, their beliefs are different than our own but are based on a similar underlying logic, namely that of B-series time. His definition of B-series is flexible enough to allow for it to be "modally uncertain and metrically uncalibrated," but it is ultimately logical: causes precede their effects, for example. Hence, he argues there is no reason to believe there is a difference between Western industrial society (B-series emphasis) and the anthropological other (A-series emphasis), despite such well-known case studies such as the ritual calendars of Bali:

> There is no fairyland where people experience time in a way that is markedly unlike the way in which we do ourselves, where there is no past, present, and future, where time stands still, or chases its own tail, or swings back and forth like a pendulum. All these possibilities have been seriously touted in the literature . . . but they are all travesties, engendered in the processes of scholarly reflection. (Gell 1992:315)

This "fairyland" is something of a straw man for Gell. Part of Gell's argument is that all humans experience A-series time as the (logically underpinned) time of everyday practice (Bourdieu 1977; cf. Gosden 1994:114-126). Thus, while it may be argued that the B-series time is similar to a generative grammar of temporality, and accordingly time does not run backwards, Gell would probably agree that the diversity and immediacy of social times is gained through "being in the world," and that it is these *perceptions* of time (which includes "natural" cycles and rhythms) which have import for material culture, site formation, and other matters of archaeological interest. The question therefore devolves to what effect the times and motions of social practice have on the archaeological record and interpretive approaches to it (cf. Shennan 1993).[28] Interestingly, Ingold resolves the A-series: B-series dichotomy by asserting that the latter is merely an aspect of the western

commodification of time. Drawing on ethnographic studies of both hunter-gatherers and British Rail locomotive drivers, Ingold notes that both spend much of their time in pursuit of apparent leisure activities (chatting, napping, playing cards) rather than subsistence pursuits (hunting, driving trains), to the dismay of Capitalist commentators.[29] Ingold's (1995:5) conclusion is that "clock time is as alien to us as it is to the people of pre-industrial societies: the only difference is we have to deal with it." "Free time" (the time of consumption) in western discourse is defined in contrast to "work," (the time of production). Ingold (1995) explicitly casts the contrast as being between a "dwelling perspective" and a "commodity perspective," a point which will be reiterated in the following chapters.

### 3.7 Conclusions: Time and space in the archipelago

The temporal and spatial constraints of the environment contribute to, but do not determine, the "choreography" of daily life. This choreography is the "entire ensemble of tasks,[30] in their mutual interlocking (Ingold 1993:158)," in other words, the "taskscape." It is the totalised ethnographic accounts of the taskscape which have been used to create the dichotomy of "complex" and "simple" hunters and gathers. The discipline of the clock has been falsely embedded as a stage in the discourse of progression from simple to complex. So, if it were possible to inform a time-geographic or other quantitative geographical application with the social-time representation of practice or dwelling, it would become a "scale model" of the taskscape. In its austere abstraction of experiential time and space, the scale model would be to the real taskscape as a musical score is to the performance, as the performance of painting is to the painted picture, and as the act of dwelling is to the landscape itself. Yet, such an approach to time geography perhaps answers Ingold's (1993) call for archaeologists to do what they do best: investigate the temporality of the non-Capitalist landscape, and not just create idealised scores or designs for dwelling. The following chapters start to implement this program, firstly by discussing the role of mobility in the perception of the environment, and subsequently by discussing the nature of the built environment in a Fjordland archipelago. From there, an empirical investigation of mobility within such an environment is outlined and discussed.

---

[28]. Shennan's approach to social practice is via game-theoretic modelling in which time passes as a series of decisions and their consequences and space is abstracted.

[29]. Ingold (1995:24-25) notes that the Anthropologists' Zen-affluent characterisation of the hunter-gather lifestyle coincides with the view of the English gentry that the working classes were indolent, un-foresightful, profligate, kept irregular hours, and were bent on instant gratification and merriment.

[30]. Ingold elsewhere (1995:6) defines a task as "an activity embedded in a social relation."

# CHAPTER 4—ARCHAEOLOGY AND THE ECOLOGICAL APPROACH TO VISUAL PERCEPTION.

## 4.1 Introduction

The previous chapter outlined some ways of looking at time and space in relation to hunter-gatherer life in coastal archipelagos. This chapter introduces the ecological approach to visual perception and discusses some areas in which it may be able to inform archaeological method and theory. In particular, the emphasis placed by the psychologist J.J. Gibson (1979) on routes and paths through the environment, and on the gaps between these routes, is suggested to be relevant to a spatial approach combining network and locational analysis, location-allocation modelling, and geographic information systems. Details of this proposed approach are discussed in subsequent chapters.

## 4.2 An introduction to the ecological approach to visual perception

James Gibson (1979) presents a unified theory of visual perception that has wide implications for other disciplines, including archaeology. It is impossible to condense all aspects of his argument in this section. Rather, that aspect which is of most immediate interest will be discussed: his assertion that real-world visual perception cannot be understood without acknowledging that the eye swivels in the orbit, that the orbit is attached to a swivelling head, and that the head is supported by feet and moves through the environment. Depth is perceived mainly via the occlusion of surfaces and edges as objects and observer move in relation to each other, rather than purely as a result of binocular vision. The whole body, including the orbit and the nose (which form the most basic occluding edge and which unify the environment with the body) is a total visual system. Constant motion of the eye is the rule, and the fixed point of observation, the norm in most laboratory experiments on visual perception during which the head is immobilised, is a rare exception which should properly be conceived of as a pause in locomotion (Gibson 1979:75). Indeed, he notes that people actually see *better* during locomotion:

> Seeing the world at a travelling point of observation, over a long enough time for a sufficiently extended set of paths, begins to be perceiving the world at *all* points of observation, as if one could be everywhere at once. . . . Each object is seen from all sides, and each place is seen as connected to its neighbour. The world is *not* viewed in [single point] perspective. The underlying invariant structure has emerged from the changing

perspective structure . . . (Gibson 1979:197; emphasis in original)

Gibson believes that movement is central to perception, that the "meaning" of things in the environment can be *directly* perceived (the theory of affordances), and so the environment becomes known through direct meaningful input, as a person or a person's eye traverses (and visually samples) paths or routes through that environment. Thus, there is no fixed point of observation, but rather paths of observation, which can be conceived of as unifying movements during which the invariant structure of the environment is revealed through a flowing perspective.

Combining the above with other aspects of his theory, Gibson (1979:219-222) concludes that perception should not be conceived of as "snapshots" that somehow get melded together in the brain, but as a diachronic, continuous process in which the observer is, in effect, in more than one place of observation at any given time. This seeming paradox is resolved if one accepts Gibson's argument that perception itself is in a real sense a timeless phenomenon.[31] A corollary of this argument is that the environment can be (and usually is) perceived from the point of view of another observer:

> The common assertion, then, that 'I can put myself in your position' has meaning in ecological optics and is not a mere figure of speech. To adopt the point of view of another person is not an advanced achievement of conceptual thought. It means, *I can perceive surfaces hidden at my point of view but unhidden at yours.* This means *I can perceive a surface that is behind another.* And if so, *we can both perceive the same world.* (Gibson 1979:200; emphasis in original)

So "public knowledge" (Gibson 1979:200) of the environment is not solely based on communication, but on what might be called *learned,*[32] *shared co-perception*: a new theory of information exchange. It is important because Gibson's definition of the environment is relational to individuals. The environment is defined as the surroundings of those organisms that perceive and behave. The words *animal* and *environment* make an inseparable pair, each term implying the other.[33] The "space" of the

---

[31]. Gibson does not use the terms, but it is clear that perception occurs outside of the A- and B-series temporal categorisation (see Chapter 3).

[32]. In the sense of the ontogeny of perception discussed elsewhere by Gibson (1979).

[33]. Consider Rival's (1996:148) description of hunting with the Huaorani: "One's body takes the smell of the forest and ceases to be extraneous to the forest world. One learns to perceive the environment as other animals do. One becomes a 'dweller' deeply involved in a silent conversation with surrounding plants and animals."

environment must be understood in terms relevant for the animals it surrounds; Gibson (1979:7-44) argues that these are not the terms of physics, mathematics or philosophy, such as planes, points and vectors, but terms which more adequately describe the experiential world, such as surfaces, places and paths. Collectively, the surroundings of an animal are the same as those of all, but in their specifics they are different: resolution of this contradiction lies in consideration of any animal as a unique, but *moving*, point of observation.

Nevertheless, that individuals are the centres of their own private environments and that they figure in the surroundings of other individuals immediately raises the question of social behaviour. Social relations are enveloped within the theory of affordances (Gibson 1979:127-146). An affordance is something (or someone) in the environment *and* the value or meaning of that thing, and so can only be known relative to an observer. While the physical world and its invariant structure is real enough, the experiential environment of value and meaning can only be understood by reference to the animate being that perceives those meanings:

> But, actually, an affordance is neither an objective property nor a subjective property; or it is both if you like. An affordance cuts across the dichotomy of subjective-objective and helps to understand its inadequacy. It is equally a fact of the environment and a fact of behaviour. It is both physical and psychical, yet neither. An affordance points both ways, to the environment and to the observer. (Gibson 1979:129)

People are defined (Gibson 1979:135) as "detached objects with topologically closed surfaces," whose rich and varied affordances for each other cumulatively comprise the total realm of social significance for the humans. Social interaction between people is understood as the irreducible, reciprocal and direct perception of situational, mutual affordance.[34] Such perceptions are inevitably much more complex than those between people and inanimate objects. "Behaviour affords behaviour," and the subject matter of the social sciences is an elaboration of this basic fact (Gibson 1979:135).

If these concepts are accepted, then one may start to grasp what a Gibsonian view of society might entail, apart from the banal realisation that we all live in the same world. All social action is embedded in "behavioural loops:"

> What one animal affords the observer is not only behaviour, but also social interaction . . . An understanding of life with one's fellow creatures depends on an adequate description of what these creatures offer, and then on an analysis of how these offerings are perceived. (Gibson 1979:42)[35]

But Gibson is vague on what constitutes society. This is presumably for two reasons. Most importantly, spoken language is critical to social interaction, but it falls outside the realm of visual perception, although there is presumably an aural analogue to the ambient optical array. It is a debatable point how much symbolic activity can occur that is not mediated or informed by language. This is not to suggest that language is the only form of symbolic behaviour, but it is surely a crucial one. Second, writing and art (which are both visually perceived) are considered as a special class of objects which display "mediated" (rather than direct) knowledge. It is these devices, insofar as they are durable, which permit "the storage of information, and the accumulation of information in storehouses, in short, 'civilization' (Gibson 1979:42)."[36] A glimpse into a Gibsonian view of society is his comment (1979:141) that children start to be socialised when they can perceive affordances for others as well as for themselves.

In placing so much weight on the individual, Gibson is merely following an ecological agenda, as is explicit in the title of his book, and so he cannot be faulted for that alone.[37] Nevertheless, by failing to explicitly discuss the collective nature of societies, group interaction, communication and ritual, corporate interests and so forth, Gibson makes it difficult to apply his theory in a social context. It is a humanistic ecology based on the individual, but one that fails to sufficiently *socialise* either the ecology or the human. Nevertheless it may provide the framework for more humanistic social studies (Reed 1988:123).

For example, the social anthropologist Tim Ingold has taken a Gibsonian approach to hunters, gatherers and

---

[34]. This relates to the discussion of complexity and egalitarianism in Chapter 2. In a hierarchical system these affordances will be reduced for those above and below one, as the stratification reduces the day to day social negotiation. In an egalitarian system, the affordances of one's peers might be so complicated by the rules that keep them equal that an effective upper limit on the size of the social universe would result. This is a novel variation on the usual scalar stress group size limitation arguments, or other such arguments.

[35]. It is interesting to note that Gibson does not seem to make a qualitative distinction between animals and people (cf. Reed 1988). Hence, to the extent that shared co-perception is a kind of communication, people and animals can share a degree of public knowledge and can be said to communicate.

[36]. These devices may also permit cohesive human groups to expand above the magic number thresholds supposedly imposed by information processing or memory management constraints (e.g., Kosse 1990).

[37]. See Smith and Winterhalder (1992:39-41) for a discussion of methodological individualism in relation to the social sciences; also see Bell (1994: 281-311) and Rocha (1996).

pastoralists. He notes, echoing Gibson, that "we need a set of terms to describe the geometry not of abstract, isotropic space, but of the substantial environment in which humans and other animals move, perceive and behave (Ingold 1986a:147)." By defining mobility in terms of routes through the environment (understood in a Gibsonian framework), Ingold reaches a categorisation of three different kinds of tenure:[38] the zero-dimensional tenure of places, the one-dimensional tenure of paths and tracks, and the two-dimensional tenure of the earth or ground surface. The last kind of tenure is said to be characteristic of agricultural groups (cf. Schlee 1992). More interestingly, in his discussion of one-dimensional tenure Ingold stresses that there is no implication of areal control or appropriation. Rather, nature is appropriated vectorally: "the hunter appropriates only those animals whose path he succeeds in crossing (Ingold 1986a:151)." Thus, tenure among hunters and gatherers consists not of surface areas but of "sites and paths within a landscape (Ingold 1986a:153)." Boundary formation or maintenance behaviours may therefore be unnecessary—and, if present, act as "signposts rather than fences" (Ingold 1986a:156)—and a controlled permeability of inter-group ranges is introduced. The implication for archaeology, once again, is the necessary adoption of regional perspectives to which these mobility processes are subordinate, and in particular, the avoidance of unjustified creation or imposition of hard-edged social or spatial boundaries.

In summary, this section has introduced some aspects of Gibsonian ecological psychology and noted an anthropological application of it. The major points are as follows:

(a) People perceive their environment with a total (corporeal) visual system, which constitutes a *continually moving* point of observation.

(b) Understanding mobility is likely to be central to understanding the perception of and relationship with the landscape in a hunter-gatherer society.

(c) Some paths or routes of mobility (and hence of perception) are more common than others. There is a bundling of individual mobility vectors (as discussed in Chapter 3), and therefore "empty spaces" between paths are defined by default.

No conclusions have yet been drawn about the usefulness of a Gibsonian approach in archaeology, although it has been used in archaeological studies of art (Molyneaux 1991), material culture (Graves 1990) and Palaeolithic society (Gamble 1995). The following sections attempt to establish two different points of utility of ecological psychology: creating a more sophisticated understanding of

the environment, and helping inform more traditional forms of archaeological spatial analysis.

## 4.3 Empty spaces or vacant places? Thoughts from the Archipelago.

A general emphasis on paths and routes, nodes and networks, of mobile peoples and their well-trodden (or well-paddled) paths cannot be fully realised without due consideration to those parts of the world which are less well-trodden, or, indeed, untrodden. While the favourable routes on a coastline or coastal archipelago are largely determined by the inherent or actual directionality of the landscape (Chapter 3), that which lies between these paths, i.e. the "empty spaces,"[39] must also be considered. This section is a preliminary discussion of these empty spaces, with particular attention to archaeology in archipelagos, rather than in less directional environments. In particular, the key distinctions of *place* vs. *space* and of the prehistoric *occupation* vs. the resultant *material record* will be discussed, as well as the perennial question of *scale*. Finally the implications for one key ecological measurement, population density, are briefly considered.

### 4.3.1 Empty space and vacant place

If the theories of the ecological psychologist James Gibson are used as a starting point for the discussion of hunter-gatherer behaviour, the term "empty space" must be abandoned. For Gibson, space is an abstract concept and cannot be part of an environment, for an environment only exists reciprocally to an observer (Gibson 1979:7-10, 43). Instead, just as a plane is a geometric concept with a surface as its environmental analogue, space is analogous to "a medium" which in the case of humans is air, and in that of fish, is water (Gibson 1979:33). The continuous, timeless, "holistic" perception of the environment (Gibson 1979: 253-255) means that there can be no true emptiness in an environment, only locations of relative hidden-ness, paucity of affordance, or vacancy. The reciprocal of *nothing is perceived* is not *nothing is afforded*. One cannot talk of empty spaces as affordance-less: the variety of potential affordances of these places could include subsistence, healing, communication with ancestors, burial, or fulfilment of any number of human agendas. However, being both limited in affordance and seldom perceived means, they will not likely have a large variety of meanings. Nor are such places necessarily distant or obscure: they can equally include "under the floorboards" or "the horizon;" "the distant mountain-top" or "the bottom of the sea." Rather than *empty*, a better term is *vacant*. For

---

[38]. Ingold (1986a:157) contrasts tenure with territoriality. Territoriality is practical behaviour intended to manage the exploitation of resources in a given area, and is essentially co-operative. Tenure, by contrast, concerns the social appropriation of nature, manifested as exclusivity of access, the casting of nature in a temporal continuum, and the imputation of creative potency to it.

[39]. It is important not to characterise these in any sense as negative spaces, but as places not necessarily full of affordances or behaviours, or the archaeological sites that may result. The dispute over the Stein River valley in British Columbia, where a lack of archaeological evidence along the valley trading trail was used to claim it was empty of prehistoric occupancy and thus could be logged (Wickwire 1992:61-62) shows that this question of vacancy is not merely an abstract problem.

Gibson, there is a large difference between vacancy and emptiness. The former would be known either through previous direct perception or indirectly known through predication, which respectively produce either explicit knowledge or tacit knowledge (Gibson 1979:260). In contrast, emptiness is a philosophical abstraction that not even an astronaut experiences, being enveloped in a portable environment. By definition, empty space would be both unknown and, quite literally, meaningless.

Gibson's broad term for locations is "places:" a location in an environment as contrasted with a point in space. Hence, a place by definition can only be within an environment, and the habitat of an animal is made up of many places. Places need not have sharp boundaries, and can be nested at many scales (see below). Nevertheless, it may be possible to look for natural or other breaks in the patterning of places, and network analysis may be able to help describe and analyse these patterns (Chapter 6).

### 4.3.2 Vacant places and fjordland archipelagos

The above theoretical discussion can perhaps be better put into focus through the device of an idealised maritime society living in a fjordland archipelago, in which transportation is almost exclusively by watercraft. Essentially, these people live on only one plane: sea level. They have limited direct perception of either the forest or the submarine environment.[40] Movement is through an archipelago of vistas and barriers: perception is of a complex sequence of going-out-of and coming-into sight.

Not only *mobility* but also *the view* is channelled. In an archipelagian maze of occluding edges, there will naturally be many places that are hidden at any given time: the far sides of islands, bays behind headlands, and so forth. Despite their transient hidden-ness, these are part of the bundle of well-paddled routes, and could well be an "occupied point of observation" at any time, only the occupant is someone other than the self. They are not necessarily vacant. What *is* of interest in this section are the routes and places which are normally vacant. There are at least three kinds of normally vacant place in this idealised archipelago: the inland terrestrial surface, the submarine and benthic environments, and vacancies along the coastal strip. Each bears brief mention.

First, the most obvious vacancies from a maritime viewpoint are the interior land surfaces of the islands and mainland which form the archipelago. These are relatively seldom visited. Furthermore, heavy vegetation cover can conceal the forest floor and all that occurs there. Hence, in day to day coastal life, most of the land is, in effect, invisible: its multiple affordances only hinted at by the even

sea of trees.[41] The layout of the forest is relatively invariant, the locations of the trees and berries and medicine and the other affordances change only at a very long temporal scale or to the regular rhythm of a seasonal cycle. The crowded mass of visual solid angles and the relative lack of good eating for animals make it an unattractive place to hunt. People thus tend to penetrate the forest only when they have a specific task in mind, and there is transmitted knowledge of what and where the forest affords. Navigation is at a premium, although reconnaissance will surely be embedded in it.

Second, the underwater medium is similarly concealed. While occasionally conditions may be right to see deeply into this environment, and while some of its more mobile or buoyant inhabitants may make a surficial appearance, there is much more hidden than visible. It bears a superficial resemblance to the sub-vegetational terrestrial environment, but the submarine environment is much more complex. It is home to a much wider range of life and hence a richer variety of affordances, which include staple subsistence.[42] For humans it is, in effect, a substance, whereas for its inhabitants it is a medium (Gibson 1979:21-22). Except in the most superficial and transient way it cannot be visited by humans. Knowledge of it is gained by perceiving its affordances indirectly from surficial phenomena, or by probing it with fishing gear or other instrumentation. The submarine environment is to a large extent known (the fishing grounds and the make-up of the bottom, for example), but through what sense is it perceived? How does one perceive a halibut lying on the bottom? It could be argued that fishing (at least with a line) is both an act of subsistence and an act of perception, that one is embedded in the other, and hence to understand one is to approach an understanding of the other. This is, I believe, a good example of Ingold's (1993:158) concept of the "taskscape:" "the entire ensemble of tasks in their mutual interlocking," embedded in sociality and temporality.

Third, the coastal zone is punctuated by places of lesser and greater affordance. At the extreme of few affordances, a place may be *de facto* vacant. Even if such a place is frequently perceived, it seldom or never constitutes a point of observation. Nevertheless, it is part of the fabric of flowing perspective that orients people to their routes and

---

[40]. In fact, the affordances of the forest are absolutely essential to First Nations of the Northwest Coast: transportation, shelter, storage, clothing, medicine, subsistence and spiritual communion. For simplicity's sake, this is overlooked at present.

[41]. It is ironic that the canopy of the forest is its most perceived yet least visited aspect.

[42]. Here there is a crucial distinction between the sub-marine layout (physical fabric and non-mobile species), which is relatively persistent, and the behaviour of the detached objects (i.e., fish), which are mobile. As Gibson (1979:199-200) notes, the position of displaceable detached objects must be re-learned (or monitored) continually. Out of this monitoring will grow knowledge of the habitual or characteristic behaviour of the species. A special example of this is knowledge of migratory animals, especially those, such as fish, which are largely hidden. In this case, a distilled knowledge of the habitual bundles of routes, or of secondary indicators, of the animal is what matters. The apparent lack of affordances of the given interception spot must be over-ridden by expectation based on culturally transmitted knowledge. This need not be directly verbal, it could be via the display of art or the display of built facilities, or embedded in myth.

places. In the archipelago, the patchy landform of *continuous* and *discrete* spaces (Santley 1992) means some places will be highly favoured for certain kinds of activity. Critically for the regional archaeological record, one important kind of place is a shoreline that affords landing a watercraft. The terrestrial environment may be accessed by a limited number of these "bridgeheads," which act as doors in from the marine passageways, and may be correspondingly likely to have archaeological sites. On the other hand, some places are vacant precisely because of what they afford, such as actual or supernatural danger.

### 4.3.3 Vacancy and scale

In common with any other place, a place defined as vacant on the basis of relative unaffordance or for explicit cultural reasons may be of any size. It is through a consideration of scale that two current issues in archaeology come into focus: landscape or off-site archaeology, and the definition of bounded cultural units. The spatial patterning of people's action in the world does not necessarily equal the spatial concentration of material remains. Doubtless Foley (1981) is right in stating that the archaeological record is spatially continuous yet not homogeneous, and that the homogeneity results from both behaviour and site-formation processes. This is equivalent to the debate of how and where to define an archaeological site (e.g., Dunnell 1992, Binford 1992). But Foley's Figure 1 (Foley 1981), for example, suggests a direct link between the well-trodden paths and the pattern of material remains, whereas it is by no means clear that repeated travelling on routes, especially those representing day-trips, will leave any lasting archaeological record. Does one consider the multiple points of observation in the same way that a landscape archaeologist looks at artifacts scattered across the terrain? Or, does one look at the clusters and define them as sites, in which case one is looking for bundles or nodes of perception (routes and occupied places)? Dunnell (1992:36) criticises the use of the notion "site" because, amongst other reasons, as a multiplex archaeological construct a site's most important attribute, its location within a landscape, is often lost. A more sophisticated approach would be to try to understand the locations in the landscape with no reference, at least initially, to where archaeological sites are. Gibsonian theory offers a way to understand locations in the environment in terms of their reflexive relationship with humans.

At a broader scale is the kind of vacancy discussed by Upham (1992:139): "empty spaces in regional and pan-regional systems are those areas between major population centres: areas without obtrusive or distinctive evidence of occupation." This definition is based on relative density of archaeological remains, yet Upham shows how these "empty spaces" helped integrate societies at the pan-regional level. Upham (1992:140) further states that the neglect of empty space is mirrored in an emphasis on either core or periphery, but not the in-between places, which "leaves large rural underclasses without history." In his Chacoan case study, Upham (1992) suggests that hunters and gatherers occupied the apparently vacant gaps in information space between the more sedentary communities. "Empty" spaces thus create an important dynamic in regional, pan-regional or world systems. He claims they are not amenable to analysis by the usual sort of spatial techniques. Yet, it might be possible that a more subtle understanding of emptiness versus vacancy in perceptual terms might aid analysis of these "non-regions," and bring them fully into a core-periphery or spatial interaction model. Marginalisation of groups living at a lower intensity or producing less durable material culture could be a problem almost anywhere such archaeological variation exists, including, at some scale or degree of resolution, coastal archipelagos occupied by hunters and gatherers.[43] It is worth noting that many prehistoric hunter-gatherer environments—especially fjordland archipelagos—are broadly riddled with vacancies, because transportation technology did not allow much crosscutting of the inherent directionality (Chapter 3). This is important because, as Ingold (1986a:157) suggests, to ignore the areas between sites is to turn somewhere into *nowhere*, and thus deny a satisfying notion of indigenous land tenure.[44]

In a previous section it was briefly discussed how a view of territoriality that focused on routes and paths necessarily made it more difficult to think in terms of geographically bounded social groups. Such boundaries that actually do exist may be much more permeable than commonly thought, with boundary sign-posting along the routes being more common than perimeter marking (Ingold 1986b). With a model of routes through vacant places, boundaries between groups become even more nebulous. Most of the border will in fact consist of adjoining vacancies. Again, this is not to say there is no knowledge, interest in, or traversal of these vacant areas, merely that clear demarcation in the absence of consistent occupation or direct perception is something that needs to be explained rather than assumed. For example, the apparently well-defined territories of the Northwest Coast, and the interest in private ownership of rights to places (Richardson 1982) could be at least partially an illusion. With the paths (seaways) so well ingrained, ethnographers could have mistaken the "signposts" along the linear routes as "territorial markers" and connected them through the interlying vacancies into a non-existent two-dimensional system of tenure. It would be necessary to question what sort of precision was used indigenously to delineate territory off these routes, in the interior of the islands or in the more open ocean, and to consider whether such off-

---

[43]. At a broad scale, the Northwest Coast could be seen as a linear core, with a large continental periphery, a case, perhaps, of the centre at the edge.

[44]. Thus grounding the network approach developed later in this thesis in an ethically satisfying contemporary social context, as it is enabled thorugh simultaneous consideration of material evidence *and* the non-materially evident constraints on human life.

route demarcation more closely resemble Ingold's (1986a) understanding of territoriality and tenure.

### 4.3.4 Routes, vacancy and population density

Population density is usually calculated as the number of people per unit area of land, as discussed in Chapter 3. In that chapter, some obvious problems with this areal approach to "carrying capacity" were noted. To summarise:

- animal resources exist in a natural ratio whereas needs are cultural, for example, acquisition of sufficient meat may still result in a deficit of hides;

- measurement of the unit area into which the number of people is divided is problematic, as is the census, since both rely on a simplistic view of bounded territorial and social units; and,

- carrying capacity might logically be considered in longer terms of biological reproduction, hence the baseline scale terrain unit for calculation of carrying capacity should relate to the connubium, rather than some population unit otherwise defined. The problem reverts to, "how is it bounded?" And, thus similar questions of definition and circumscription arise.

To these points can now be added the new problems raised when one starts to conceptualise territory as routes and vacancies: even if there were bounded territorial units, then the internal exploitation of these may be differentially patterned. Two areas of the same size might have quite different route structures. The actual bundles and nodes of occupation which determine the density or intensity of occupancy might be quite different yet archaeologically indistinguishable, especially in a site-based approach. This is most clearly exposed on the coast, where land area is much less relevant for carrying capacity than the length, involution and productivity of the coastal and fluvial ecotones. It is the heterogeneity of the occupation, the effective bundling and routinisation of daily habit that constitutes the exploited area. This will differ according to the terrain and the cultural practice, making *any* inter-group comparisons problematic, a problem compounded for archaeologists by taphonomic and other preservational factors.

A better understanding of mobility, using Gibson's and Ingold's theories as a starting point, may enable the simplistic and moribund ecological variable of population density to be either revived with new vigour, or laid to rest altogether. For example, range size is said to be restricted by mobility costs, supposedly limiting the radius of the range to a distance that can be covered round trip in a day (Mandryk 1993:43). This relationship is said to be so close that evidence of large range sizes can be taken as evidence of increased mobility (Rigaud and Semik, in Mandryk 1993), and carries an implication of lower population density. In a Gibsonian scheme, larger ranges imply a lower density of paths per square unit area. But, does this mean an un-braiding of the bundles of mobility, or fewer

bundles, or fewer strands in each bundle? And what is the effect on the vacancies? It could be that "population density" is effectively the same, only with more holes in the route network. Equally, this will require an understanding of the animate environment, and how a reduction in routes will affect strategies of its "vectoral appropriation (Ingold 1986a)," some of which strategies may leave distinct archaeological signatures.

## 4.4 Gibsonian psychology and locational analysis

The previous sections have introduced Gibsonian psychology and discussed its potential relevance in anthropological studies. This section will discuss points of common interest between the ecological psychology of James Gibson (1979) and spatial analysis in archaeology, particularly the locational analysis of prehistoric hunters and gatherers as expounded by Martin Wobst (1976).

Wobst begins his 1976 paper by challenging the primacy of the "site" as an archaeological unit of analysis, suggesting that a more appropriate scale is one that corresponds to such constructs as "society" or "population." Using a site as the boundary for data collection, limits the researcher to investigating a single scale of social relations. Constructs with larger boundaries, such as the mating network (connubium), allow for different scales of social relations to be investigated, and allow a strength of the archaeological record (its spatial and temporal scope) to be exploited.

Despite its apparent scope of tens of thousands of square kilometres, Wobst's (1974, 1976) spatial analysis is rooted in the simulated decision making and life histories of individuals. These decisions are made according to statistical likelihoods (such as mortality and fertility rates) or from rules analogised from ethnography (such as the incest taboo and variations on exogamy). The effects on the group are the sum of the individual events, and of their interactions. For example, the death of a spouse may have a ripple effect on the group demography as the survivor re-enters the mating eligibility pool. It would be a mistake to naïvely collectivise these individual actions or decisions, as Wobst elsewhere notes:

> The potential danger is that these newly coined entities, such as the minimal mating network, are treated as operational units in their own right. At least for most hunter-gatherers these entities have behavioural relevance only to the extent that they link *individuals* horizontally and temporally. (Wobst 1981:222; emphasis in original)

One obvious problem would be to start ascribing agency or corporate identity or collective will to these heuristic entities,[45] while perhaps a less obvious danger is the simple act of interpreting the hexagons as bounded social groups which have a direct link to a parcel of land. Regardless of their derivation from ethnographic "magic numbers" (which in any case are suspect), at issue here is the complicated problem of the closure of ethnic groups. The intent of Wobst's analysis, and that of similar studies such as Mandryk (1993), is to model information flow across an idealised socio-geographical model. Wobst attempts to show the relationship between individuals acting within cultural and demographic parameters and the large scale, long term implications of these cumulative decisions. However, a tighter link between individual decisions and their social context would be helpful. Gibson, apart from his above noted statements on public knowledge, does not attempt to discuss the effects of individual perception on groups, or vice versa. By contrast, Ingold carries his idea further, arguing that direct perception and information pickup is essential to a shared sense of "being-in-the-world,"[46] and hence sociality is:

> Given from the start, *prior* to the objectification experience in cultural categories, in the direct perceptual involvement of fellow subjects immersed in joint action in the same environment. (Ingold 1992:47; emphasis in original)

The direct perception of the affordances of other people bypasses the filter of social rules and categories, although these are fundamental to the way "in which we call others' social action into account . . . social life without rules is not chaotic (Ingold 1992:54)." Just as nature is a second-order construct only enabled by self-consciously disengaging from the experiential world, so society as the orderer of human behaviour stems from seeing human nature as either inherently disorganised or as mere potential (Ingold 1992:54).

In summary, Wobst works from the (partially socially determined) actions of the individual, but with the intent of building an understanding of larger scale processes. Communication is conceived of as an even flow over idealised social and other landscapes. In Gibsonian analysis, the individual is central. Nevertheless, the approach works inwards from the total visual system to dissolve the mind: body distinction and outward to dissolve nature:culture and other divisions (Gibson 1979:141, Ingold

1992). Gibsonian theory accounts poorly for communication, except as either co-perception or visual display.

Neither approach has impact at the medium social scale that corresponds to household or local group social structure. For Wobst, this medium scale is considered only as a grid for rules, such as exogamy and the incest taboo. The survival of the group across generations is important, as it is an expression of multiple individual life histories, but is subservient to the survival of the mating network as a whole, which is independent of any one group's survival. Wobst is not interested in the (habitation) site, which is arguably the most coherent archaeological expression of this social group. In a Gibsonian approach, the paths taken by individuals in groups form bundles of co-perception, and are critical for the formation of public knowledge and an unspoken consensus of reality. The most intense and complex affordances are those of one's closest fellow humans, who are also important in the process of socialisation to the perception of culturally specific affordances, although Gibson pays little attention to this ontogeny of perception.

At a still broader scale, Wobst considers the connubium crucial to archaeological analysis because inter-group interactions shape intra-group behaviour at individual settlements (1976:49), and thus influence the archaeological record. Gibson does not discuss these broad scales but there is no reason why one cannot extend the bundles of familial or local paths to connect with each other.

Differing notions of geographical scale are used by Wobst and by Gibson. The latter comments that the layout, and the environment in general, is characterised by scalar phenomena in which environmental units nest within larger units:

> There are no atomic units of the world considered as an environment. Instead there are subordinate and superordinate units. (Gibson 1979:9)

Gibson limits himself to the scale of the directly perceivable, only eliminating objects which require a telescope or a microscope, or which require pictures or writing to apprehend. This list thus appears to exclude maps, or any form of bird's-eye or aerial representation of the environment. A map is said to be a useful artifact, but it is a mistake to not separate the artifact from the state of mind it is produced by or produces. Instead, composite pictures of the environment are built up, but not as the stitching together of remembrance. Rather, a notion of temporally and spatially non-specific direct perception is introduced, in which the environment is continuously perceived from all places/paths at once (Gibson 1979:198-200, Ingold 1992:45. Even temporarily hidden places are directly perceived. Unlike either a cognitive or a paper

<hr>

[45]. Wobst (1976:55) appears to do this himself: "to counteract these disruptive tendencies, several social mechanisms are available to the society in question." The jump from a pattern produced by individuals to the feedback mechanisms that maintain group survival is by no means clear. This is particularly apt in light of Wobst's concern with finding the appropriate archaeological scale for understanding large-scale processes that effect behaviour at settlements.

[46]. Ingold (1993) elsewhere takes this seemingly simple notion of existence and, unnecessarily in my view, cloaks it in the philosophy of Heidegger.

map, there is in no sense a circle labelled "you are here." Rather, "you are everywhere."

This sort of analysis at first glance appears to have little in common with Wobst's approach. However, a key point about locational analysis is that it is largely about social or information geography. The use of isotropic surfaces and regular hexagons is a simplifying convenience, an aid to thought about the sorts of trade-offs that must be made between costs and benefits of gaining information and turning that information into substance. In this case the "substance" is mates, modelled with a landscape of demography, simple mating rules and population density. Thus, the use of hexagons cannot be critiqued as an oversimplification of the terrestrial environment because the plane is more a representation of behavioural space than of terrestrial space, although it does have implications (given certain assumptions derived from ethnography) for real world spatial situations. It would be a mistake to interpret the hexagons as territorial boundaries: they are graphic conveniences in a model that is based on prehistoric social groups defined by social/information criteria. It may be more appropriate to think in terms of networked "social fields" (Lesser 1961) with permeable boundaries rather than in terms of closed boundedness, at least in some contexts or at some scales. The discovery of such scales is discussed in Chapter 7.

Thus, although the eye is drawn to the hard edges and formalised boundaries of Wobst's hexagons, not too much should be read into them. The heart of the 1976 paper rests on an assumption of permeable social boundaries between the groups and it is the resulting vectors (which could be analogised to well-trodden paths) of communication which define or produce the relative social boundedness of the group. Furthermore, the network as a whole can be more or less open or closed. While Wobst may assign a leading role to group size and density, his scheme is not as rigid as it graphically appears, nor far removed from Ingold's one-dimensional tenure concept. It may be possible to "drape" a locational model over an environment understood in Gibsonian terms of surfaces, mediums, places, and so forth, which could be a first step towards a humanistic human ecology.

Temporally, Gibson (1979:11-12) limits himself to events at a human scale, in the course of a discussion which dispenses with "socialised time" as being irrelevant to the study of visual perception. In contrast, Wobst runs his model one year at a time, building up a long term pattern which in its totality is outside the limits of human perception or apprehension. Nevertheless, as with Gibson (1979:12), he might agree that "the flow of abstract empty time . . . has no reality for the animal. We perceive not time but processes, changes, sequences, or so I shall assume." The question is, how does the perception of these sequences initiate behavioural responses if the long-term result is never apprehended? In other words, there is a

difference between a trend and stochastic fluctuation. This is relevant in small group demographics where minor declines in reproductive success can lead to long-term reproductive failure and extinction of the local group (Wobst 1974). Gibson's emphasis on the relatively short term of human lifetimes may be difficult to reconcile with the temporal resolution possible in the Palaeolithic. On the other hand, the "timelessness" of his theory of perception leaves it flexible enough to accommodate a variety of approaches to the nature(s) of time.

In summary, it has been shown that there are some interesting similarities and contrasts between Wobst's location-centred approach and Gibsonian ecological psychology. Specifically, a parallel approach unifying both might be able to:

• help introduce or refine the crucial element of mobility, which is otherwise a dependent variable in Wobst's analysis, a refined view of mobility which leads to alternate conceptions of territoriality and may be congruent with Wobst's permeable hexagons;

• ground a locational and/or network approach in a humanistic framework, in which such cross-culturally difficult dichotomies as nature:culture and mind:body are dissolved.

However, the connection between the individual and society is problematic in both approaches. Gibson largely avoids the question, whereas Wobst has cultural rules and demographic facts but little interest in "cultural negotiation" or "dialectics" or any other sort of dynamic social process. The solution may be to adopt a regional perspective in which individual behaviours are interpreted at a large enough scale that middle order social process is subordinated. Indeed, Wobst (1978) has argued that it is this connection that allows escape from the "parochial" model of hunters and gatherers, and hence from the "tyranny of the ethnographic record."

### 4.5 Conclusions: perception, mobility, and the archaeology of archipelagos

Gibson's theory of visual perception can help structure thinking about several important aspects of the archaeology of hunters and gatherers. Gibsonian psychology asserts, above all, that mobility is crucial to active engagement with the world as an *environment*. But patterns of mobility are not random. They are braided together into bundles in different ways at different scales. This may be the daily or yearly activities of an individual or of a group, and it may constitute routes through daily space of individuals or supra-regional space of multiple individuals. Either way, some patterns of movement may be favoured, because of habit, the landform, the built environment, ritual topography (Schlee 1992) or a variety of other reasons. The effect is to linearise or multi-linearise mobility within the environment.

The insight into routes is well suited to inform both time-geographic approaches to human ecology and network or locational analysis of spatial patterning. It may offer a way to humanise human ecology, because while it is centred on the individual, it is individuals who are intimately and actively engaged in their environment (Ingold 1992:44). Rather than reifying culture as a prescriptive agent or passive product of human ecology, it "leaves it out of the equation (Ingold 1992:53)." Cultural construction of the environment is understood as a second-order phenomenon founded on human discourse, an optional *epilogue* rather than a *prelude* to practical action (Ingold 1992:52).

The insight into routes and mobility that Gibsonian theory allows is particularly appropriate for the study of maritime hunters and gatherers, whose mobility may be constrained to waterways. These waterway routes, as discussed in Chapter 3, have the crucial attribute of being *known*. Thus, rather than starting from a site-based perspective and imputing routes of communication between the sites, with all the uncertainty this necessarily entails, it becomes possible to start with the known routes and, with the body of theoretical support outlined in the subsequent chapter, develop hypotheses about the human ecology of an area, which will then perhaps be testable against the known site structure. Critically, known site locations and ethnographic information are not introduced until later stages of the analysis. As outlined in Chapter 6, the method of such an analysis will include using a geographical information system to help create and analyse a schematic network representation of the study area.

# CHAPTER 5—MOBILITY, BUILDING, AND SOCIAL PRACTICE ON THE NORTHWEST COAST

## 5.1. Introduction

Previous chapters demonstrated that coastlines should not be stereotyped as linear environments (*contra* Wobst 1976). Rather, a surprising degree of planarity or multi-linearity can be achieved through the presence of inlets and islands. The implication for archaeological spatial analysis on coastlines is that the demographic and social costs, which Wobst claims are produced by the shape of the physical/social environment, are re-opened as problems for investigation. It is suggested that these costs cannot be derived from cross-cultural ethnographic analogy (made operational through locational analysis) alone. Locational and many other archaeological spatial analyses employ an idealised geometry of the world. These models are populated by individuals mainly known through empathy, common sense and through naïve applications of the principle of least effort. The arguments in Chapter 4 regarding the individual and the environment led to direct criticism of these models, yet held out the hope for their rehabilitation in a modified "humanistic human ecology." It is suggested here that a mutualistic relationship between the individual and the environment needs to be framed in an anti-cognitivist, anti-Cartesian world view. Such a framework avoids the inherent problems in uncritically universalising either:

(a) the second-order construction of nature as a neutral geometric space to be entered and adapted to; or,

(b) the rearward projection of any particular historical or ethnographic worldview, i.e., the "tyranny of the ethnographic record" (Wobst 1978) expressed via simplistic applications of the direct-historic approach.

In this chapter these two lines of argument (the importance of the active individual rather than the mere automaton, and the structuring features of the environmental geometry) will be brought together under the umbrella of Gosden's (1994) concept of the "landscape of habit." It is suggested that social theories of practice and the *habitus* (Bourdieu 1977) are relevant to the archaeology of the Northwest Coast (NWC), particularly as they can be applied to improving our understanding of mobility. Further, it will be shown that it is reasonable, even necessary, to think of the NWC landscape as a *built environment*, with implications for spatial and historical analysis of the archaeological record. Taken together, this discussion will then lead to a specific program of analysis of archaeological data from the West Coast of Vancouver Island, implemented using a Geographic Information System as described in Chapters 6 and 7.

## 5.2 Mobility and practical mobility

Hunters and gatherers have long been characterised as mobile peoples. Accordingly, archaeologists have usually considered mobility as a collective strategy or response to environmental circumstances. In a processualist archaeological paradigm, mobility is normally considered as an adaptive strategy, with the implicit assumption that its actual pattern relates to optimal exploitation of naturally existent resource structures (Kelly 1983). The ensuing settlement pattern - logistical or residential (Binford 1979) - then imposes certain conditions or possibilities on other "cultural subsystems." Indeed, mobility has been considered something of a prime mover in hunter-gatherer societies, responsible for their simple and lightweight material culture, their small settlements, and other characteristics of "simple band society," as critically reviewed in Chapter 2 (see, for example, Kelly 1983; Torrence 1983; Keeley 1988; Renouf 1991).

However, rather than being necessary social features of a particular way of life, these can be seen as the pragmatic effects of the time-space-energy constraints on the human body (listed above in Chapter 3). Some of these constraints can be relaxed with technical application or innovation, such as the use of untended facilities or watercraft, but, as noted, many of the inherent constraints of the human body form a universal baseline of time-space activity. Thus, the mobility of *individuals*, while inevitably occurring within a culturally-specific settlement and subsistence milieu, is intrinsically important. For example, Ingold makes a compelling case for re-conceptualising mobility. He notes (1986:179-81) that it is not enough to simply look at the amount of travel that people do but the patterning of that travel, and discusses the actual implications of hunter-gatherer mobility patterns for their relationship to both the landscape and to the natural world. To recap, Ingold distinguishes between land *tenure* — the appropriation of planar, two-dimensional tracts of land — and *territoriality* — the activity of people along one-dimensional paths, between zero-dimensional places, with the appropriation of nature occurring during encounters and interceptions. The paths and tracks that people follow "impose a habitual pattern on the movement of people (Jackson in Ingold 1993:167)," yet they are also *a result* of that movement across the landscape. Thus, it is argued that mobility produces not only the "muscular consciousness (Ingold 1993:167)" of practical activity, but also sediments into the landscape a network of paths and tracks which cumulatively represent the activity of a community. As will be outlined further below, such a mobility network is part of "the taskscape made visible (Ingold 1993)," and is an important tool to bring shape and scale into the heart of an archaeological spatial analysis. A highly directional environment routinizes mobility and implies a partially knowable prehistoric landscape of habit. Thus, there is an opportunity to escape from the bird's eye view, map-oriented Cartesian spatial analyses critically featured in Chapter 4.

## 5.3 Mobility, the *habitus*, and the practical mastery of space

As discussed in earlier chapters, it is customary to rely on maps in archaeological spatial analysis. Maps are models of all possible routes, and show a Cartesian space (Gell 1985:273). However, "practical way-finding (Gell 1985)" is mapless and is conducted in terms of co-ordinates centring on the agent. Arguing that the cognitive theory of mental maps conflates the map-as-artefact with the state of mind that it produces, Gell suggests that people orient to the environment through *mapless practical mastery*, a concept derived from the work of the French sociologist Pierre Bourdieu (1977). Bourdieu, of course, does not directly address hunter-gatherer mobility. However, he does (1977:73-78) discuss the notions of "practical mastery" and "strategy," and these are relevant insofar as they help one to understand the patterned movement of people through space. By taking an individual-centred view of mobility, the concept of mobility as collectivist strategy is implicitly rejected in this thesis. For example, the foraging vs. collecting dichotomy has been reified as categorical options that *groups* of people choose, rather than descriptions of what they do. Bourdieu indirectly criticises such totalising categories in his often-quoted criticism of the analogy that culture is like a map:

> It is the analogy which occurs to an outsider who has to find his way around a foreign landscape and who compensates for his lack of practical mastery, the prerogative of the native, by the use of a model of all possible routes. The gulf between this potential, abstract space, devoid of landmarks or any privileged centre—like genealogies, in which the ego is as unreal as the starting point in a Cartesian space—and the practical space of journeys actually made, or rather of journeys actually being made, can be seen from the difficulty we have in recognising familiar routes on a map or town-plan until we are able to bring together the axes of the field of potentialities and "the system of axes linked unalterably to our bodies, and carried about with us wherever we go," as Poincaré puts it, which structures practical space into right and left, up and down, in front and behind. (Bourdieu 1977:2)

Thus, practice is centred on the body, and it is possible to see Gibsonian ecological perception and the theory of affordances (Gibson 1979; Chapter 4) as, in a sense, the proximal mechanism for practical activity in the world. Bourdieu considers it unhelpful to think of goal directed behaviour as the realisation of the "explicitly stated purposes of a project or plan (1977:72)," a fallacy he terms the "finalist illusion" because it reduces historically situated and socially contingent social practice to a mechanical reaction. In other words, the purposeful projects of the individual are always modified by their embededness in the *habitus*.[47] The concept of the *habitus* does not readily lend itself to summary. Bourdieu (1977:72) defines it as "structured structures predisposed to act as structuring structures . . . history turned into nature." Or, as Gell (1985:273) puts it, "the set of inculcated dispositions [cf. Bourdieu 1977:214, fn. 1] to respond to situations in an unreflective, socially patterned way." In effect, the *habitus* is a highly subtle concept that describes how the generator, or structurer, of an individual's social practice is simultaneously structured by that practice. After disposing of the "finalist illusion," Bourdieu goes on to criticise the opposite extreme, which is that individuals are bound by rules. What is left, then, is the rich middle ground of the *habitus*:

> The *habitus* is the source of these series of moves which are objectively organised as strategies without being the product of a genuine strategic intention. (Bourdieu 1977:73)

It can be suggested then, that mobility patterns are intrinsically part of the *habitus*.

To start a different approach, we must discuss where the "fallacy of the rule" comes from. According to Bourdieu, rules described by informants are a form of rationalisation for the behaviour that the *habitus* predisposes. When queried about a behavioural arena over which they have "practical mastery (1977:19)," informants become "semi-theoretical (1977:18)," a state of discursive self-delusion concerning their own actions in the world. In this, the anthropologist or "learned questioner" and the informant share a similar thought process, although their derived constructs will, of course, differ:

(a) behaviour is observed, or reflected upon.

(b) a rule is concocted which fits the behaviour.

(c) the mistaken assumption is made that the rule that fits the behaviour actually guides it.

(d) the conclusion is reached that the behaviour is caused by the rule.

Rather, Bourdieu believed that the true nature of *practical mastery* is "learned ignorance, a mode of practical knowledge not comprising knowledge of its own principles (1977:19)." The importance of this for the apprehension of mobility is that mastery of space is not based on mental

---

[47]. Presumably the *habitus* differs from "tradition" in that it is double ended: both a structuring and structured structure.

maps, which are central to a Cartesian ego-centric, "mechanical-cybernetic (Gell 1992:263)," cognitive model of the individual. As noted in the previous chapter, ecological psychology rejects the theory of mental maps in favour of the non-cognitivist framework of places, paths, and encounters. It may be possible to assert, then, that ecological psychology constitutes the proximal mechanism by which practical activity in the world is enabled.[48]

Barrett (1994:13) describes the relevance of the fallacy of the rule to the archaeological analysis of a monumental landscape. He notes that there is no use in applying or imposing a "descriptive geometry" of the landscape and then looking for the underlying "generative geometry," because Neolithic monuments such as Avebury were never conceived of as a single project. As all episodes of this re-fashioning and renewal were re-workings of what had gone before, the fallacy was to convert regularities in material culture to a rule. Thus, in accordance with *habitus*, neither absolute free will nor simple goal-directedness was responsible for the archaeological landscape. This sort of analysis is of obvious importance for all archaeological spatial analyses of built environments and will be revisited below, in a discussion of where the line should be drawn between *natural* and *built* environments and, indeed, if such a line should be drawn at all. Throughout, it must be realised that, as formulated by Bourdieu, *habitus* is essentially a temporal concept, but with a latent spatiality. Gosden (1994) has attempted to draw out some of the spatial implications of Bourdieu's theory of practice with his concept of the *landscape of habit*. If the *habitus* is to be of use archaeologically, then it must be linked to both material culture and to space. As noted above it is useful in the analysis of built environments. The following sections discuss the notion of a built environment, starting with a definition of a *building*.

## 5.4 The built environment

In the previous chapter the concepts of place, path and vacancy were shown to be critical in understanding mobility within a framework of humanistic human ecology. In this section, it will be further argued that the landscape of places and paths can be known archaeologically, and be considered as a "built environment," even when they are represented by the ephemeral and discontinuous material remains of a hunter-gatherer archaeological record. A building is defined as "any durable structure in the landscape whose form arises and is sustained within the current of human activity" (Ingold 1993:169). Thus, it does not refer only to architectural structures, but also to the accumulation of material items resulting from human activity. Environment continues to be defined only in relation to an observer, as discussed in Chapter 4. Minimally, then, the *built environment* has a rich meaning

of the durable record of practical and other activity in the world.

Further, even the distinction between buildings and non-buildings should not be seen as absolute. Rather, this is another recreation of the false dichotomy between nature and culture, referred to earlier. Ingold (1993) illustrates this point with reference to a landscape painting by the artist Pieter Bruegel the Elder, showing peasants in the medieval Netherlands at harvest-time. Within the landscape, the church, the fields and the paths are all self-evidently part of the built environment, in that they are durable and arise out of human action. Less obviously, when comparing the tree with the church, Ingold (1993:170) suggests that "the form of both is an embodiment of a developmental or historical process," and that the people are "as much bound up in the life of the tree as the tree in the lives of the people." Thus, buildings and trees both emerge from the continual self-transformation of the world. It is gathered into the taskscape because of its affordances (fruit, shelter, etc.) yet, as a point of reference, it is itself a place and gathers the landscape into it.

Explicit recognition that the hunter-gatherer environment is a built environment is over a decade old, with some of the implications now being widely recognised. For example, Conkey echoes Bourdieu (whom she does not cite) when she writes that,

> Humans have become masters at environmental structuration: "a transformed environment is a good alternative to a bigger brain (Wagner 1972:xi)". Not only do humans structure their environments, but these structuring acts structure humans, from object manipulation to the architecture that obviously constitutes a built environment. Environmental structuration is sociospatial in its genesis and in its perpetuation. (Conkey 1984:266)

Further, she goes on to note that hunter-gatherers are not often thought of as contributors to a built environment, partly because on the whole they do not construct relatively permanent architecture or other structures. However, she suggests that they certainly do generate a structured environment, "if only by means of the differential deployment of personnel throughout the landscape and of the locations that they settle and use" (Conkey 1984:267). Conkey suggests that a "settlement system" itself is a form of building, but a building that is an emergent property of process, not as the result of a plan or blueprint. Thus, Conkey is arguing against the imposition of the fallacy of the rule. This line of thought edges the material record of sites closer to the non-material record of structured (and structuring) mobility within a constrained landform.

---

[48]. The importance of this remark will become clearer in Chapter 7.3.3.

34

Kenneth Ames echoes this when he notes that the settlement system itself is a kind of artificially created landscape:

> Both sedentism and semi-sedentism might be better thought of as particular kinds of social geographies (Conkey 1984) or as particular kinds of artificially constructed landscapes in which residential patterns and associated social and cultural patterns become fixed and maintained at certain places for some period of time. *In a sense, residential sites become part of the furniture of the landscape* [emphasis added]. (Ames 1991a:109)

Ames carries on to discuss the *longue durée* aspects of mobility strategy and resource distribution on the Columbia River Plateau, but it is important not to see the hunter-gatherer built environment as a mere reflection of ecological structure. As a prelude to arguing against this point, Gosden (1995) recapitulates it: the built environment could be said to be nothing more than the residue of economic activity, and it does not really structure action" so much as it is structured by environmental ("non-cultural," though culturally perceived) patterning in resources. In the course of discussing why the hunter-gatherer:farmer distinction has become distinctly unhelpful in Australian and Papua-New Guinean prehistory, Gosden notes that primary emphasis on the "requirements" of subsistence leads to environmental and economic determinisms, such as,

> the requirements of the subsistence round are said to determine the nature and pattern of movement or sedentism, while the products derived from subsistence influence the levels of population possible and the amounts of trade or exchange, craft specialisation, etc. . . . Subsistence is the base on which all other elements of social life must be built. (1995:807)

To avoid this determinism, Gosden proposes that the starting point be, in effect, the built environment:

> Food and drink are a vital consideration when creating a world, but they are a necessary, rather than a sufficient condition in this *shaping* [of the world] [emphasis added]. (Gosden 1995:807)

Gosden's critique bears strong import for much Northwest Coast ecologically-oriented culture history, while in the previous chapter the cross-disciplinary convergence of anti-

dualist thinking about the environment was noted. Inherent in this was a criticism of the concept of "ecological niche" as something that exists independently of the organism, as something *out there*, waiting to be filled. The niche is more properly seen as an active construction of the organism:

> *Organisms assemble their environments out of the bits and pieces of the world.* Indeed, an environment is nature organised by an organism....*organisms alter their environments.* It is a fundamental feature of life that organisms both create and destroy the conditions for their own existence by physical alterations to their milieu [emphasis in original]. (Lewontin 1982:160)

This is evidently congruent with Gosden's (1994:82, following Bourdieu 1977) comments that each generation is born and socialised into "a particular landscape and this becomes something that [they] are." People never approach the world "from without, as a foreign object," rather, they are *always* within it:

> A familiar landscape is not nature in opposition to our culture, but a web of connections which people have become used to warping in special ways. (Gosden 1994:82)

By *landscape*, Gosden does not mean purely cultural or symbolic constructions, rather, landscapes are:

> Spaces carved out by patterns of action, which then help to pattern future action. The symbolic aspect of the landscape is derived from the actions carried out within it: a conscious gloss on unthought practice. (Gosden 1994:81)

Thus, even the most ephemeral archaeological sites, and even those sites at which interaction occurs but no material remains develop, are included within the landscape. A further extension to this argument is to add other features. The construction of a social landscape (Gamble 1995), for example, results in a network of significant people, who through their (moving) occupation of space, can be conceptualised as named, meaningful *places*.

### 5.5 Example: what might it mean to reject the "Fallacy of the Rule" in a spatial analysis?

A central theme of this research is the importance of theorising the relationship between individuals and landscape. In a locational model (e.g., Wobst 1974, 1976), this relationship, while central, is completely rule-bound. A set of "cultural assumptions governs all [computer simulation] runs" (Wobst 1974:165). Amongst these are such normative prescriptions as: (a) a mate searches for the closest available partner; (b) the regional population is 100% endogamous; and (c) members of a minimum band move only if they marry, or need to either divide or amalgamate with neighbouring groups.

Clearly, these prescriptions were a necessary evil to facilitate the computer programming. Indeed, some of them may well reflect cross-cultural norms. But crucially for Wobst's model, the people abide by the rules until certain thresholds are crossed, when new rules abruptly replace the old. The most important of these thresholds, and the one of most interest to Wobst's general conclusions, is the actual *extinction* of the local groups or, cumulatively, of the connubium. Wobst holds that this demographic crash-landing results from the interplay of fertility, mortality and group size, played out according to the functionalist rules of the simulation. However, the model is actually dependent on the type of individual modelled: lemming-like, they blindly follow normative rules over the demographic cliff.[49]

It is very difficult to think of a way in which the *habitus* could be modelled in such a simulation, which was meant to consider demographic variables, and was not meant as a holistic simulation of society. It would not be enough to have the program assess the historically arrived-at present, "look" several generations into the future and then choose the present move that maximises future success. A program that looks ahead, like a chess player, would merely be a refinement of optimisation studies and would, in effect, be a teleological version of Wobst's simulation in which the computer program was specifically designed to not only behave according to normative rules but to reproduce pre-ordained anthropological constructs. Working towards definitions in this way would not necessarily be of much novel interest. It might seem counter-productive to attempt to model a construct such as the *habitus*, as this might require the inappropriate imposition of rules onto an essentially rule-less arena. Nevertheless, it is worthwhile to take on board the essential ideas of the dialectic between objectivist and subjectivist structures.

The recent paper by Maschner and Stein (1995) illustrates this point. The authors describe a GIS application in the Alexander Archipelago of the Southeastern Alaskan "panhandle," traditional territory of the Tlingit people. The authors compared site micro-environment (slope, drainage, cardinal and climatic exposure, island size and distance to fresh water) and a measure of intensity of use (site area),

using a GIS-implemented logistic regression model, in an attempt to build a predictive model of site location.

They found that all the midden sites were on flat, well-drained places: but crucially, they did not explore whether this is a description of the midden itself or of the affordance of its place. In other words, the midden-as-building (built through long-term practical and other activity) is wrongly mixed into the model as an environmental variable. This matters, because one element in the model that could not be explained was "site area." They conclude in no uncertain terms that,

> intensity of occupation by Native Tlingit inhabitants was completely independent of these [environmental] factors . . . we still have no understanding of the variables that influenced how long, or at least with what intensity, a site will be occupied. (Maschner and Stein 1995:932)

The answer to their problem probably lies in their failure to take a built landscape approach. Instead, they combine the locational aspects of the sites in relation to the landform and to the affordances of the environment (including other sites), and the reflexive consideration of the regional *habitus* (the landscape of habit). This resulted in some shell midden sites becoming more intensely used than others. This is to say that a combination of network and locational analysis performed within the space of the built environment might have added significantly to their findings. Their apparent and repeated (cf. Maschner 1997) failure was to neither consider more than one scale of analysis, nor more than one sort of space, nor more than pragmatic site-specific decision-making; but to only consider the neutral space of nature, and the scale of the site's immediate micro-environment. Thus, there may be reason for considerable interest in building a network of habitation sites to explore their locational relationships at a more macro-scale. To do so it is necessary to conceive of the Northwest Coast landscape as a built environment. The built environment is an unfinished edifice, and as such cannot be the simple result of decision making variables and their proximal effects.

### 5.6 The Northwest Coast as a built environment

Looking at the varied and substantial archaeological sites of the Northwest Coast leads one to the conclusion that the landscape as a whole is aptly considered as a built environment. These sites include both deliberate special purpose constructions (e.g., fishtraps, rock art, canoe skids) or the less deliberate—but substantial—residues of everyday life (e.g., shell middens; beach lithic scatters).[50]

---

[49]. This is a break from the usual criticism of Wobst's approach (e.g., Bettinger 1980): that it depends too much on idealised group social constructs and undifferentiated space.

[50]. If the interest is in the *habitus* these should not be considered simply as "archaeological sites" but as agglomerations of material aspects of the

These are briefly described immediately below, while their interest from a landscape perspective of these will be discussed in subsequent sections.

(a) Village sites and middens. These are located somewhat pragmatically according to the affordances of the landform. This siting is surely enhanced by the midden itself, which normally constitutes a flat, well-drained terrace. In any case, as discussed below, an important question is not so much exactly why any given site is where it is (micro-environmental questions of drainage, slope and so forth having been investigated and found important by Maschner and Stein 1995), but what influences the inter-site spatial patterning and regional site hierarchy. They are a purely archaeological type, with the activities—general habitation—which lead to their formation having only the discard of mollusc and other shells in common.

(b) Defensive sites. These frequently contain shell middens themselves. These are similar in derivation to the above, but are even more constrained in location by the exigencies of defence. They may have a reflexive relationship with the location of middens: i.e., some villages are located near defensive positions, while other defensive sites are located near villages (Moss and Erlandson 1992).

(c) Canoe skids. These are cleared pathways for landing canoes through a cobble/boulder shoreline. They are often associated with middens, but not always: they offer gateways from the maritime environment to the general terrestrial environment as well as to sites. They probably persist even after any associated sites are abandoned or change use, and thus have a different use-life within the built environment.

(d) Fishtraps/weirs. As is the case for canoe skids, these may be pragmatically sited (they must be in appropriate places to catch fish). They presumably required an initial planned and organised construction, followed by some degree of routine annual maintenance. Some individual fishweirs in Alaska are known to have been used over a thousand year span (Moss *et al* 1989).

(e) Culturally Modified Trees (CMTs). These are trees (living and dead) which bear evidence of bark stripping, plank acquisition, house frame and canoe-log acquisition and medicinal uses. In essence they are quarries for organic products. These are numerous, and can be surprisingly durable, with one recently discovered living cedar from Barkley Sound bearing a bark-strip dating to over 800 years before present (Eldridge, pers. comm.).

(f) Human Burials. Burials are widely recognised as potentially of immense significance in the landscape, and, in other parts of the world, provoked the construction of monuments. On the Northwest Coast, burial caves are probably a historic phenomenon and burials within middens are of limited interest in the assessment of built environment. In some areas, mortuary poles and grave houses were erected. "Burials" in trees, away from other

sites, are potentially of a great deal of interest from a landscape perspective.[51]

(g) Rock art. Pictographs and petroglyphs are common in some areas, though not on the west coast of Vancouver Island. They are of obvious importance as durable and occasionally highly visible alterations of the environment (cf. Conkey 1984).[52]

(h) Further, there are those phenomena that arise from the activities of people but might not be considered as archaeological sites themselves. For example, tree felling may encourage berry growth and the scrap wood left from plank acquisition may make a useful supply of spare parts (expedient wedges, skids, workspace clearings, scaffolding) and thus encourage further utilisation of a certain area. The impact could also be negative, as bark-stripped trees, while they continue to live, are usually unsuitable for plank, post, or canoe-log acquisition. Another example is Monks' (1987) suggestion that fishtraps acted to enhance the local trophic productivity and thus altered the distribution of resources, quite apart from their functional role in catching fish. Shell middens themselves, even when abandoned, remain for centuries as large, unnaturally flat, well-drained areas with different vegetation. In these and other ways (very briefly reviewed by Ames 1991b:942), the resource structure of the environment was intentionally or otherwise manipulated. Insofar as it is a durable alteration, arising and sustained in human activity, this qualifies as a building of the environment, regardless of the degree of intentionality behind the process.

The pragmatic siting at a micro-environmental scale of many of the above is not a problem when arguing for a built environment. Constraint in site location is of most immediate interest if attempting predictive modelling (see discussion of Maschner and Stein 1995 above), or indeed any spatial analysis with a model of *unconstrained* opportunity for site location and which then directly compares ideal or optimal location to actual location. The difference in treating the Northwest Coast as a built environment is the introduction of the archaeological sites themselves (in the broader sense of "buildings") as structured/structuring features of the environment.

## 5.7 The built environment and the "Fallacy of the Rule"

Having defined the Northwest Coast environment as a built environment, it is critical we not conceive of it as having arisen from a plan. Rather, a regional archaeological record is an interrupted process. Maschner and Stein are therefore subject to Barrett's criticism that some archaeologists utilise a *descriptive geometry* when conducting spatial

---

taskscape. That is, they should not necessarily be conceived in site-typological terms.

[51]. The practice of tree burial would be an opportunity for an examination of the relationship between the body and the landscape: the body is taken out of the social sphere and put in the "natural" environment, which probably could be analysed as a re-mapping or inscription process.
[52]. Perhaps equivalent in some ways to a monument, or to the church in Ingold's (1993) discussion—it qualifies as a building.

analyses, and then go looking for the underlying *generative geometry*. This is said by Barrett to be erroneous because it starts with an assumption that, in his example, monuments were conceived of as a single project:

> [Avebury] is the physical remnant of a number of abandoned projects and not the culmination of a series of planned phases. These projects were undertaken at different locations within the landscape, and at these *locales* actions and exchanges between people created the material conditions which then helped, in turn, to sustain these particular human relations. (Barrett 1994:13; emphasis in original)

The fallacy was to convert the regularities in material culture into a rule as, in accord with *habitus*, neither unalloyed free will nor simple goal-directed behaviour was responsible for the archaeological landscape. Barrett is mainly concerned with the built archaeological (indeed, primarily monumental) landscape, but a similar point is given earlier and more relevant exposition by Conkey (1987). Criticising the use of regional/temporal labelling of mapped archaeological distributions, she notes (1987:67) that "this places emphasis on sites (or bone harpoons, etc.) as products, as cultural outputs, rather than as processes." In fact, the privileging of form over process, of the products of action over the action itself, is part of a "western meta-narrative" (Ingold 1993).[53] Ingold's solution (1993:158) is to emphasise that the "landscape" is really just the "taskscape congealed." The taskscape is "the entire ensemble of tasks, in their mutual interlocking . . . it is to labour what the landscape is to land" (Ingold 1993:158). It must be right, then, to consider mobility patterns, which define the space-time geography of the constitutive tasks of dwelling, as a part of the landscape. If this is accepted, then the built environment (as "mutualistic process," not "dualistic form") is conceptually inseparable from (or, at least, logically includes) the directionality of the landform.[54]

The concept of the built environment is therefore useful because it allows the integration of patterned activity over time with the environment in a way that does not emphasise product over process, nor set up a false dichotomy between nature and culture. The applicability of such a critique to the Northwest Coast is obvious in the case of such normative analyses as Maschner and Stein (1995), and Donald and Mitchell (1994:115), who suggest that "there

was a cultural response to this variation [in salmon distribution and density]. Territories grouped streams together in a way that not only reduced the variation in resources . . ." In their example, the descriptive grammar of salmon escapements is used to generate cultural projects of risk-buffering resource stabilisation.

## 5.8 The built environment and moveable material culture

While Jeanne Arnold makes some interesting points,[55] in an effort to avoid both technological determinism and a denial of the importance of technical innovation, she assigns prime mover status to "aggrandisers" (Arnold 1995). With their personalities lifted straight from the ethnographic present (almost entirely from Drucker (1951) *The Northern and Central Nootkan Tribes*), these individuals engage in labour control, capital investment, and power, deploying technology against a strongly deterministic natural environment. Thus, the historical particularities of her case studies (Nuu-chah-nulth Vancouver Island and the Chumash Channel Islands of central California) are united: "Where raw materials[56] appropriate for the construction of large boats overlapped with such [complex-archipelagic] zones, conditions were conducive to the adoption of reliable watercraft" (Arnold 1995:35). Reliable watercraft are then noted to be crucial in a descriptive catalogue of NWC subsistence and social pursuits—from fishing to trade to marriage proposals to dentalia procurement. Accordingly, Arnold (1995:743) concludes that differential ownership of these reliable boats is an important contributor to NWC social complexity in general and that the regional patterning of resources is thus crucial in the observed spatial heterogeneity in relative levels of "complexity," across the NWC as a whole. The twist in this version of the cultural-complexity argument formulated elsewhere by Arnold (e.g., 1992, 1993) is that she suggests that advanced watercraft were part of a strategy of elite domination.[57] However, I would not give priority to the particularities of the transportation technology, but rather discuss the ways in which technology alters the perception of the environment. While I have noted in Chapter 3 that the directionality of the environment can only be assessed

---

53. Another archaeological illustration is presumably the recent discovery of the importance of behavioural use-life histories for lithic analysis, and the escape from the mental-template (form-privilege) stereotype.

54. And thus one once again arrives at a powerful critique of Maschner and Stein (1995), whose GIS-enabled predictive model of site location only considers localised micro-environmental variables.

55. For example, in passing she descriptively notes some issues of coastal configuration, such as locational disadvantage and coastal "gateways" that are of much potential interest to this thesis. I would argue that she needs to think much more about these issues before launching herself into a just-so Marxist tale of aggrandising, wealth and power, especially as she seems to have read little literature from the Nuu-chah-nulth area she discusses, apparently confusing, for example, Puget Sound (Seattle area) with Nootka Sound.

56. An argument reminiscent in some ways of other ecological prime movers, such as the climax cedar-forest determinism of Hebda and Mathewes (1984).

57. In principle, I am not opposed to the idea of "aggrandises." It is a welcome focus on the individual and on factionalisation that helps call into question another NWC stereotype, that the winter village was a unified social grouping or a collection of competing kin-ordered factions. This is useful to remember given that winter villages leave as residue the largest and most impressive middens.

relative to technology,[58] a stronger suggestion could be made that the transportation technology itself, along with the mobility patterns it both structures and is structured by, form an integral part of the landscape of habit. To return to Gosden:

> A humanly created world has the same dimensions as the physical world it occupies. It has extension in space and depth in time. Extension in space depends upon the regular movements that people make in carrying out tasks and maintaining social connections. . . . Movement and connection always have material dimension, depending on mode of transport and the use of material, including food to bind and divide groups. (Gosden 1995:807-08)

Arnold would embed transportation technology in a rearward projection of ethnographic culture. It might be more useful (initially at least) to see it embedded as one of the material correlates in a *habitus*. Indeed, the concept of the *habitus* explicitly defeats teleology (Bourdieu 1977:73). More concretely, as Gosden (1994:24) notes, the density, arrangement and connections between human groups underlies social life, arises from past social formation and helps create future formation. This echoes Conkey's point above, that part of environmental structuration is the differential deployment of personnel, a view that is virtually Time-Geographic/Giddensian. Watercraft, as movable material culture that facilitate further movement, can be seen as part of the built landscape, rather than as passive objects responding to human need. Indeed, they are movable parts of the environment, almost extensions of the body, and can easily be conceived of as technology that blurs the division between the body and the environment. Further, by defining the spatial extent and character of the landscape of habit, watercraft act as a bridge for the extension of the built environment to include the routinised patterns of mobility in a social geography of the archipelago. The notion of landscape should be extended

> so that landscapes and seascapes are considered jointly and seen to have different powers of separation and connection at varying periods of history. The sea is not necessarily a bridge or a barrier: it is what people make it. Just as the land can be made and remade by human influence, so can the sea. (Gosden and Pavlides 1994:170)

## 5.9 Conclusions: the maritime landscape of habitual action

The built environment matters to archaeological theory. The *habitus* can act as a unifying concept to link behaviour with the spatial patterning of material remains without implications of either deliberate optimisation or naïve totalisation of decision making. A foundation of the research that follows is that the vectors of mobility in the archipelago are knowable, and are important because,

> the fact that islands are always connected to other areas provides a challenge to the notion of landscape when applied to insular situations. Individual island landscapes respond to the network of connections in which they are enmeshed and the demands that these networks create. (Gosden and Pavlides 1994:169)

Unifying the lines of thought outlined in Chapters 3, 4 and 5 leads to a new and potentially useful approach combining social theory and network-analytic tools that can be implemented through a Geographic Information System. The next chapter introduces a case study that implements this theoretical approach.

---

[58]. For example, the directionality of the NWC environment is both "inverted" to some extent (transportation switches from sea to land), and fundamentally different (islands are inaccessible) in the absence of watercraft.

## CHAPTER 6—INTRODUCTION TO THE CASE STUDY

### 6.1 Introduction

The previous chapters have outlined the general theoretical direction of a research program designed to investigate the relationship between individual action, perception, and the physical environment. A unified language of discourse in which the environment is conceived as a network of places, routes, and vacancies helps bridge the gap between the individual and society. The distillation of practical activity across that network, as proximally measured by the density of shell midden accumulation, permits investigation of certain aspects of the landscape of habitual action. This chapter outlines how the research program is put into practice through iterative location-allocation modelling in a Geographical Information System (GIS). Discussion of certain aspects of the method and theory of GIS is followed by an introduction to the case study and the nature of the available data. Finally, the method and theory of location-allocation analysis is outlined, alongside its practical application to the case study. The results and discussion are mainly concentrated in the following chapter.

### 6.2 Geographical Information Systems and archaeological "tacking"

Geographical information systems were first developed in the 1960s by Canadian geographers (Martin 1990:29). Burrough (1986:6) defines a GIS as a "powerful set of tools for collecting, storing, retrieving at will, transforming and displaying spatial data from the real world for a particular set of purposes." Savage (1990a:23) suggests that the creation of new data via the transformation of existing data is what separates a GIS from a computer assisted mapping or drafting system. The spatial data entered into a GIS describes objects from the real world in terms of:

    (a) their position relative to an established co-ordinate system of any scale,

    (b) their attributes which are unrelated to their position, such as colour, elevation, cost, incidence of disease, or any other attribute measurable at any scale, and

    (c) the spatial interrelations between these objects, i.e. their topological relationship (after Burrough 1986:7).

In effect, then, a GIS functions as a relational database with the capability for graphical display and statistical analysis in which data are referenced to geographic co-ordinates (Curran in Martin 1991:45). Green (1990:4) suggests that GIS have been adopted by archaeologists because traditional methods of archaeological spatial analysis faced an intractable set of four problems:

    (a) statistics are difficult to use for describing and analysing continuous, spatial data,

    (b) spatial data often have no boundaries, so that classic set theory cannot be applied,

    (c) there are usually no known, inherent, internal partitions to enable the prior establishment of nested spatial units, and

    (d) traditional statistics are not equipped to deal with the simultaneous description and correlation of multiple forms over space.

Faced with these problems, a GIS offers both methodological solutions and theoretical feedback in the course of an archaeological analysis (Green 1990:4). Both Kvamme (1989:142-143) and Marble (1990:16-17) note that much of the value of a GIS is to speed both measurement and graphical display of spatial patterning, which can come from any source. Marble (1990) cites the example of the geographer Hägerstrand , who in the 1950s had a team of graduate students manually encode real and simulated spatial data cell by cell for an area of southern Sweden. Such an intensive effort could be reproduced in a matter of weeks on a small GIS, with superior results. Similarly, Carlstein's (1982) exhaustive work applying time-space "prisms" could translate into an interesting GIS-enabled approach (O'Kelly 1994:71), as could the transportation geography outlined by Lowe and Moryadas (1977). Marble's point is that a GIS is interactive because it is fast and provides feedback. This helps both exploratory data analysis and the development of hypotheses in a way strikingly reminiscent of Wylie's (1993) philosophical reflections on archaeological research.

Wylie (1993:23) proposes an analogy that scientific argument is more like a cable than a chain:

> The arguments used to evaluate incommensurable theories typically proceed not by a linear [link-by-link] movement from premises to conclusions or from individual 'facts' to generalisations, but rather by exploiting multiple strands and diverse types of evidence, data, hunches, and arguments.

Stabilisation, or what Hodder (1992) terms "coherence" of these sorts of argument, is then achieved by tacking back and forth between the theory and the data, with the latter giving a regular "reality check" and preventing the archaeologist from disappearing into either a nihilistic relativism or a model-induced virtual reality. Furthermore, on both sides of the tack there is what she calls "vertical tacking," reinforcing the strands of the argument-as-cable. It is here that the bridging argument outlined in the previous chapter is situated: a strand tacked in to connect two other strands (Ingold-Landscape (Ingold 1993) and Wobst-Network (Wobst 1976) on the theory side. As Wylie notes, the more of these strands the better:

> It is the independence of sources, and therefore of the constituent arguments about evidential significance, which

ensures that the strands of the resulting cables are not just mutually reinforcing, but are also, and crucially, mutually constraining. (Wylie 1993:25)

Thus, rather than condemning research projects that are, at least occasionally, "data driven," Wylie (perhaps making a virtue of a necessity) argues that tacking back and forth between theory and data leads to a gain in knowledge at each stage. Her position is based in a middle ground between objectivism and relativism (Wylie 1993:25). Essentially, this amounts to a stance of philosophical realism (cf. Bhaskar 1989; Gosden 1994:10-11): our complex presuppositions are not all-pervasive, but are tempered by the resistance of the data. Such resistance can occur, but does not necessarily occur, within a framework of formal hypothesis testing. It is a recognition of the non-plasticity and/or inconsistency of the data that provokes a corresponding willingness to re-examine core beliefs and suppositions and, by implication, acknowledges that there *is* a real world.

The research presented in this and the following chapters occurs mainly in the second stage of this process, in which a case study provides an external reality to challenge and provides a platform for a return tack to theory. The "core beliefs and assumptions" at hand[59] are those relating to environment and landscape and to the bridging arguments presented in Chapter 5. One object of the research is, therefore, to examine these core beliefs in a realist context. Kvamme's (1989) and Marble's (1990) conclusion that GISs are particularly suitable for exploratory data analysis also makes them particularly useful for implementing Wylie's generalised research philosophy. More specifically, a GIS-enabled spatial interaction analysis should be an iterative exercise that cycles back and forth from visualisation and analysis to the operating assumptions behind the model, an essential process that O'Kelly (1994:71) notes is often replaced by expressive, yet futile, "handwaving." Prior to discussing the specifics of this research orientation, it is useful to look briefly at three other relevant areas of theoretical debate in current archaeological applications of GIS.

## 6.3 GIS and the conception of the individual

Many spatial approaches either have a rule-bound, rational decision making individual as an input (e.g., Wobst 1976), or else seek to explain observed patterning of archaeological data in these terms (e.g., Renfrew 1973; Irwin 1985), and some GIS-based approaches are no exception (e.g., Maschner and Stein 1995). The arguments have been made in previous chapters why these models of

the individual are unsatisfactory. In this section I will look at some of the alternatives, with reference to GIS implementations.

Landscape approaches to prehistory may involve an explicit consideration of the perspective of individuals (e.g., Thomas 1993; Tilley 1994, Llobera 1996). In GIS-based implementations such an individual-centred approach may also be tendered, but with the attributes of the individual disguised. For example, cumulative viewshed analysis (e.g., Wheatley 1993, 1995) emphasises the intervisibility of monuments. The basic unit of visibility is, and can only be, what an individual human perceptor can see from any given vantage point, or, as more often formulated, the set of places from which a given point can be seen. Practitioners of such approaches hope to discover patterns of inter-visibility, which give clues to the cultural motivation for the siting or form of monuments (Gaffney *et al* 1995). The approach may be vulnerable to the charges of totalisation and the fallacies of the rule, as previously outlined, although it does hold promise for bypassing economic determinisms and trivial ecological associations, thereby accessing an emic cultural landscape. Furthermore, one advantage of such approaches might be the creation, through viewsheds or some other individual-centric approach, of a justifiable analytic region or scale of analysis which itself is independent of material culture, although it may be defined relative to monuments or other items of material culture. The importance of deriving such *a priori* spatial-analytic units should not be underestimated.

These approaches are clearly related to Renfrew's (e.g., 1994) cognitive-processual archaeology of the mind, a central tenet of which is that people's actions are patterned by belief. Through the archaeological study of the material correlates of these beliefs, inferences can be drawn about prehistoric cognition (cf. Gaffney *et al* 1995:51-61). The possibility remains open, however, that such individual-centred approaches can be improved by simultaneous consideration of such contextual factors as the landscape history; by more subtle models of technology, such as the *chaîne operatoire* (Leroi-Gourhan 1993); and, I would argue, by consideration of the constraints and freedoms offered by the interplay of environment and *habitus*.

While ambitious, this does not go as far as some researchers, who have argued for applications that seem unattainable. Stead (1995:314), for example, argues that "perception surfaces," representing past perceptual frameworks, "could be used to distort Cartesian maps into an ethnocentric map base for the study period and culture." In other words, Stead suggests maps could be "rubber-sheeted" to represent or fit specific cultural perceptions of the environment, such as a mariner's impression of the size and shape of the coastal environment, or other such "mental map" conceptions.

---

[59]. None of these could be said to be core beliefs for most Northwest Coast archaeologists.

## 6.4 GIS, environmental determinism and landscape history

For all their utility in analysing spatial problems, GISs perform rather poorly at explicitly accounting for temporal variation (Stead 1993:42). Most GISs employ multiple overlays at "snapshot" intervals to represent a sequence of events, analogous to a movie film. The number and interval of sequential time slices (frames) offers the illusion of movement through time. This presents the dual problems of oversimplification (via elimination of potential alternatives at any stage) and huge data storage and processing requirements with ensuing complexities.

Geographers are particularly concerned with temporal representation and modelling when investigating such phenomena as hourly or seasonal changes in resource use or distribution. Clearly, at the temporal scales usually employed in archaeology this may not be a problem as many kinds of archaeological data have insufficient temporal resolution to make the time-slice effect a problem. Stead (1993) suggests it might be possible to include a fourth variable when encoding for each data element, giving dimensions $x$, $y$, $z$ and $t$), and it is in this general direction that technical advances are being made (for a full discussion, see Langran 1993). Whether because of technical unsophistication or theoretical shortcomings, it is still the case that, as Martijn van Leusen summarises during his lively debate with Gaffney (Gaffney and van Leusen 1995:379), the time-slice effect of GIS crushes the landscape history into two dimensions, and "makes us forget about the previous history of the landscape and the fact that it is part of the living social system."

However, there is a solution to problems stemming from both a lack of explicit temporal data (which is unlikely to ever be satisfactorily solved in the archaeological case) and to technical shortcomings. The solution is to abandon the efforts to reproduce chronological time in a model and, instead, to *focus on aspects of the archaeological record which implicitly have a social temporality*. Normally, chronological control is difficult to attain over larger regions because, even in the relatively rare presence of multiple well-dated sites, fine scale (e.g., annual) contemporaneity or seasonality of site, use is difficult or impossible to demonstrate. Both contemporaneity and seasonality require considerable excavation and site interpretation, and, even then, missing data from unexamined, unknown or destroyed sites remains a problem. It is normal that there are many more known sites of unknown age than there are of known age: site location is easier to ascertain than site chronology. Since we have seen through the work of the time geographers that human spatial and temporal behaviour is inherently linked, there would be clear advantages for regional analysis in archaeology if such a linkage could be utilised for archaeological research. As outlined in Chapter 5, the concept of the built environment provides such a link by explicitly incorporating the spatiality of *habitus*, the temporality of the landscape and the archaeological record. In other words, the aim is neither a statistical description of a data set, nor a model of cognitive understanding of the environment (van Leusen 1995:380). Rather, this research accepts the compression of time at a shell midden as a cumulative sedimentation of general activity, and thus an inscription of how "social being" (Gosden 1994) builds the environment.

## 6.5 GIS, technological determinism, and archaeological research.

Archaeologists have usually worked with available spatial data sets. In particular, they have almost always worked, as this research does, with existing digitised map coverages or map sheets. The production of these sheets—planometric, elevation models, vegetation, drainage, and so forth—is vastly time consuming and expensive. In any case, it has usually already been done within other disciplines or by government agencies, such as geography, forestry, energy resource management, and so forth. Even in government, where there has been a great deal of interest in archaeological GIS as a tool for predictive modelling and site-record management, archaeologists have often worked under the umbrella of broader programs, using generic spatial data and adding such archaeological data as they already possess or actively seek in the course of their research. This has meant that GIS archaeologists have been, more than most archaeologists, consumers of data. Combined with their consumption of GIS technology, usually in a relatively off-the-shelf way, and with their utilisation of existing archaeological data, it is fair to say that, more than most fields of archaeological research, GIS in archaeology is a consumer of data, theory, and method. In all three areas, there is the possibility for unthinking or constrained adoption of inappropriate tools. For example, Kvamme (1995) notes the high price of top-end UNIX-based GIS platforms, software, and peripherals, implying this channels researchers into using cheaper desk-top systems such as IDRISI, which, with their fundamentally different data structures and capabilities, may influence the research design. Furthermore, analytic needs specific to archaeology may not be met by commercial packages, and the insignificant market that archaeologists represent to the manufacturers means their needs probably never will be met, except by customised programs. The archaeologist is thus forced to accept either a non-ideal analysis, or to delve further into the remote and abstract world of computer programming. This can, of course, have the positive benefit of detailed understanding, but is not an option open to all archaeologists who wish to implement a specific research program with a GIS, rather than implement a specific GIS-based research program. In contrast, Stead (1993:42) lists four current areas of research in which archaeological data are used that also advance general GIS method and theory. These are: diachronic studies, cost-surface analyses, cultural perceptions of the environment, and the problem of GIS "over precision" (cf. Claxton 1995).

This tendency towards technological determinism does not apply to the GIS-based attempt to implement the program set out in chapters 3, 4, and 5 for several reasons. First, the problem is inherently spatial, and not one in which the spatial aspects are given primacy because of a desire to use a GIS. This is obvious in the case of the discussion of environmental constraint and linearity, and locational approaches. These fall well within conventional geographical approaches and a GIS is self-evidently suitable for their investigation. Furthermore, it can be argued that key aspects of the temporality of the landscape, such as the paths, places and process of building, are more readily understood through their archaeological spatial components, in this case study because of the "knowability" of the landscape and the nature of shell midden sites. Space is treated as a unifying dimension for the purpose of a wider analysis of more varied topics, including individual behaviour, perception, mobility, and social practice. The GIS-space is not considered to be a necessary mapping of social space: in other words, the fallacy of the rule (descriptive geometry = generative geometry) is avoided. Second, and more specifically, the use of network and location-allocation analysis is primary. Arc/Info, a widely-used commercial Geographic Information System was chosen to implement the research design because it contained network and spatial interaction modules, rather than network analysis being performed simply because Arc/Info could do it. The conception or modelling of society as a network has a long history in social anthropology and archaeology (Firth 1951, Lesser 1961, Hannerz 1992, 1994; cf. Chapters 4 and 5), although its adoption here stems from its perceived utility as a novel way of implementing Ingold's programmatic papers on mobility and landscape, and unifying them with the environmental-constraint arguments previously reviewed. Arc/Info provides an ability to seamlessly combine the network of environmental constraint with the actual archaeological landscape. Other GIS programs would be unable to implement a network analysis themselves, while free-standing network analysis program modules such as UCINET (Borgatti and Freeman 1992) have no spatial analytic capability apart from the implied algebraic spatiality of a connectivity matrix. Finally, a GIS can be a very visually-oriented analytic tool, which has worked to its detriment: critics may disparage it as nothing but pretty pictures while practitioners may be seduced by the visual display possibilities of what may be otherwise sober and solid research (Kvamme 1995:6-7). Ideally, as Kvamme points out, formal statistical methods and visual presentation should be in parallel evidence, allowing a more rounded assessment of the research program. In the present research, the archipelago is understood as, and

represented by, a two-dimensional planimetry of continuous and discrete space, from which network features can be derived. Under these circumstances, nothing would be gained by illustrations which showed the network against, for example, the three dimensional digital elevation model of the study area, or some other visually striking but irrelevant construction.

**6.6 Outline of the case study**

The study area is located on the west coast of Vancouver Island, from Point Owen, immediately north of Port Renfrew, to the southwest corner of Kyuquot Channel (Figure 6.1). From south to north it includes the major topographical features of the Nitinat Lakes, Barkley Sound and Alberni Inlet, the Long Beach area, Clayoquot Sound, Flores Island, Hesquiat Harbour, Nootka Sound and associated fjords, and the Nuchatlitz Inlet/North Nootka Island areas (Figure 6.2). While the study area measures 250 km in length by 50-80 km in width, the length of coastline in the archipelago is much greater. The study area was chosen because it has seen considerable archaeological research, and so has a reasonably extensive record of archaeological sites. It also offers a varied topography of several archipelagic sound complexes connected by, or leading to, much more linear stretches of coastline or fjords. It is thus useful for examining the coastal properties outlined in Chapter 3.

There exists a substantial ethnographic record for this area, which will not be drawn on until the discussion. Major sources include Drucker (1951) and Arima (1983), while a recent summary is found in Arima and Dewhirst (1990). Summaries of the regional culture history include Mitchell (1990) and Matson and Coupland (1995), the latter also summarise a general Northwest Coast culture history.

The data used in this study are from two sources kept at the Archaeology Branch of the Province of British Columbia (AB): digitised base maps and an archaeological site inventory database. The former are produced by the Provincial government in the course of its overall resource management strategies. The latter derive from a number of separate archaeological survey projects, most notably, Haggarty (1982); Marshall (1993); Arcas Associates (1986; 1987); Mackie (1983); and McMillan and St. Claire (1982). A complete bibliography on disk, *Archaeological Field Research in British Columbia*, is available on demand from the AB, updated quarterly. Almost all of the references are to unpublished reports, theses and other grey literature. A series of digitised maps of the study area was provided by the AB. While notionally at a scale of 1:250,000, these maps have much better spatial resolution and accuracy than that suggests. They correspond to the Government of

Fig. 6.1 Study Area.

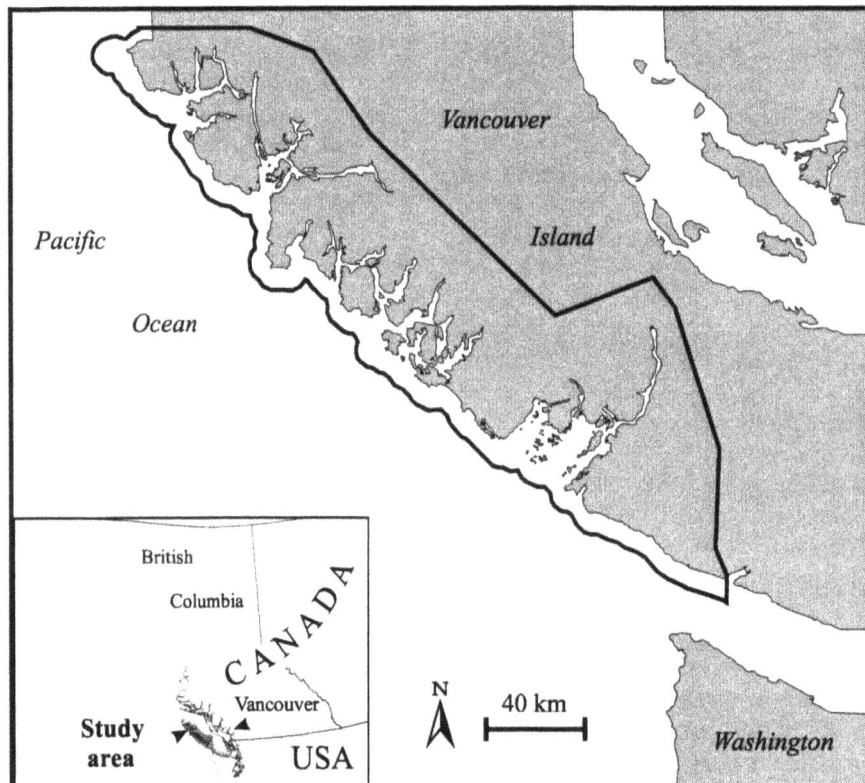

Fig. 6.2 Study area with major named regions as *per* Appendix A.

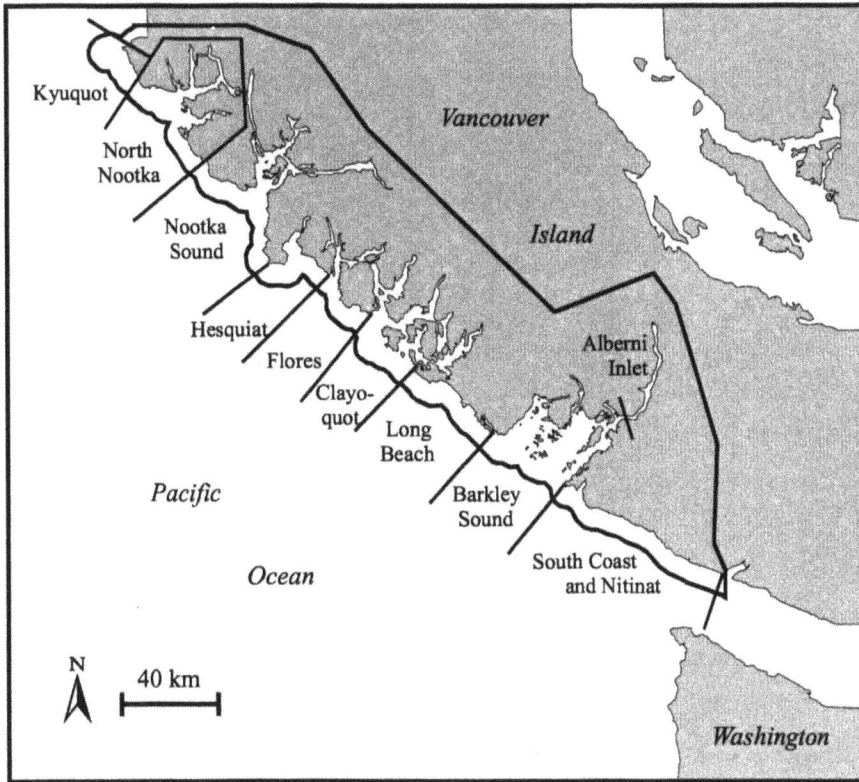

Canada sheets 92C, 92F, and 92E. Each digital mapsheet was composed of a number of separate layers. Of these, the coastline, island and archaeological site location layers were of the most use. Drainage, water body, and place name layers were used mainly for illustrative or referencing purposes. Other natural layers, such as vegetation and elevation, and modern feature layers, such as roads, towns, picnic areas, and so forth, were not used.

The archaeological site layer shows the sites as discrete point features, regardless of their actual polygonal size or shape. At the scale of analysis of this project, this is not considered to be a problem—the largest site is less than 500 metres in maximum diameter. Associated with this layer was minimal identifying information about each site, mainly the site record number and its map grid (latitude and longitude, and UTM) location. This layer was carefully corrected for errors and omissions against the site database (see below). In cases of discrepancies, third party sources or AB staff were consulted.

All the map sheets and layers were provided in digital format exported from the Arc/Info 6.1.1. geographical information software release. They were re-imported into Arc/Info release 7.0.3. running on a Silicon Graphics Indigo workstation operating under IRIX 5.3. The relevant mapsheets and layers of the map coverages were linked

together in a way suitable for this analysis. Some features, such as mudflats, were manually eliminated, and some cleaning of false polygons and dangling vertices was performed. Control reference was to paper copies of the appropriate hydrographic charts, which provide a highly accurate rendition of the coastline and coastal features.

Much more information about each site was contained in a separate database. These data are originally derived from a multitude of different archaeological projects, including the major surveys noted above and many minor surveys or informal recordings. The database is maintained by the Archaeology Branch as part of a nation-wide archaeological site record, the Canadian Heritage Information Network (CHIN). CHIN data are a subset of data held in the site record files at the AB. Some important information is missing from CHIN, notably site maps and photographs. The information taken from CHIN was in the form of a text file that could be imported into commercial spreadsheet or database programs.

The quality of information on CHIN is variable, reflecting the original site recording process. Some sites are extremely thoroughly recorded, while others have little more than site type and location. Furthermore, in terms of spatial exhaustiveness, the site record for the study area is by no means complete (see Eldridge and Mackie 1993 for a general discussion of the quality of the British Columbia archaeological site inventory). Nevertheless, taken together, the site location and attribute information form a remarkable and surprisingly comprehensive data source for this lengthy stretch of coastline which is, after all, mainly remote and inaccessible. Relevant problems in the site inventory will be discussed further below.

The combination of digitised maps, archaeological site location and a database of archaeological site information enabled the use of a geographic information system. The system chosen as most suitable was Arc/Info, described below.

## 6.7 Implementation of the case study

The following sections describe the GIS, and the data used in the case study.

### 6.7.1 Arc/Info and the Geographic Information System

Arc/Info is a commercially produced software for use in a Geographic Information System. A non-technical (if dated) description of its basic features is given in Peuquet and Marble (1990). Mainly designed to run on UNIX and related workstations, a DOS version is also available, which is considerably less powerful. A fully capable version of Arc/Info 7 is forthcoming for high-end Pentium PCs. Arc/Info is the most comprehensive and versatile of GIS software packages, having sophisticated modules for both vector (point-line) and raster (grid) data formats. Importantly for the goals of this research, it has an advanced ability to handle both graph-theoretic topologic matrix structures (networks, route systems and dynamic segmentation) and spatial interaction models (including the family of gravity models and location-allocation analytic tools). Such analyses can therefore be done in a cartographic setting, rather than in a non-graphic mathematical matrix, which aids intuition, exploratory data analysis, error correction, and the cross-checking of results. Drawbacks to this software include expensive licensing and system requirements, a difficult user interface and an idiosyncratic terminology that is at odds with most GIS packages.

### 6.7.2 Data: description and pre-processing

The following sub-sections describe the derivation of the data used in this study, and some steps taken to make it suitable for the questions at hand.

*Midden Definition.*

Sites in CHIN are classified into a number of different site types, arranged hierarchically in a format delimited by commas and semi-colons. Thus a single place in the landscape may be categorised as: "general purpose, habitation, shell midden; resource procurement, tree, bark strip; petroform, canoe skid." Each of these features may have a different site number, or, they may all be subsumed under a single site number. The AB site management

process has recently seen steps taken to increase the consistency of site type assignment and site designation, mainly by splitting complex, multi-purpose sites into separately numbered single feature sites, which may have overlapping boundaries. Nevertheless, it was possible to read through the complete CHIN file for each of the sites within the study area, selecting all those with any shell midden component, regardless of whether this was the recorded primary site type or was merely noted in a memo or other field.

All sites with a shell midden component were included in the general category of "shell midden." Inevitably, this may have included some special purpose sites, such as lookouts, defensive sites, or shell processing stations. Similarly, some general purpose sites may well have been eliminated, such as lithic scatters and inter-tidal sites, not to mention all the general activity sites which do not lead to lasting material remains. It was felt that, apart from the reasons for focusing on shell middens discussed in Chapter 5, consistency of comparability was gained by limiting the study to shell middens. For example, whether compared with each other or to shell middens, the site areas of fishtraps, rock art, burials and lithic scatters are probably irrelevant in terms of intensity of use of the landscape. A different research program could doubtless be devised which included all site types, but it might well have difficulty using simple site area as a meaningful variable.

*Midden Clustering Procedure.*

Site definition and the meaning of the notion "site" is of widespread concern in archaeology, and is at the core of both landscape and off-site archaeology (e.g., Foley 1981, Dunnell 1992, Binford 1992). Many of the shell middens were extremely close together, yet were officially designated as separate sites on the basis of discontinuous deposits. Others were large, but there was no record of sufficient testing to establish continuity of deposit across the entire area designated as "site." In order to mitigate this problem, individual shell midden sites were joined together into shell midden "site areas." The methodology used to determine midden zone areas was to buffer each site (which are represented as a point, regardless of their actual size) with a circle of 500m radius. All sites with intersecting buffers were then considered as a single midden zone, within which the areas of included single shell midden was totalled into a measure of cumulative midden area. In many cases, no other sites fell within the buffer zone, while in one extreme case, 46 sites chained together to create a macro cluster area. These data are summarised in Appendix A. The result was to reduce the number of sites from 576 individual middens to 238 midden zones. This was desirable not just because it simplified the network, but because to some extent it reduced the emphasis on the notion "site." In other words, since the shell middens are all to one degree or another "general purpose" sites, the effect of the buffering was to identify zones of general purpose activity within the archaeological landscape.

Although some of these zones contain only a single site, they are still comparable as the usefully ambiguous concept of "general activity" dissolves the intra-site:inter-site dichotomy.

Finally, the centroids of the polygons produced by the intersecting buffer zones were calculated, and were used as nodes for the site network (see Figure 6.3, p. 48). In zones with a single site, the centroid node was, by definition, the same as the site location, while in zones with multiple sites, the centroid could be in a non-site location, including locations on the water or inland.

*Shell Midden Site and Zone Areas.*
Of the 576 known shell midden sites in the study area, site area is known for 526. The missing values are mainly due to incomplete site recording or site destruction. In some of these cases, a qualitative assessment of the site size is possible. For example, some site records note that there are multiple house platforms present (suggestive of large size), while others employ qualifiers suggestive of small size, such as "pocket midden." While these are suggestive, the site area of these sites was left coded as "unknown" and such qualitative assessments are only referred to in relevant discussion. When gathered into site cluster areas with the procedure described above, 21 of the 238 midden zones have no areal data (Appendix A).

For consistency, all site areas were taken from the CHIN database site area field. This field is calculated by multiplying length times width, taking no account of the shape of the site polygon, i.e., whether it is trapezoidal, curved, or otherwise irregular. In some cases this field was manually calculated from CHIN length and width data. Further information was sometimes available in archaeological reports. While in some cases this may objectively have been more accurate, it was also certainly less consistent, reflecting the idiosyncrasies of individual recorders, some of whom calculate site area without obvious reference to length and width. In any case, accurately recording the size of a shell midden is a difficult task on the Northwest Coast, requiring considerable shovel testing and soil probing (often through deep, root-laden overburden), and usually performed in conditions of dense, vinous undergrowth (see Mackie 1986 on coastal survey techniques, and Stein (1992) or Claassen (1991) on shell midden structure and taphonomy).

### 6.8 Establishment of a network of sites

As argued in Chapter 3, the highly constrained physical topography of the Northwest Coast means that the shape of the prehistoric transportation environment is, in the main, knowable. Following from this, and assuming the existence of watercraft, the spatial relations between the midden zones can be schematically represented as shortest-path distances across the water. In linking the zones together

this manner a network is created, enabling the application of network analytic tools to the topological relations between sites.

The method of linking the zones was simple, but entailed some unavoidable applications of judgement. All zones are joined to all others, at least through intervening ones. In other words, any two midden zones are linked by one or more paths, and so the network is described as "connected" (Wilson 1984:4). The nodes of the network are midden zone centroids (single sites or clustered sites), while the vertices are routes connecting zones with each other, and so the network describes the travel space of midden-oriented general activity. No limit was placed on the number of vertices that could join a node. Direct connections were made between sites unless an indirect path via another site did not appear to be significantly shorter. Such decisions were made by judgmental assessment, as some sites had many possible path combinations and it was not possible to qualitatively assess each permutation. However, in most cases, it was obvious which links should be added. Unlike Bell *et al*'s (1988) case study, there were no external indicators of how the network might be structured,[60] nor direct evidence in the form of built roads. Nor was there evidence for which direct routes might be absent, unlike Milicic's (1993) case study, in which historic trading and parish records were used to build a network model of the Venetian period Dalmatian archipelago. In the absence of such direct evidence (which, in any case, runs the risk of building circularity into the model), the simple procedure used in this case study is the most defensible. Overall, the site network is a reasonable and internally consistent schematic representation of the spatial relationships between sites. The whole network and its details are shown in Figures 6.4, 6.5 and 6.6 to give an idea of its construction. Figures 7.9 - 7.16 (pp. 69-72) also show the whole network. The vertices of the network are measured in metres and kilometres. If reliable data existed on average speed of travel by canoe, it would be a trivial task to convert the units of measurement into minutes, hours and days, thus transforming the network into a schematic of "travel time space" (Bell *et al* 1988; Gorenflo and Gale 1990), assuming that all units of distance were traversed in the same units of time. It is more reasonable and cautious to assume the isotropic planarity of the water surface than to enter into a (necessarily difficult) assessment of relative difficulty of movement, as dictated by wind, tide, distance from shore. Such assessments of prehistoric seamanship and perception would be arguable at best and, in any case, would likely even out at the scale of analysis employed in this study. If the isotropy of travel over water is accepted, then travel time and distance are linearly related, and only require calibration vis-à-vis each other.

---

[60]. Spanish Colonial maps showed that large centres were more directly connected to each other than simple topology would indicate. Further, they used a formula to relate land slope to walking speed in order to calculate travel time, a refinement not necessary in the current study.

Fig. 6.3 Detail of creation of the site network. Shaded circles are site buffers which define midden zones; dot represents the centroid of those zones which is used as the node for network creation.

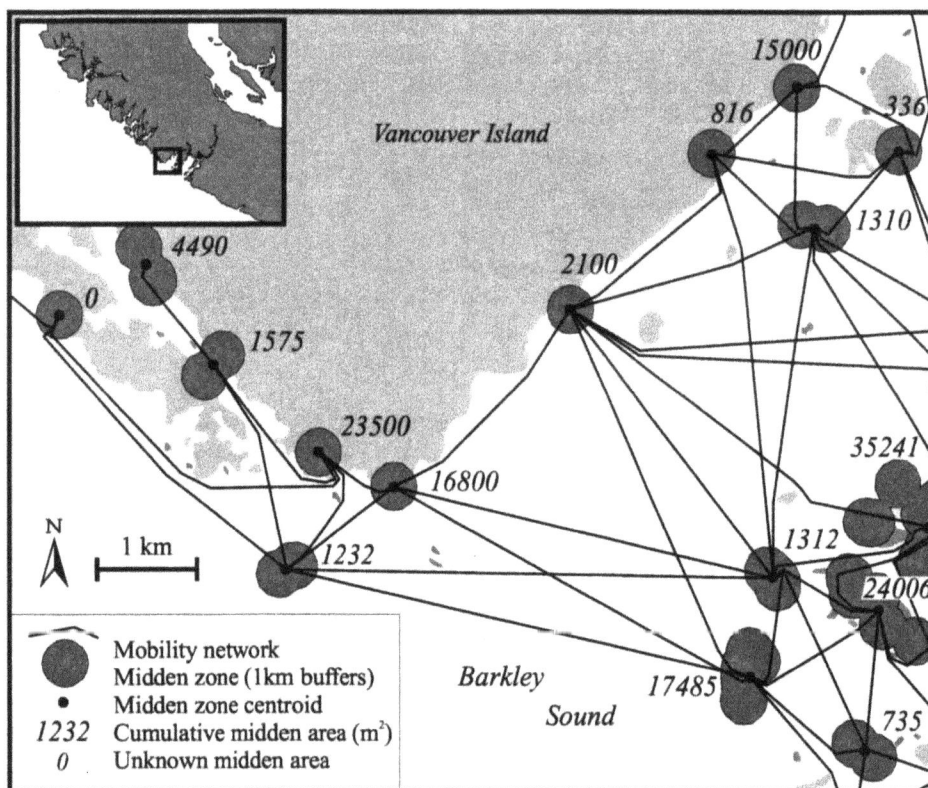

Fig. 6.4 Detail of the north area of the site network.

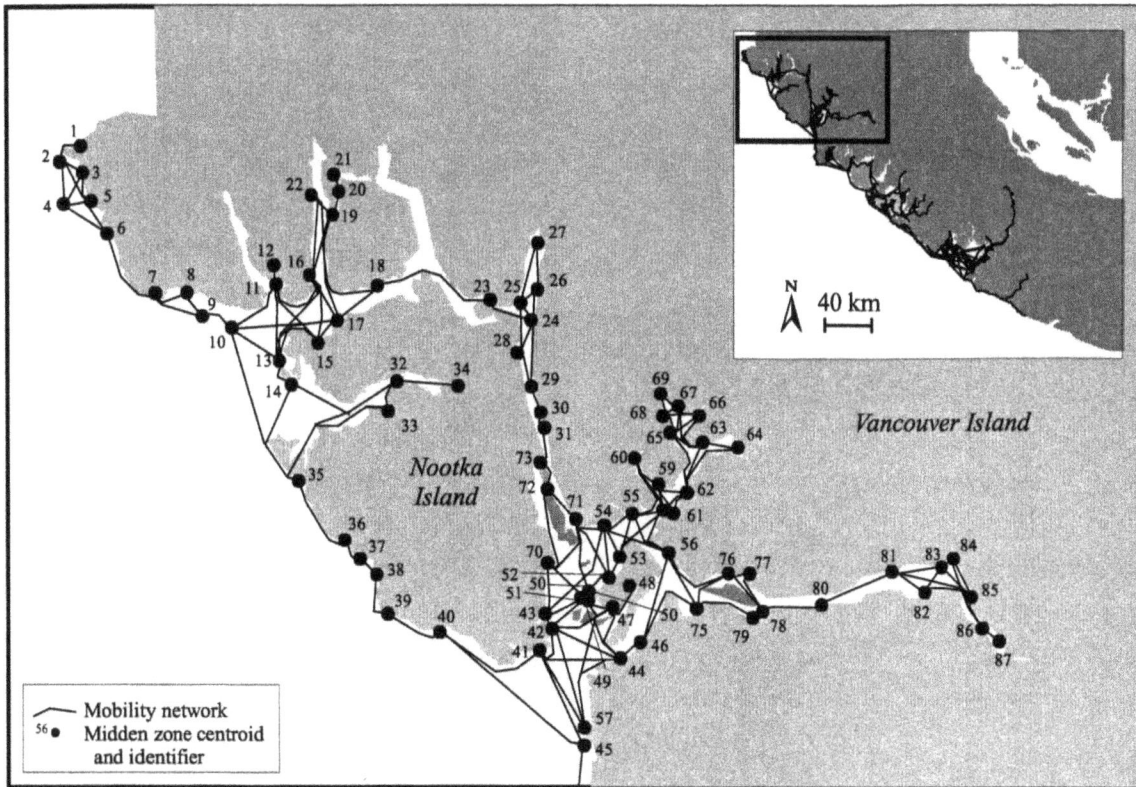

Fig. 6.5 Detail of the central area of the site network.

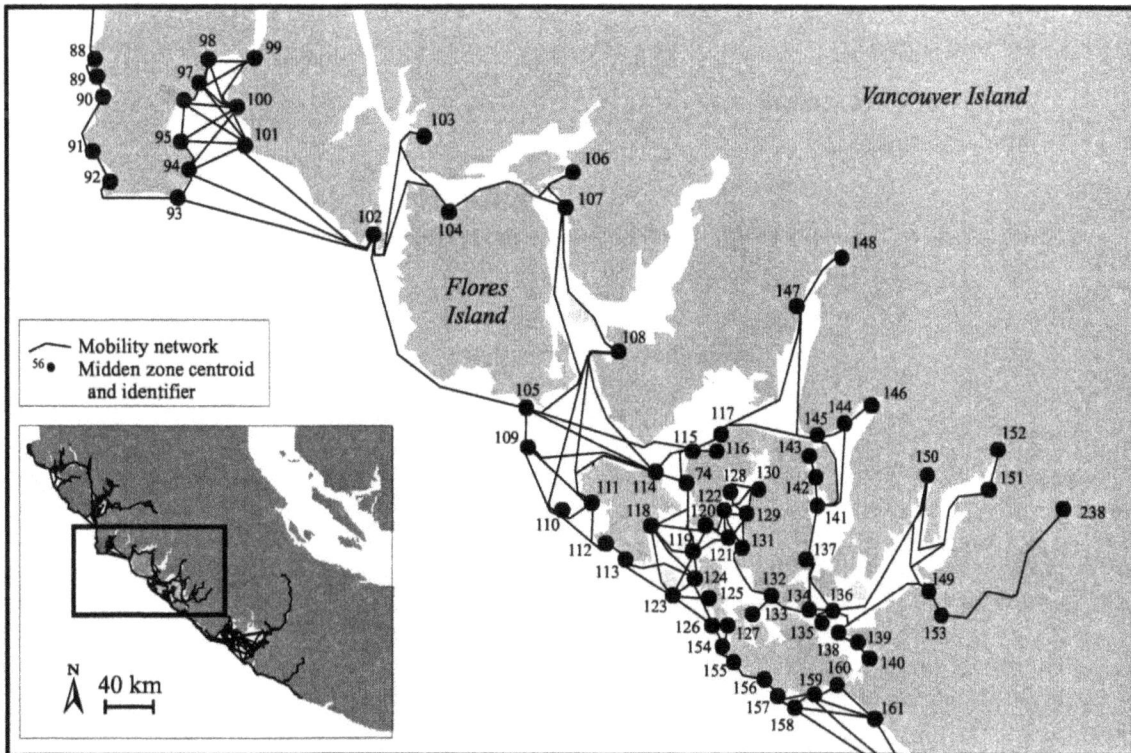

Fig. 6.6 Detail of the south area of the site network

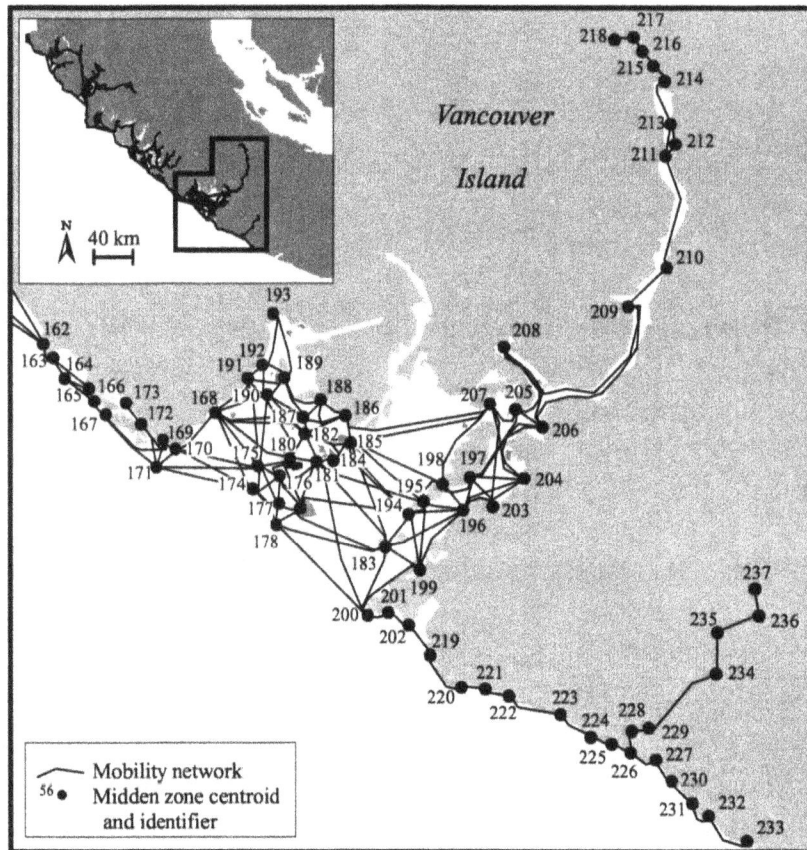

## 6.9 Location-allocation analysis

The following sections discuss location-allocation analysis and its implementation in the present study.

### 6.9.1 Introduction

Location-allocation is a type of spatial interaction analysis. Spatial interaction methods minimally deal with at least pairs of points or areas in space between which there is posited to be some sort of flow of people, goods or information (Bailey 1994). The most commonly used general spatial interaction model is the family of gravity models (Haynes and Fotheringham 1984). These were widely used in geography and archaeology on an intuitive, "even metaphysical" (Tobler and Wineburg 1971:40), basis before being theoretically justified as the general solution to an entropy maximisation problem (Bailey 1994:34-35). In the gravity model, interaction between pairs of points or places is related to both their relative sizes and their relative distance apart. It is important to realise that size and distance do not necessarily have to be physical mass nor linear distance, but can refer to

population, capital, goods, cognitive (perceived) distance, distance expressed as travel time, even frequency of place names (Tobler and Wineburg 1971).

Location-allocation analysis was developed to help solve site selection problems in the public and private economic sector for facilities such as retail outlets, schools, fire stations and medical facilities; namely, in situations where an organisation needs to obtain the most efficient distribution of a system of facilities according to various (market or non-market) criteria. For example, rules can be applied, such as: no child should live more than two kilometres from a school; no house should be more than five minutes from a fire-hall; or hamburger outlets should be optimally sited with reference to lunch-time traffic. The unique aspect of location-allocation is the ability to solve the problem for *all* facilities in the system at the *same* time (despite using pair-wise comparisons), thus incorporating the *inter*dependence of central places with each other into the solution. For example, the location of one school or one fire-hall necessarily affects the potential location of all others.

In location-allocation modelling, a set of points or places is assigned to a centre or to a set of inter-dependent centres in a way that optimises some objective function, such as minimisation of total distance travelled from places to centres. The process is described in more detail below, in which reference is to the simplest model, the $p$-median, used in this analysis. The following terminology is employed, which reflects the model's origins in modern retail, service, and transportation geography. Terminology is given for the network implementation of location-allocation, which can also be implemented for a continuous surface.

### 6.9.2 Terminology used in location-allocation analysis

An origin node is a node on the network that contains the potential for interaction with a centre. This might be a household with a quantified desire to purchase hamburgers or a certain number of school-age children; or it might be a more abstractly defined notion, such as "potential for interaction" (ESRI 1995). In this case study, the midden zones are the origin nodes. As records of general human activity, they are witnesses to actual interaction. In the location-allocation model, their only attribute of interest is their location on the network.

The simplest implementation is that all origin nodes contain the same potential for interaction, i.e., potential interaction is homogenous across the network nodes, influenced only by relative separation. This is equivalent to asserting that, for example, all households had an equal desire to buy hamburgers. The possibility exists to weight the potential by some external variable: survey data might show that residents of some areas purchased more hamburgers, and this could affect the location of the hamburger restaurant. While in some archaeological applications such weighting might be possible (see Bell *et al* (1988) for such an example), in this study of prehistoric general-purpose activity location, no such variable was considered plausibly knowable. Thus, potential interaction is unweighted and equal across the network, except as affected by distance.

A candidate node is a node on the network deemed suitable for the possible location of a centre (see below). In retail or other contemporary implementations, criteria such as zoning laws, unsuitable infrastructure and other logistics will rule out some locations. Thus, of many vacant lots in a city, one subset may be considered suitable for locating a school, while another (likely different) subset may be suitable for a recycling facility. An external-criterion-free implementation is used in this study: all origin nodes are also candidates for the designation as a centre. In most applications in prehistoric contexts there will be little or no *a priori* knowledge of what external criteria might apply, although the identification of such criteria is itself a major topic of research through predictive modelling (for Northwest Coast examples, see Maschner and Stein 1995; Beattie 1995; Eldridge and Mackie 1993).

A centre node (usually referred to in the location-allocation literature as a "facility," occasionally as a "destination node") is either a fixed candidate, or a mobile candidate chosen on the basis that it optimises the objective function. In the case of a single-centre solution in the $p$-median model, the candidate node that minimises the total distance travelled across the network will be selected. In the case of a two-centre solution, the chosen candidates will be those which together minimise this objective function, and so forth. It can be seen that centres will influence each other's location, and that centrality is thus measured *relatively*.

In the process of solution, mobile candidates are free to either enter the solution set, or not to enter it. Whereas fixed candidates *must* be part of the solution, non-candidates are, of course, unable to be designated as centre nodes. Fixed candidates are used in applications where some facilities already exist. For example, given the existence of nine hamburger outlets in a city, location-allocation can find an optimal location for a tenth. In such an application, the nine existing restaurants would be designated as fixed candidates, while the set of suitable places for the tenth outlet would be designated mobile candidates, and the optimally located one of these would be chosen according to its maximising properties relative to the objective function. A similar process could be used to simulate prehistoric colonisation or other landscape in-filling processes, as discussed in the next chapter.

The objective function summarises the goal of the formula used by the location-allocation model. It incorporates the objective (such as to minimise distance or to maximise coverage) and any constraints. For example, the objective function of the $p$-median model, used throughout this study, is to minimise the total distance between all origin nodes and a set of centres (Hillsman 1984). Put another way, it is to determine the location of a designated number, $p$, of centres, such that the total distance between origin nodes and these centres is minimised (ESRI 1995). All origin nodes must be assigned to a centre. This process can be visualised as a method of calculating all the possible paths between all the origin nodes, and then finding the unique combination of centres that together maximise the objective function. By contrast, another model, the maximal covering model, determines the location of a designated number of centres such that the number of origin nodes within a certain distance threshold of the centres is maximised. Not all origin nodes need be covered. One can visualise this model as the process of placing a designated number of disks of a pre-determined diameter over a set of nodes, shifting them around until the maximum possible number of nodes are covered.[61] This model has seen occasional use in archaeology (Bell *et al* 1985, Church and Bell 1988, Bell and Church 1987 and 1988; Steponaitis

---

[61]. The distance covered by the disks would, in a network application, be measured along the network paths, and thus the disks wouldn't be round in the normal sense of the word.

1978). Other models include various permutations of constrained, nested, distance-powered, distance-decayed versions of the above, and attendance models. All of these require *a priori* constraints (e.g., non-linear distance effects or ascribed catchment radii) as inputs; in a prehistoric archaeological application these constraints will necessarily involve argument. While the *p*-median model is certainly not assumption free, it is based on much more general principles of least effort and entropy maximisation, and not on case-specific constraints imposed by the investigator. Mathematically, all of these models ultimately devolve to the *p*-median model (Hillsman 1984:307). Nevertheless, they have quite different assumptions, require different input knowledge sets and produce markedly different solutions.

### 6.9.3 The *p-median* and other location-allocation models

The *p-median* problem is solved in Arc/Info by the following formula (ESRI 1995):

$$\text{Min } Z = \sum_{i=1}^{n} \sum_{j=1}^{m} w_i * d_{ij} * x_{ij}$$

subject to the following constraints:

1. $\sum_{j=1}^{m} y_j = p$ : restricts the number of centre nodes to *p*.

2. $\sum_{j=1}^{m} x_{ij} = 1, \forall i$ : ensures that every origin node *i* is served.

3. $y_j \geq x_{ij}, \forall i, \forall j$ : node *i* can assign only to *j* if there is an open centre node at *j*.

4. $y_j = 0,1, \forall j$ : centre node location decision variable.

5. $x_{ij} = 0,1, \forall i, \forall j$ : allocation decision variable

where:

$i$ = location of origin node
$j$ = location of candidate centre
$n$ = number of origin nodes
$m$ = number of candidate centres
$p$ = number of central nodes to locate
$w_i$ = weight at origin node *i*
$d_{ij}$ = shortest distance between origin *i* and candidate *j*
$y_i$ = 1, if facility is located at site *j*
   = 0 otherwise
$x_{ij}$ = 1, if demand location *i* is served by a facility at site *j*
   = 0 otherwise

The solution set is found from Arc/Info with the command LOCATEALLOCATE. Before this command can be issued there are a large number of steps necessary to make operational this procedure, such as constructing network topology, creating centres files, and assigning candidature. These cannot be detailed here without recapitulating the

manual and introducing an immense technical vocabulary specific to Arc/Info. One technical point of interest to anyone contemplating applying this analysis is that Arc/Info uses heuristics to find the total set of shortest paths. Computation of actual shortest paths on a network (the "travelling salesman problem") is a computationally intensive problem, used to test, and even to calibrate, super-computers. Heuristics give a comparable solution to over 98% accuracy, but in a fraction of the time (ESRI 1995; cf. Hillsman 1984). However, the program that implements the default heuristic (not the heuristic code itself) in Arc/Info 7.0.3. is faulty, and will not accept a mix of fixed and mobile candidature. For consistency it is therefore necessary to use an optional, and equally accurate (ESRI 1995), heuristic, but this means the procedure cannot be run through Arc/Info's graphic menu interface. This problem may be fixed in future Arc/Info releases.

### 6.9.4 Previous uses of location-allocation in archaeology

As noted, location-allocation was developed within the context of modern spatial decision-making and there is a wide literature covering geographical examples (ESRI 1995). Archaeological examples are much less common (see Steponaitis 1978; Bell and Church 1985; Bell *et al* 1988; Gorenflo and Bell 1992; Church and Bell 1988). This is presumably because many permutations of location-allocation analysis require data that are not readily available in archaeological case studies, whether because detailed cultural motives or practices cannot be reliably summarised, or because there may be insufficient relevant locational data. A good example is an archaeological analysis of the Aztec Period Basin of Mexico (Bell *et al* 1988), which mixes archaeological, ethnohistoric, historic and experimental data to build a model of subsistence and information flow.

### 6.9.5 Summary of the application

The site network defines the basic inter-site topology. All shell midden zones have the same potential to be chosen as a central place, and any number of nodes can be assigned to any central place. The application is not concerned with differential "demand" across the network, nor with the capacity of central places to meet that demand. Both of these factors are assumed to be constant. Rather, the application, finds subsets of the midden zones that are "centrally located." The definition of centrality is a quantifiable measure of the total network distance-minimising properties of the location, a measure that, furthermore, includes optimisation relative to other central places.

As there is no prior reason to assume that any given number of central places within the study area is the "right number," the application was run iteratively for different numbers of central places. In this application, an iteration is a solution set for a given number of centres. If all origin nodes are mobile candidates, then the solution set is said to be optimal, and will constitute a descriptive geometry of centrality. If some of the candidates are fixed, then the solution set is termed sub-optimal.

Midden area within the midden zones (origin nodes) does not enter the calculation of centrality. Cumulated midden area, as a measure of intensity of site use (Maschner and Stein 1995) can therefore be held as a dependent variable, against which the solution sets can be compared to see if there is a relationship between a location-allocation solution set of interdependent centres and the intensity of the use of these central places.

## 6.10 Conclusions: site networks, location-allocation models, and the archaeology of archipelagos

The spatial relationships between sites within the study area can be represented as a network, which provides a quantified, schematic representation of the structure of some aspects of prehistoric general-activity. Location-allocation is a potentially useful procedure for partitioning the region-wide general activity into any number of sub-regions, based on travel distance. These partitions consist of a subset of the midden zones. One midden zone in each partition is identified as a central place, based on its distance-minimisation centrality. In the following chapter, more detail on these solution sets of central places will be introduced, and further characteristics of the midden zones will be discussed.

## CHAPTER 7—RESULTS AND DISCUSSION

### 7.1 Introduction

Locational and attribute data on 1,069 archaeological sites — including 576 shell middens — from the study area described in Chapter 6 were entered in a Geographic Information System. Due to the constrained and directional topography of the study area a justifiable set of mobility/transportation links between the sites could be established, thereby forming a site network. The topological relationships between the shell middens were analysed using the $p$-median location-allocation (spatial interaction) model. It was found that some solution sets of sites (identified as central sites in terms of distance minimisation) were significantly larger than expected. Features of this model and the resulting sets are discussed in depth, and conclusions are drawn concerning scale of analysis. Further discussion follows in which the result is explained as an example of the utility of incorporating social theories of the *habitus* and the built environment in order to avoid the totalising fallacies of the rule. This result is then placed into a wider archaeological context in Chapter 8.

### 7.2 Implementation and results of the case study

The case study employs the following methodology. Twenty-five iterations of the $p$-median location-allocation model were run on the site network to find optimal solution sets for one centre node through 25 such nodes. Outputs were converted from native Arc/Info IRIX format to spreadsheet (Microsoft Excel) files for analysis. All origin nodes were equal in their potential for interaction. The areas of midden zones were not an input in the model and thus had no influence on the choice of centre nodes. Similarly, all candidate nodes were considered to have an unlimited ability to accommodate interaction to them, regardless of their area or any other attribute of the known archaeological record at that node. The model resembles simple non-hierarchical partitive spatial clustering procedures in that the solution set of central nodes is chosen which best minimises total distance "travelled" across the network, unaffected by the characteristics of origin or central nodes, nor by any distance exponent other than 1 (ESRI 1995). It is thus similar to k-means clustering, except clusters form in a network topology rather than in a multidimensional attribute space, and it is the cluster centroids (central places) which are of most immediate interest, rather than cluster membership. As in k-means, the investigator asks for a certain number of clusters, and the procedure creates them whether or not they truly exist (Shennan 1988). Caution in the interpretation of any particular solution set is therefore essential. Patterning or trends exposed by multiple iterations of the model under different parameters are assessed (cf. Shennan 1988; Orton 1980; Hillsman 1984; Bell and Church 1985; Church and Bell 1988), or the resultant clusters are validated according to external criteria. The procedure followed in the current study is further discussed in the following paragraphs.

In each iteration there was no constraint on which origin nodes (midden zones) could be considered as potential centre nodes. That is, all demand locations were also candidate locations, and were designated as mobile candidates in all runs. Each set of selected centres was then compared to the data on cumulative site area within the midden zones. The results are shown in Appendix B and graphically as Figure 7.1 (p. 55). In the latter, the X-axis records the number of centres asked for in the iteration. The Y-axis shows the averaged site areas of the selected set of chosen centre nodes. Thus, the first symbol on the left shows that in a single centre node solution (Iteration #1), a midden zone with an area of 46,376 square metres is chosen. In the following iteration, two midden zones with an average size of 6,816 square metres are chosen, and so on. Each solution set is optimal in respect of simple distance-minimisation, and there is no necessary carry-over of selected sites between iterations, although such carry-over is free to occur, and does occur. Figures 7.9 through 7.15 (pp. 69-72) show the solution sets for one, three, and five through nine centres, respectively. Figure 7.16 (p. 71) shows all midden zones selected at least once in the 25 iterations.

While Figure 7.1 is visually persuasive, the result needs to be assessed in terms of statistical significance. Table 7.1 (p. 58) and Figure 7.2 (p. 55) show the results of the test of significance on the set of iterations. Student's $t$-test was used, but, because the sample is not drawn from a population with a normal distribution, the values for the midden area were converted to their natural logarithms. This approximately normalises the log-normal distribution of midden zone areas (Appendix A, Figures A1-A3) and allows the use of a parametric difference-of-means test such as Student's $t$ (Mueller *et al.* 1977:399, 434; Shennan 1988:108-113). The lowest gridline on Figure 7.2 is the 0.05 threshold of statistical significance, and so solution sets which fall below this line are statistically significant in terms of the average size of the selected central midden zones. The symbols track increasing iterations from left to right, thus the leftmost symbol represents Iteration #1 (the solution for a single centre), and so forth. It can be seen that the selection of Midden Zone 74 as the single set is statistically significant, despite it consisting of only a single case. The implications of this are discussed below. More interesting is the sequence of significant results from the solution set of five centres through the solution set of nine centres. After the solution set for nine centres and thereonwards, the $p$-median model does not produce sets of middens which are significantly larger than might be

Fig. 7.1    Results of 25 iterations of the location-allocation model.  Each symbol represents the averaged area of the midden zones selected within each solution set.

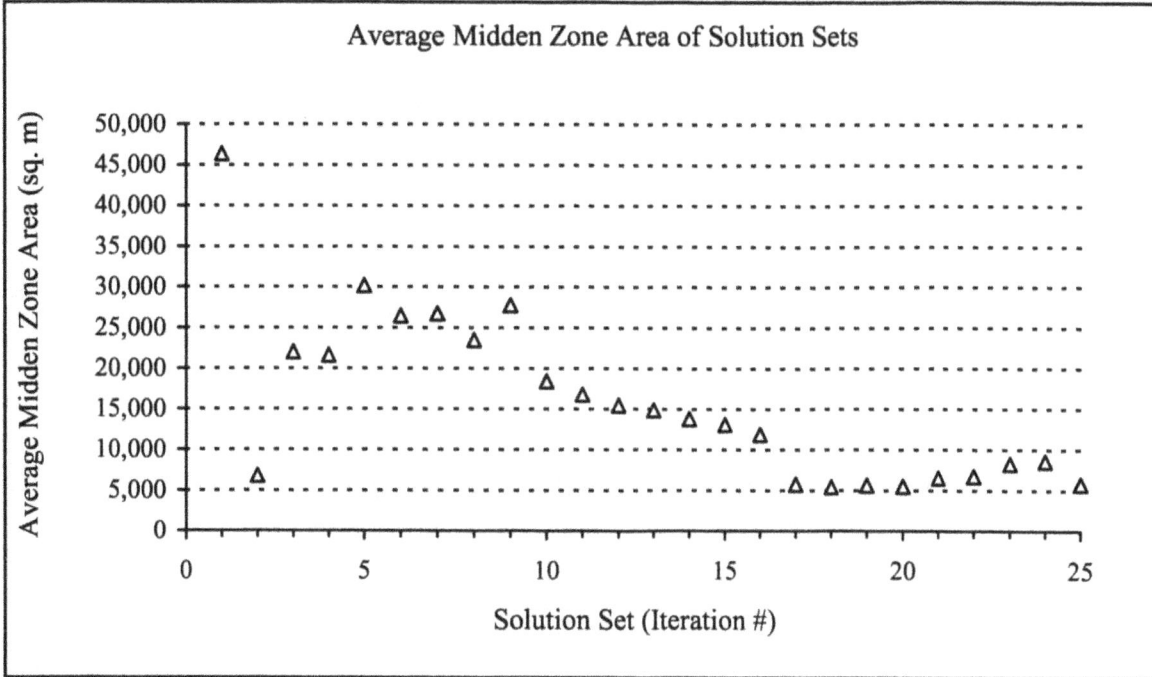

## Average Midden Zone Area of Solution Sets

Average Midden Zone Area (sq. m)

50,000
45,000
40,000
35,000
30,000
25,000
20,000
15,000
10,000
5,000
0

0        5        10        15        20        25

Solution Set (Iteration #)

Fig. 7.2    Plotted tests of significance of size of Solution Set midden zones.  Calculated using Student's t-test, values given in Table 7.1.  All sets where $p < 0.05$ (lowest grid line) are statistically significant.

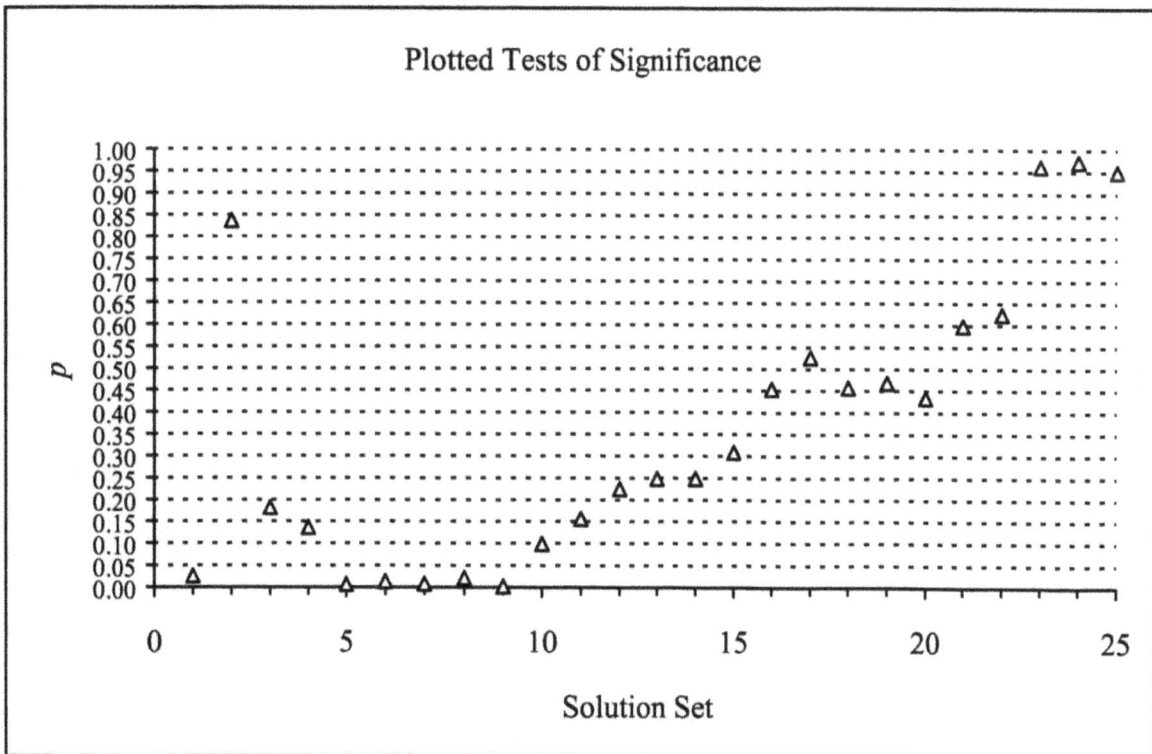

## Plotted Tests of Significance

$p$

1.00
0.95
0.90
0.85
0.80
0.75
0.70
0.65
0.60
0.55
0.50
0.45
0.40
0.35
0.30
0.25
0.20
0.15
0.10
0.05
0.00

0        5        10        15        20        25

Solution Set

expected by chance alone, although it does continue to select some large middens. It is my contention that these five sets bracket a scalar property of the cultural environment, the nature of which will be discussed further below. By comparison, Figure 7.3 (below) shows the results of a 25-step iteration in which Midden Zones were chosen at random. While this is only a single set of random iterations, it does illustrate how far the actual result deviates from a chance occurrence.

Fig. 7.3 Results of 25 iterated solution sets chosen at random. Each symbol represents the averaged areas of the midden zones selected within each solution set. Note the lack of patterning compared to Fig. 7.1.

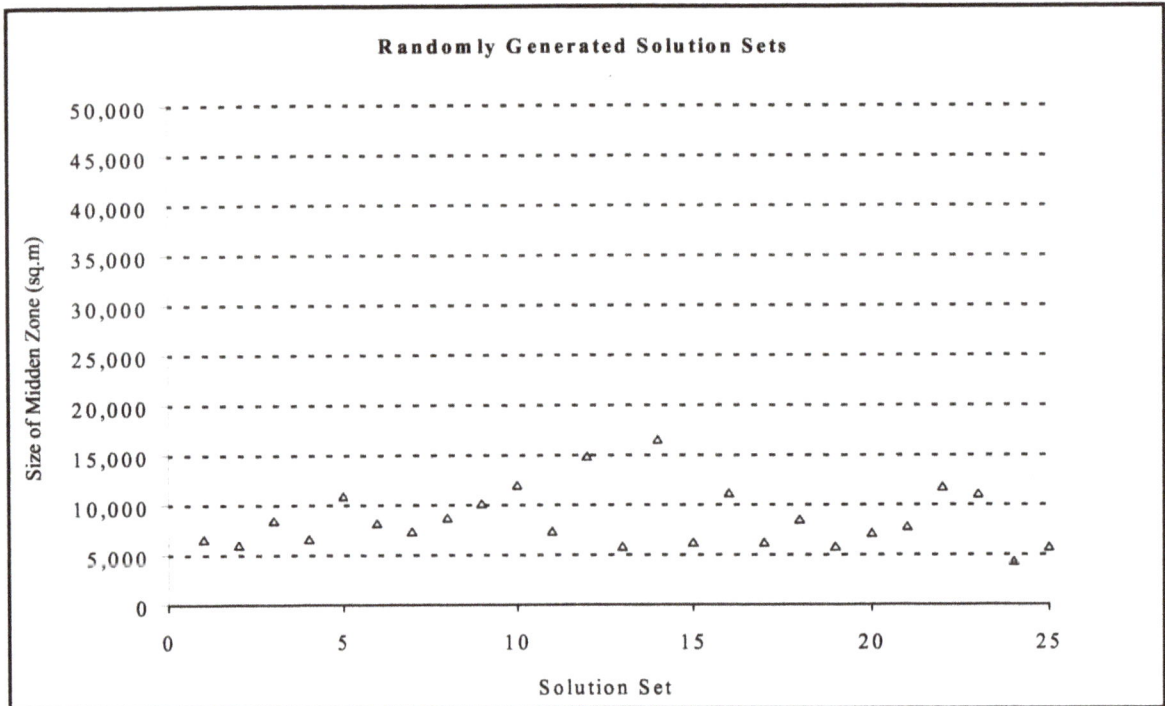

Having established that these solution sets have independently verifiable significance in terms of the size of the general activity zones, the sets can then be compared back to the objective function of the model, i.e., distance minimisation across the network as a whole. The probability scores of the solution sets are plotted against the objective function (average distance travelled from the candidate zones to the central nodes) in Figure 7.4 (p. 57), the values of which are listed in Table 7.1. Setting aside the anomalous solution set for a single centre, it is possible to bracket off a between-centre distance range within which centrality of location is correlated with intensity of use. For solution sets 5 through 9, this range is from approximately 12 to approximately 19 kilometres. In other words, at average travel distances across water of under 12 kilometres factors other than relative centrality are probably more important determinants of site location and/or site size. Within the scope of the present study it is impossible to determine exactly what these other factors might be, but likely candidates are listed in the general discussion, below. At distances of over about 19 kilometres the observed patterning is more difficult to interpret. The lack of significance may be a result of the smaller number of centres (< 5) present in these early iterations, meaning midden zones of even larger areas would need to be selected to establish statistical significance - i.e., an even higher size threshold would need to be crossed for the pattern to obtain statistical significance, as conventionally defined at $p < 0.05$. Equally, the lack of statistical significance may be a genuine threshold effect in the culturally perceived environment. The average distance "travelled" in a set of three centres (the solution set at which the start of the five through nine centres trend is judgementally observed) is 27.9 km (Table 7.1). In any case, given that the upper threshold is defined by categorising the steep end of the objective function's logarithmic distribution (Figure 7.5, p.57) it is probably best not to strive for over-precision at this end of the bracket. Figure 7.6 (p.58) shows that there is no relationship between non-*inter*dependent centrality (as measured by network "accessibility" as defined by ESRI (1995), and site size.

Fig. 7.4 Average distance "travelled" within each solution set. Leftmost symbol is Iteration #1, increasing rightwards. The grouping of symbols in the upper right is the set of significant solution sets. Distance "travelled" refers to the average distance from node to centre within each solution set

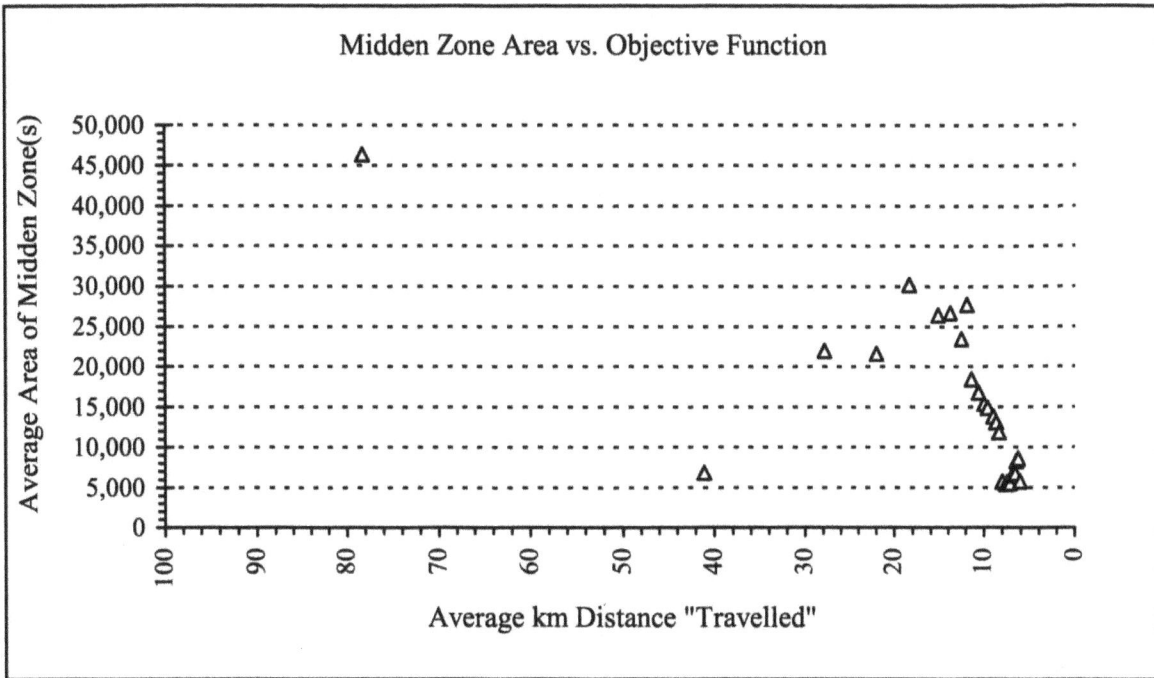

Fig. 7.5 Plot illustrating optimization of the *p*-median model's objective function (minimization of total distance travelled) through 25 iterations.

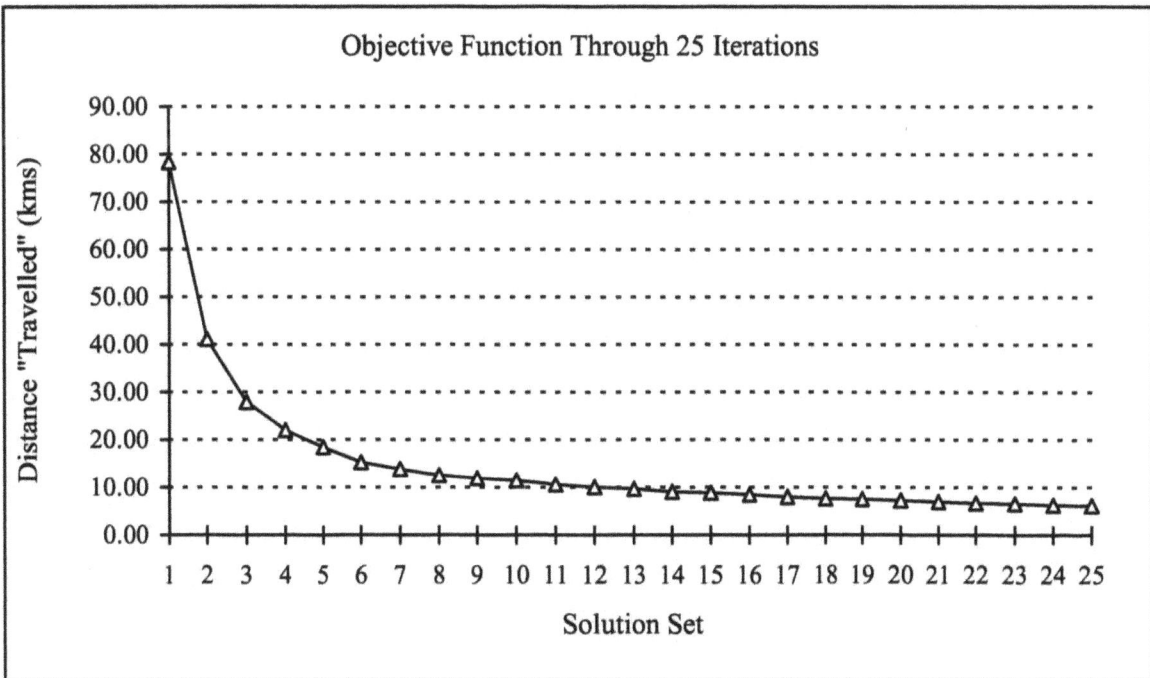

Fig. 7.6 Scatterplot of independent network accessibility of midden zones versus their size. Increasing values of the x-axis indicates greater accessibility of the midden zone on the network.

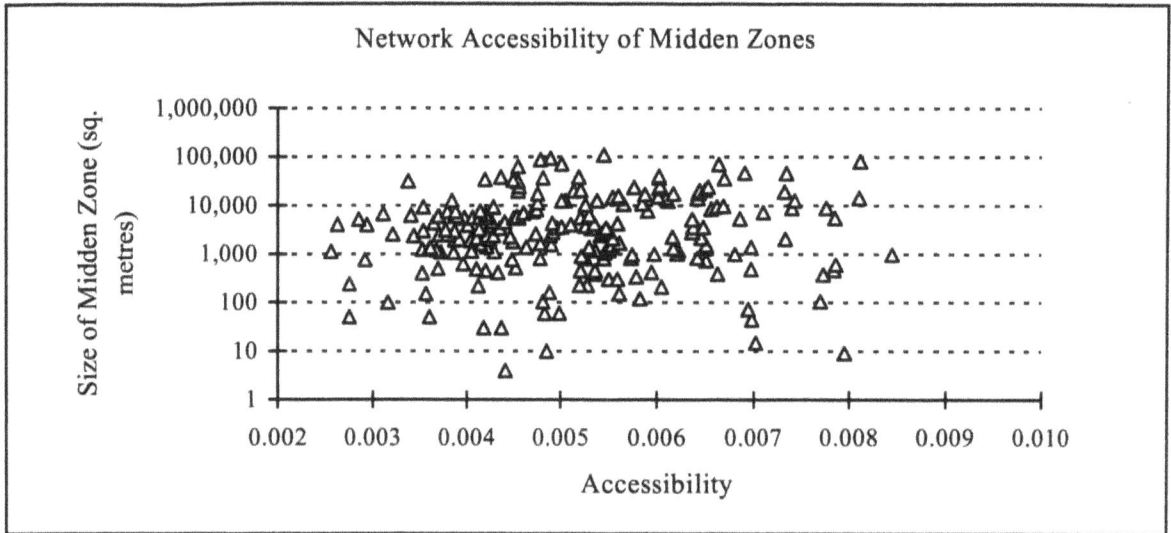

Table 7.1 Results of tests of significance by solution set and table of distances "travelled."

| Solution Set | M Z A rea (sq. m etres) | A verage D istance "Travelled" (km s) | $p$ |
|---|---|---|---|
| 1 | 46,376 | 78.32 | 0.03 |
| 2 | 6,816 | 41.12 | 0.84 |
| 3 | 22,014 | 27.92 | 0.18 |
| 4 | 21,637 | 22.04 | 0.14 |
| 5 | 30,174 | 18.46 | 0.01 |
| 6 | 26,445 | 15.23 | 0.01 |
| 7 | 26,709 | 13.84 | 0.01 |
| 8 | 23,484 | 12.52 | 0.02 |
| 9 | 27,743 | 11.92 | 0.00 |
| 10 | 18,300 | 11.43 | 0.10 |
| 11 | 16,766 | 10.56 | 0.16 |
| 12 | 15,408 | 10.03 | 0.22 |
| 13 | 14,872 | 9.65 | 0.25 |
| 14 | 13,810 | 9.05 | 0.25 |
| 15 | 13,097 | 8.86 | 0.31 |
| 16 | 11,855 | 8.45 | 0.45 |
| 17 | 5,712 | 7.95 | 0.53 |
| 18 | 5,420 | 7.62 | 0.46 |
| 19 | 5,604 | 7.50 | 0.47 |
| 20 | 5,504 | 7.18 | 0.43 |
| 21 | 6,508 | 6.95 | 0.60 |
| 22 | 6,711 | 6.65 | 0.62 |
| 23 | 8,252 | 6.51 | 0.96 |
| 24 | 8,563 | 6.27 | 0.97 |
| 25 | 5,759 | 6.10 | 0.95 |

KEY:    MZ = Midden Zone

$p$ = two-tailed probability from t-Test (bolded are statistically significant)

## 7.3 Discussion of results

The following discussion has three parts:

- Discussion of Solution Sets 1 through 4, i.e., those below the zone of statistical significance,
- Discussion of Solution Sets 10 and above, i.e., those above the zone of statistical significance,
- Discussion of Solution Sets 5 through 9, i.e., those which are significantly correlated with Midden Zone areas. This discussion flows into a more general discussion of the significance of the result to the theories outlined or developed in previous chapters.

### 7.3.1 Solution sets 1 through 4

The statistical significance of Solution Set 1 probably reflects the number of large sites in Clayoquot Sound; the selection of this large (46,376 $m^2$, 96th percentile of known Midden Zone areas) site is to some degree a result of the chance occurrence of Clayoquot Sound in the middle of the study area. In other words, this significant selection is probably an artifact of the arbitrary study area boundaries. Indeed, the site in question, Midden Zone #74 (the important Kelsemaht village of Cloothpitch (Drucker 1951) on Meares Island) is never again selected in any solution set.[62] Solution Set 2 is also composed of two zones (#171 and #42) which are never again selected, but these sites are only of average size, suggesting they bear little relationship to interdependent network centrality across the archipelago. With Solution Set 3, all three central nodes are of greater than 14,000 $m^2$, and are in the top 18% of all sites with known areas. While not statistically significant, this is suggestive that the 19 km threshold (i.e., from Solution Set 5 downwards) should not be taken overly literally, and the threshold could, perhaps should be set at Solution Set 3. Looking at Figure 7.5, it can be seen that if statistical significance were to start with Solution Set 3, then the upper size limit of the bracket of significance would be a radius of approximately 30 kilometres travel distance, rather than one of 19 kilometres.

### 7.3.2 Solution sets 10 through 25

After Solution Set 9, the model has passed through the group of solution sets which are significantly correlated with midden zone area as zones are added to the solution sets with each iteration tend to be no larger than expected. The meaning of the bracketed significant solution sets will be discussed further below; at this point discussion will be limited to why there might be a "threshold" beyond which iterations of the model lose their significance.

First, it is important to dispel any impression that all big sites are picked, and that after the threshold is passed there are no further large sites left to pick, and thus the model is

forced to pick solution sets with smaller and smaller sites. Thus, it is worth noting that 198 of the 238 midden zones are never picked in any solution set, including those ranked 1st, 3rd and 5th by size. While this dispels the notion all large zones are picked, it also indicates factors other than interdependent centrality affect intensity of use.

Second, it is very unlikely that underlying data problems prevent the selection of a larger number of significant solution sets. In order for this to be the cause of the decline in statistical significance, incompleteness of the data would have to be systematic. In other words, one would have to argue that there was an underlying pattern present beyond Solution Set 9, but that this pattern was obscured because of systematic data skew. The main potential sources of data skew, as outlined in Chapter 6, include simple measurement error, the use of differing criteria by different archaeologists in recording the size of sites, and incomplete coverage of the study area. While these factors are acknowledged to influence the study area data-set, there is no reason to believe the data is systematically skewed in a way that would produce a false result of the sort encountered. Indeed, the identification of this real and replicable result from a large and heterogeneously derived data set is in itself an indication that these data, for all their faults, are not skewed.

Third, it is possible that above the upper threshold of significance micro-environmental variables become relatively more important determinants of intensity of site use compared to site network centrality. For example, local environmental factors such as proximity to fresh water, presence of suitable beaches for canoe landing, and exposure to prevailing winds are known to be important ethnographically (Drucker 1951, Arima 1983), and have been shown to be important for archaeological predictive modelling in the similar environment of Southeast Alaska (Maschner and Stein 1995, Maschner 1997), as reviewed in Chapter 6. Similarly, singular strategic resources may be important determinants of site location. Marshall (1993:100-146 describes a number of relatively local environmental and social factors with inferred importance for site size in Nootka Sound. For example, proximity to defensive sites, to salmon streams, sheltered waterways, and to other localised "tethering" resources may increase intensity of local general purpose activity, as may "jostling" for position on the outer coast. It is possible that after a certain spatial threshold is crossed, interdependent network centrality (as defined in the *p*-median model) may matter less for site location than more local factors. The problem with this explanation is that it implies that conscious decision-making behaviour produced the pattern observed in Solution Sets 5 through 9. As this pattern consists of sets of *interdependent* centres, then it follows that decision-makers must have had both an apprehension of the study area as a whole *and* had sufficient control to collectively intensify behaviour at those optimal places. It is worth

---

[62]. It may well be interesting that Clayoquot Sound has a large number of large sites, although it is beyond the scope of this study to speculate what factors - Culture Historical, data inconsistency, or culturally-relevant centrality, is responsible for this apparent pattern.

noting again that the location-allocation model did not have any environmental or cultural variables as an input, only relative site location on a schematized transportation network.

Fourth, the annual round may mask the effect at a local scale. It is well known (e.g., Drucker 1951:36-51, Mitchell and Donald 1988) that, ethnographically at least, indigenous people in this area made at least two seasonal moves.[63] At the broad scale this might not influence the result because fewer solution sets than ethnographically-documented local indigenous groups are being selected. Once this threshold is passed, then each local group will have two or more foci of intensity of use (a winter one and a summer one) and the model will be projected onto a binary space of discontinuous occupation.[64] In other words, emphasis on shell middens as *general* activity occupation sites may mask some other patterns that would be reflected in more specific site typology. On the other hand, the emphasis in this study is on general activity across a region as a whole: it is impossible to explain all aspects of human activity, and probably undesirable to try.

Fifth, there might be either historical connection to places which over time became non-optimal within a continuously modified built environment, or such places might become circumscribed by cultural landscape-infilling. Significant components of the built environment are added at locations which were once optimal, but are no longer. This scenario has appeal for explaining the lack of significance at the narrower scales as it doesn't call for a simple underlying environmental determinism of site location, but accounts for historical process.

Finally, it must be noted that all or some of the five explanations above may be acting in combination to produce the 12 kilometre threshold of significance. As Marshall (1993:119) notes, some large Nootka Sound sites are in especially favourable *local* conditions while "others definitely [are] not, suggesting factors other than physical terrain were directing the selection of [large] site locations."

In summary, it seems probable that, for reasons which cannot be wholly explained at present, the relationship between site size and *p*-median centrality does not hold after the archipelago is partitioned into more than nine interdependent regions. Yet, within the brackets of Solution Sets 5 through 9, the relationship *does* hold.[65]

This pattern is real, and regardless of uncertainty in determination and description of its upper and lower thresholds, the meaning of the observed pattern must be discussed.

### 7.3.3 Solution sets 5 through 9

Some reasons for the bracket of significant relationship between Midden Zone size and *p*-median network centrality are discussed below.

First, as above, one may suspect that data problems or anomalies are causing the effect to be more apparent than real. This seems exceptionally unlikely as any skewing would have to be very strongly patterned in order to produce the observed pattern of selected large central Midden Zones. There is no obvious way in which the data, although incomplete in the ways previously noted, could contain such a skewing pattern, especially as the result holds for a study area which as a whole which has never previously been subject to a single archaeological analysis and whose site-survey data is unlikely to contain either a single or a systematic skewing factor.

Second, the most obvious reason for the observed pattern would be that people were deliberately, consciously optimising their movements across the study area as a whole, and thereby creating large sites at central places. While superficially attractive, this explanation is implausible because it would imply that there had been long-standing, centralised, political control over the whole study area which recognised the location-allocation type of inter-dependent network centrality, and intensified at central places accordingly. Or, at least it would imply that the archipelagian landscape of the study area was apprehended *in toto* and distance minimisation solutions were then calculated and acted upon. Both of these scenarios are implausible for logical and ethnographic reasons, and because there is no other archaeological evidence that points to such a social or perceptual unity. These scenarios would also necessarily imply that the 12 kilometre threshold is the result of "centrality no longer being important to decision-making," which shifts the burden of explanation elsewhere without solving it. The optimising explanation takes the maximisation of the objective function of the model too literally: behavioural convergence on "distance minimisation" is too easily totalised. It is best considered, in the absence of a total social phenomena that controls the optimisation of the objective function, to be a simple measure of interdependent centrality within a holistic network. It is a single-attribute *descriptive* clustering solution which should not be used to generate rule-based behavioural explanations

[63]. Although McMillan (1996:26) notes that some groups may have been dependent on local resources year-round.

[64]. There is also the possibility/probability (Haggarty and Inglis 1983) of more than two annual moves, and for regional variations in the number of moves - but the more mobile the population the less the expected skewing effect of annual round activity, in that general activity becomes more dispersed across the landscape and less systematically biased at the scale of the significant solution sets.

[65]. As with the lower threshold, it is important to note that, with reference to Table 7.1, if statistical significance is taken as *p* <0.1, then solution set

10 (*p* = 0.099) is also included in the bracket of significance. However, the argument about sample size does not hold as it should be even easier to obtain a significant result at iteration #10 than at iteration #3.

Third, in the presence of a real pattern of optimal mobility patterning, and in the absence of a plausible, rational, decision making scheme to account for that patterning, one is led to consider that this pattern was generated *non-deliberately*. In Chapter 5 Bourdieu's concept of the *habitus* was introduced. This theoretical construct was extended to include spatial and material implications by Gosden (1994) with his proposed "landscape of habit." As Gosden notes,

> *habitus*, then, is a general, concerted but unconscious harmonization of social life, a second nature. *Habitus* is not so much a state of mind, but a state of body. The human body is the nexus of the *habitus*, which organizes movements through space and time through forms of deportment and movement. As Bourdieu (1990b:69) puts it, "Arms and legs are full of numb imperatives. (. . .) what is learned in the body is not something one has, but something one is" . . . Bodily movement is also channelled through the material world, during which time dispositions are enforced and reinforced. (Gosden 1994:119)

By "material world," it is clear he means both the built and the unbuilt environments. It is obvious that the *habitus* is not just an abstract behavioural domain of structured dispositions, but it must have spatial implications as well. The landscape of action is inseparable from the landscape of consciousness (Trigger 1995), and *vice versa*. The clearest way to approach these implications is through the concept of the social *field*. This concept was introduced in earlier chapters, and tied to network analysis through the work of Wobst (1974, 1976) and especially Lesser (1961). It is therefore intriguing to see the concept of *field* become important once again at the social-theoretic end of this bridge-building thesis. Gosden, for example, discusses the spatial implications of the unconscious routinization of behaviour. The implications of the scalar thresholds identified above are consistent with Gosden's definition of a "field," which also complements the network approach to the *habitus*: "a field is a geometric space in which points are connected by a series of relationships, in which the *whole is greater than the sum of the parts* (Gosden 1994:119, emphasis added)." If we accept this holistic definition of social relations within a field, it becomes easier to understand how centrality-optimisation can be an emergent property of a landscape of habit.

In addition to the link between social fields and fields of practice, a further link to earlier chapters of this thesis can be asserted. Bourdieu's (1977) concept of *hexis* unites the individual body to the landscape via the *habitus* in a way resonant with Gibsonian Psychology. Indeed, the suggestion made in Chapter 5 that Gibsonian Psychology and the "flowing array" provide the proximal perceptual mechanism for practical consciousness now appears to have knowable archaeological implications. Further, we see that use of Gibsonian Psychology and the *habitus* is actually a form of methodological individualism, and as such avoids the problems of the reification of "Culture" and/or the ascription of agency to ill-defined special-interest collectives such as "class" or "age-grade." By insisting on an individual-centred monist approach, Ingold's (1992, 1996) distinction between environment *for* and environment *of* becomes much more useful, and indeed, applicable.

Having established that these results are most easily explained within a framework of bodily and perceptual routinization in a landscape of habit, it is interesting to note that this bodily response to macro-environmental constraint "leaves culture out of the equation," just as Ingold (1992, 1993) advises when discussing the taskscape (Chapter 5) and his exhortation to archaeologists to study the "temporality of the landscape."

Further, having abandoned "culture," at least temporarily, we are left with a subtle model of dispositions towards practical behaviour played out within scalar thresholds of the landscape of habit. This raises the issues of intentionality, decision-making and voluntarism. As Rocha (1996:21) implies, social science has been subject to a tautology of rationality, in which models of behaviour had intentionality as a silent input, rather than as a question or as a topic of investigation: "the economist only allows maximisation to be rational, thereby inserting a tautology into his argument: the individual is seeking to satisfy his satisfaction." Rocha proposes a five-fold typology of social action:

- Teleological Action: the actor pursues an end or achieves a certain desired state of affairs by choosing the most congruent means and applying them in the most efficient manner possible. In social science this is mainly modelled through simple optimising theory, and as such underpins much processual archaeology.

- Strategic Action: the actor takes the action of other actors into account. This is mainly modelled in archaeology through game-theoretic models (e.g., Shennan 1993) and human evolutionary ecology . These models were specifically designed to counterbalance the individual-actor of classical and neo-classical economics (Rocha 1996:19)

- Norm-regulated Action: actors work together to achieve ends guided by a set of common goals. In archaeology, this is the foundation of normative culture-historical explanations.

- Dramatic Action: actors participate in a series of interactions in which each is a public or spectator for the others, and the goal is achieving a desired impression on the other actors. In archaeology, this can be seen in performative analyses of power and gender.

- Communicative Action: actors collectively create texts of meaning, mediated through language, but constrained both by shared norms and imperfect individual perception of phenomena. In archaeology, this is probably best seen through the "landscape-as-text" metaphor.

Rocha's analysis of the decision-making "black box" is instructive, yet incomplete. Archaeology, with its grasp of immense time and space, must confront another sort of action: what could be termed unintentional harmonic action. It is this sort of action which I consider to be responsible for the observed pattern of Midden Zone sizes described above. Thus, to Rocha's list I would add:

- Unintentional Harmonic Action: actors have their dispositions structured by the *habitus*, with neither complete determination nor complete free will. Therefore, the taskscape is not wholly ordered by efficiency-directed rationality.

In other words, Rocha does not include habitual action within his discussion of behaviour that leads to maximisation - yet there is no reason why it should be excluded, and this thesis offers an example of how its inclusion can be relevant at the spatio-temporal scales within which archaeologists routinely work.

We have seen that Maschner and Stein (1995) could not explain variation in "intensity of use" (as measured by site area) by correlation with micro-environmental variables at the subregional scale. What sorts of explanations are left to explain efficiencies that are not rationally-directed? Ingold approaches this problem in his critique of Optimal Foraging Theory (1996). After rejecting the precepts of OFT, Ingold (1996) proposes a "received strategic framework," a construct essentially indistinguishable from the *habitus*. There is frequent confusion between an individual's capacity for rational choices of different kinds and the conception of rational choice as a *modus operandi* - reality and the optimising metaphor may have their uses, but when fused, the consequence is to impose the fallacy of the rule. As Ingold notes, one must ask whether the choices of action are real choices? If they are, they cannot be bound by past selective pressure; if they are not real, then there is no actual choice, and so actors are prisoners of enculturation. Ingold (1996:33) then echoes Bourdieu by proposing a "predisposition" to action as a middle ground to explain optimising in non-teleological terms. Indeed, as Bourdieu (1990:12) notes, the generative predictor of social practice is better conceived of as an *opus operatum* than as a *modus operandi*: the former is uncertain, contingent and fuzzy, while the latter is axiomatic, rigid and *post hoc*.

Since the built environment can now be seen as the work in progress of actors who may or may not intentionally have been optimising their behaviour by either scale-specific criteria or through habit, it is apt to revisit the comments made previously about the "fallacy of the rule." We can now glimpse an underlying truth about Marx's famous dictum that "man makes himself, but not in circumstances of his own choosing." Indeed, a similar point was made more clearly by Sartre: "what is essential is not that human beings are made, but that they make that which made them (Sartre in Rowntree 1986:)." The importance of the built environment as a structurer of disposition is precisely that it is *not* always the result of a plan, and is therefore one of the unchosen circumstances within which "man makes himself." And, since the built environment as a "work in progress" is archaeologically accessible, it cannot be ignored, as Barrett (1994) has demonstrated in his Neolithic case study. By eliminating or minimising teleological action the fallacy of the rule is avoided, both in space, and over time. For example, the arguments in Matson and Coupland (1995) concerning the "achievement of complexity" on the Northwest Coast can now be seen as assertions of long-term, teleological optimising behaviour targeted towards the ethnographic present.

It is worth considering built environments from other living domains, and how they arise from unintentional harmonic action. Stigmergy refers to "the guidance of work performed by social insects through evidences of work previously accomplished (Wilson 1975:186)." In effect, stigmergy is equivalent to a kind of communication that Wilson (1975:186) characterises as an "increase in signal duration." Take the example of termites: when building a nest termites randomly drop small balls of saliva-laden earth. A termite encountering such a ball is more likely to drop another one close by. Piling behaviour is thus reinforced, until a certain threshold of height is reached, when other termite habits start to join these together into a nest. Thus, a stochastic process plus environmental inscription allows order to emerge by structuring habits: the more order emerges from chaos, the more that order is reinforced. As Hoffmeyer (1997) puts it, "no direct interaction is necessary between the animals, since co-ordination is assured solely through the artefacts resulting from their behaviour." In other words, termites practice co-operation without communication, apart from the communication medium of the material residue of their action, and their predisposed reaction to that material. It would be a gross simplification to assert that this is equivalent to a "termite landscape of habit," yet both entomologists and archaeologists share a totalising perspective on the material products of action in the world. Just as an entomologist must learn to see the order of the termite nest as an emergent property of inculcated dispositions within a built environment rather than of collective termite design-intelligence, so must the archaeologist learn to see that, *at certain scales,* order in the archaeological landscape can result from the durable products of inculcated predispositions, as demonstrated in this thesis. Thus, to elaborate upon Bourdieu, the structured *dispositions* of the *habitus* lead to a structured *deposition*, which itself acts as a *structuring* deposition.

One current, and apt, application of stigmergy is found in the operation and control of electronic communication networks. The centralised control system for the British Telecom network consumes over 10,500 *gigabytes* of resources, and, being centralised and complex, it is prone to failure and inefficiencies. An alternative is the use of so-called "ant programs (Ward 1998)" which roam the network autonomously, each with a simple set of instructions. The ants "mark trails" across the network by increasing a value table at nodes on the network. Ants which find optimal solutions traverse the network more quickly, and so in a given time span, more ants use that trail. However, the marker signal decays over time, so there is also the possibility — indeed, the certainty — of innovative trails being pioneered once certain routes become overloaded. Data and voice transmissions are routed along these "trails" in a way that is both optimal, yet results from a diffuse, distributed process across the network not under a central control. In fact, as Ward notes, one of the most profound implications of this development in programming is precisely that the network will operate and change dynamically in a way that is impossible for a central controller (whether human or program) to apprehend. The result is an optimal solution arrived at by the cumulative activity of individual agents across a broad-scale network, with no implication of a generative grammar or totalisation on the part of the individual. Similarly, bee swarms assume an optimal tear-drop configuration, behaving like a single drop of liquid (Harris 1987:135). It is difficult, but one must be open to the possibility that at certain scales human behaviour can produce optimal solutions that look like the product of intentionality, but are no more so than a termite nest is the result of intelligence or communication. As Ward (1998:32) comments, (real-world) ant success at foraging stems not from intelligence, but from "using the world as a prompt" - a built environment of paths and places inscribed by pheromones.

In a completely different way, biologists see a notion similar to the built environment in the process of morphogenesis. Fibroblasts are the supporting cells that populate the extra-cellular matrix in adult animals. Embryologically, however, these motile cells are both the structure and the structurer of the animal's development (Stopak and Harris 1982; Harris 1987:132). The contraction of these cells as they move creates oriented ridges and furrows in the collagen that they secrete. These ridges and furrows then guide further developmental processes, such as linear patterns of muscle or feather formation. Thus, simple fibroblast traction creates a simple material effect in collagen, an effect which guides future movement, and ultimately, shapes the growth and development of the body. It is intriguing that the landscape of habit, which I argue is a product of practical consciousness enabled via direct perception, bears these

similarities to the internal landscape of the body and to unintentional communication in social insects. Body, nest and environment merge together in the rubric of non-teleological regularity. While stigmergy and fibroblast traction cannot be directly applied in archaeology, their very existence strengthens the case for looking beyond the nature:environment and mind:body dualisms, and fulfilling Ingold's exhortation to leave "culture" out of the equation. Instead, the built environment becomes a form of information storage and a medium of communication which can also act as an amplifier of such information: Schwartz's (1978:229) concept of "exthesis." Thinking of the built environment as including unconscious, but real, communication within and across generations prevents one from imposing the fallacy of the rule, as there is no way to retrodict process from product.

It also follows from the rejection of the fallacy of the rule that one must avoid totalising the environment:body relationship (cf. Chapters 4 and 5). By imposing a Cartesian dualism, and then assuming that actors operated within this dualism, the motives of the action cannot help but be mistaken. As Barnard (1990) notes, one imputes the anthropologist's view onto the people themselves. Through this imposition of etic analysis onto emic perspective the informants are turned into "naïve theoreticians" (Bourdieu's (1990) quasi-theoretical state), even in prehistoric cases with an absence of direct anthropological questioning.

Thus we arrive at another tangible benefit of this attempt to create a humanistic human ecology: the *discovery*, rather than the *imposition* of a scale of habitual action which can be transposed into the identification of more meaningful units of spatial analysis. The advantages of a fjordland maritime case study are now clearly apparent: the "knowability" of environmental constraint is the entry point into understanding the practice of mobility.[66] Having a point of entry in this case study is what allows specific conclusions to be drawn, as well as the more general speculations in Chapter 8. Ultimately, the ability to identify a scale in which habitual action makes both a *significant* and *recognisable* contribution to the archaeological signature is a significant advance in archaeological spatial analysis. As Schwartz notes,

> size is a continuous variable, but we want scale to sort itself out into levels with differing organizational and experiential implications. We should be looking for a series of levels or break points in scale, although of course we do not expect abrupt

---

[66]. More subtle renderings of this model could probably include local environmental conditions such as wind, tide, and size of landform, probably incorporated via dynamic-segmentation of the network and through constraints on the nodes to facilitate interaction.

breaks, beyond the lower end of the size dimension. (Schwartz 1978:223)

It is fair to say that the results of this thesis satisfy Schwartz's expectations.[67] Indeed, this case study points the way beyond using networks as metaphors for social spaces, and shows how networks can be made operational in an environment of non-Cartesian social geography. By allowing the investigation of the scalar principles of intentional behaviour, the possibility is that it will become possible to model and test proposals such as Gamble's (1995, 1998) regarding Local Hominid Networks and Social Landscapes. Key components of these are differences in planning and anticipatory behaviour, which come with the weighty baggage of intentionality and imposed scalar thresholds. It is intriguing to see the parallelism between Gamble's (1995:256) categorisation of material from distances of 30-80 km radius from a site as "exotic" raw material sourcing: this compares well to the ca. 19-78 km "average distances travelled" (conceived as radii of the objective function) of Solution Sets 1-4 in this study.[68] Therefore, the investigation of the scale of habitual action may be useful in finding or confirming the size of relevant spatial units of analysis. In other words, this thesis provides method by which archaeologists may be able to discover their units of spatial analysis rather than impose them, and offers attendant benefits for the confidence of interpretation through social theory and ethnography.

### 7.3.4 Robusticity of node centrality

Table 7.2 (p. 66) shows midden zones ordered by how often they entered into the 25 solution sets. The persistent selection of a site through multiple iterations with increasing numbers of sites selected offers an indication of the robusticity of the centrality of a place (Church and Bell 1985). It can be seen that the top four selections, all chosen in more than 70% of the iterations, are relatively large sites. Interestingly, the next 5 most frequently chosen sites are all very small. Figure 7.7 (p. 67) shows this pattern, on a log scale. By comparison, Figure 7.8 (p. 68), of all midden zone areas, shows that they are evenly distributed in the 1,000 to 10,000 m$^2$ range, a range which is under-represented in the set of frequently chosen centres (Fig 7.7; Table 7.2). This suggests that a bimodal pattern may hold for frequently selected midden zones which may relate to the micro-landform. Central sites may be large if they can be, but many central places are inevitably on islets which must severely constrain their size (cf. Marshall 1993:124). All sites chosen at least once in the 25 iterations are plotted as Figure 7.16 (p. 72)

### 7.4 Future interpretations of the solution sets

Having identified a subset of midden zones which are interesting because of their interdependent centrality, and having seen that this centrality is related to midden zone size, a logical next step would be to further investigate other aspects of the archaeological record which these zones might share. Such investigation would need to be undertaken with considerable caution, as discussed below.

It is initially attractive to propose that one take the set of midden zones selected, especially those that fall within the bracket of significance defined above, and examine the known archaeological information from these sites. For example, one could suggest that these central sites, if they are to some extent a "cross-roads" of the archipelago, might contain a greater proportion of exotic raw materials or of non-local faunal remains. Alternatively, if the explanation offered above is correct, the large zones were not *consciously* recognised as central places, and therefore might have an unexpectedly "ordinary" archaeological signature. Whatever the hypothesis or expectation, such research would be of tremendous interest in confirming or denying the explanation offered for the observed pattern. However, such investigation is not yet possible, for the following reasons.

It was noted previously that the case study took into account only two attributes of the archaeological record: site location and site size. While these have their problems, in terms of data validity and reliability, they are much preferable to any other existing data for the study area *as a whole*. While some sites have been extensively excavated, the vast majority are very poorly known. Most have been only visited once or twice by archaeologists for a matter of hours, or less. Thus, while the Archaeology Branch database includes many more descriptive fields than location and size, these are frequently blank. Further, even in those cases where other attributes (such as presence of features, artifacts, composition of midden, etc.) are present, the recording process has been unsystematic and variable over the long term. The study area is large, and is known from many different archaeological reports authored by many different archaeologists over a period of decades. While location and size are arguably useful attributes, there is no other single attribute which is likely to be as useful. For example, one might predict a relationship between the presence of superficial features, such as house platforms, and the centrality/size subsets of sites. However, house platforms are often difficult to see in the dense Northwest coast vegetation, are correspondingly difficult to record, and may have a limited period of visibility before they erode or disappear under overburden. This period may be less than the approximately 2,000 year frame of reference of this thesis. Therefore, the database information on this and most other attributes would have to be handled with extreme caution.

---

[67]. What is interesting, and perhaps unexpected, is that the focus on tracks and paths keeps interpretation away from simplistic imputation of bounded social units. Rather, the effect of "fuzzy" scalar breaks is to eliminate the possibility of finding such units without considerable, external sources of evidence.

[68]. Although this study differs in that distances are calculated across water with the attendant simplicities of assumption and efficiencies of transportation

Unfortunately, it is not readily possible to conduct further fieldwork to test any hypotheses which might arise from this thesis. The study area is remote and inaccessible. Virtually any place of interest is only accessible by boat, in many cases after a relatively long passage. For many months of the year such passages are impracticable or, at least, ill-advised. When the logistics of operating Northwest Coast fieldwork from England are added in, then it becomes truly impractical to carry out the sorts and scales of field research required.

Another set of expectations or hypotheses concerning the sets of selected sites might relate to the ethnographically described or modern way of life. As above, there is a certain lack of consistency in the ethnographic data across the region as a whole: some areas are better documented than others, and some may be, effectively, undocumented. A further two problems also arise. First, the ethnography of the region is particularly prone to the creation of an "ethnographic present," a "pure" cultural moment that never was. This ahistorical ethnography is not well suited to aid long term explanations in archaeology. Added to this ahistoricity are many known sources of historical distortion, such as depopulation, settlement shifting, and economic changes associated with European contact. For example, prior to the arrival of ethnographers, there was considerable depopulation due to a series of disease epidemics. One result was the aggregation of residual populations into a smaller number of large communities (Haggarty and Inglis 1983; Marshall 1993). The size and location of these was probably somewhat determined by proximity to European settlements: in either case it is unlikely that a longstanding settlement structure and mobility pattern continued unaltered up to the moment of the "ethnographic present." A second problem with the use of ethnography is more fundamental: even if the ethnographic present were "valid," this thesis describes and interprets a pattern which developed over approximately 2,000 years of unplanned behaviour. It is difficult to take synchronic ethnographic data and distil from them suitable explanations for such long-term, non-discursive behaviour. In effect, having discovered such a pattern in the archaeological record, it could be counter-productive to simplistically expect to find its explanation in the ethnographic record: while not impossible that there could be some relevant ethnographic information, its invocation would be contrary to the thrust of this thesis concerning the "fallacy of the rule" in archaeology. As above, then, ethnographic information would have to be used with extreme caution.

In summary, this thesis reaches its logical conclusion with the identification of the solution sets and the demonstration and discussion of their relationship to intensity of use. In no way is further investigation precluded, rather, this study returns to its starting point: traditional Northwest coast archaeology -- ecological, ethnographic, culture-historical -

- but with a gain in knowledge and perspective, a gain that could inform research in the years to come.

## 7.5 Chapter conclusions: quantitative post-processualist archaeology?

The results presented and discussed above show the value of an approach that identifies real spatial patterns in the archaeological record, and seeks to explain them in a way that is bound to neither simplistic application of the direct historic method nor to a reductionist reliance upon deliberate optimisation. Rather, the results show that regional archaeology on the Northwest Coast can be enhanced by the combination of quantitative geographic models interpreted through reference to social theory. Identifying a long-term, wide-scale pattern and explaining it with reference to a model of human behaviour is not a new approach. However, as Murray (1997:454) has suggested, "the archaeological record is not the subject of common-sense understandings," and so an ethnographically-distanced explanation of the observed spatial patterning was sought. Paradoxically, this interpretive *distancing*, by allowing the possibility of multiple causation at different scales, actually brings one closer to a *humanistic* human ecology.

Table 7.2 Robustness of central midden zones as defined by the number of repeat appearances in 25 iterations of location-allocation model.

| ID | Descriptor | # of occurences in 25 runs. | MZ Area (sq. metres) |
|---|---|---|---|
| 13 | NN-Greater Nutchatlitz | 22 | 33,105 |
| 226 | SC-Whyac | 21 | 31,100 |
| 214 | AB-Pt Alberni Somass S | 20 | 9,200 |
| 119 | CL-Tofino Stubbs Is. | 19 | 14,200 |
| 24 | NN-Tahsis/Esperanza 1 | 15 | 800 |
| 196 | BK-Trevor Ch | 14 | 225 |
| 134 | CL-Meares SE | 14 | 15 |
| 182 | BK-Broken Gp N 1 | 13 | 72 |
| 83 | NK-Muchalat Gold R. W | 13 | 510 |
| 5 | KY-Kapoose Ck. S | 12 | unknown |
| 107 | FL-Millar Ch | 11 | 3,125 |
| 94 | HQ-Hesquiat | 10 | 92,964 |
| 37 | NK-W. Nootka Is. 2 | 10 | 2,250 |
| 166 | LB-Ucluth NW | 9 | 1,700 |
| 100 | HQ-Hesquiat Hbr NE | 9 | 162 |
| 89 | NK-Barcester Bay C | 9 | unknown |
| 58 | NK-Tlupana C 3 | 9 | 45 |
| 49 | NK-Bligh Is. W 3 | 9 | 600 |
| 219 | SC-Pachena Bay S | 8 | 450 |
| 145 | CL-Matleset Narrows | 7 | 2,375 |
| 52 | NK-Bligh Is. NC | 5 | 1,400 |
| 19 | NN-Little Espinosa S | 5 | 1,120 |
| 181 | BK-Broken Gp NE C | 4 | 5,392 |
| 171 | BK-George Fraser Is | 4 | 4,232 |
| 138 | CL-Indian Is SE | 4 | 20,576 |
| 85 | NK-Muchalat Matchlee N | 4 | 2,985 |
| 78 | NK-Muchalat SW 1 | 4 | 6,300 |
| 62 | NK-Tlupana C 1 | 4 | 2,250 |
| 42 | NK-Yuquot N 1 | 4 | 9,400 |
| 194 | BK-Deer Gp C | 3 | 2,800 |
| 170 | BK-Chuumata | 3 | 16,800 |
| 159 | LB-Wickaninnish N | 3 | 12,332 |
| 158 | LB-Schooner Cove S | 3 | 3,600 |
| 149 | CL-Kennedy Cove | 3 | 62,900 |
| 120 | CL- Opitsit | 3 | 79,872 |
| 235 | SC-Nitinat Lk W C | 2 | 5,175 |
| 183 | BK-Deer Gp SW | 2 | 37,842 |
| 169 | BK-Tukwaa | 2 | 23,500 |
| 124 | CL-Esowista NW | 2 | 9 |
| 53 | NK-Bligh Is. NE | 2 | 1,000 |
| 114 | CL-Vargas NE | 1 | 2,800 |
| 111 | CL-Vargas Ahous Bay | 1 | 1,360 |
| 102 | HQ-Hot Springs Cove | 1 | 5,500 |
| 71 | NK-Tahsis S End | 1 | 14,000 |
| 51 | NK-Bligh Is. W 1 | 1 | 375 |
| 74 | CL-Cloothpitch | 1 | 46,376 |

**KEY (See Figure 6.2):**
KY = Kyuquot Channel South
NN = North Nootka Island
NK = Nootka Sound
HQ = Hesquiat
FL = Flores Island
CL = Clayoquot Sound
LB = Long Beach
AB = Alberni Inlet
BK =Barkley Sound
SC = South Coast & Nitinaht

Fig. 7.7    Robustness of central midden zones.  The x-axis denotes the number of solution sets the midden zone appears in (maximum=25).  Note the robust group of four central to the right, and the group of five small central zones to the left of those.

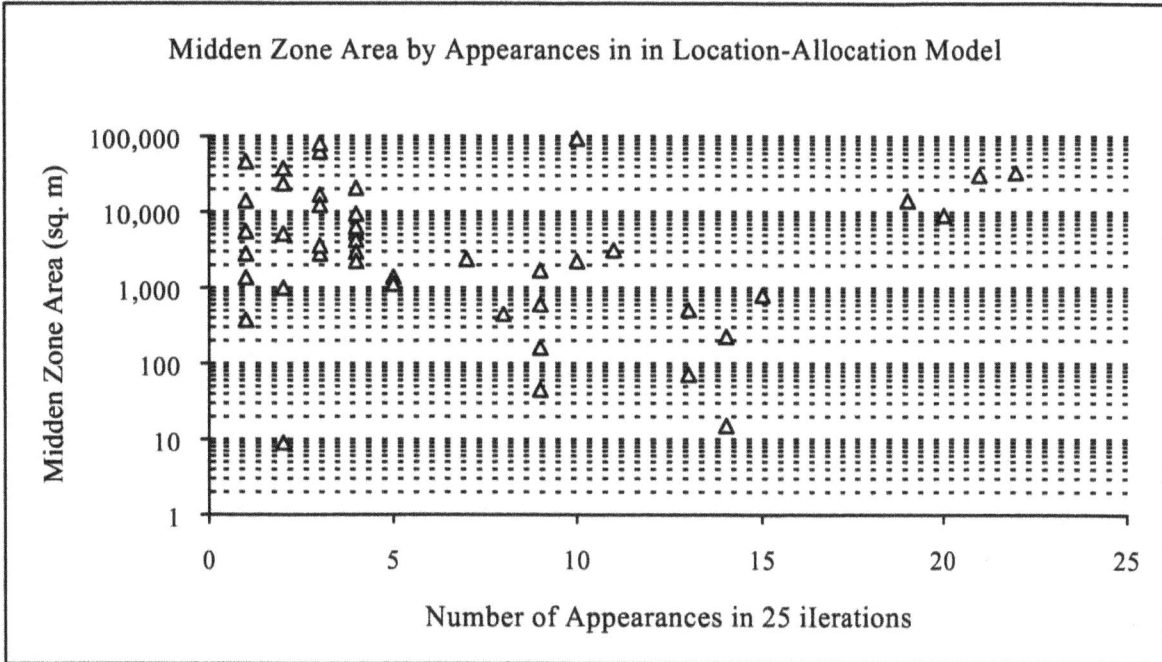

Midden Zone Area by Appearances in in Location-Allocation Model

Fig. 7.8    Distribution of all midden zones with known areas.  Note concentration in 1,000 to 10,000 sq. metre band, in contrast to Fig. 7.7 robust centres.

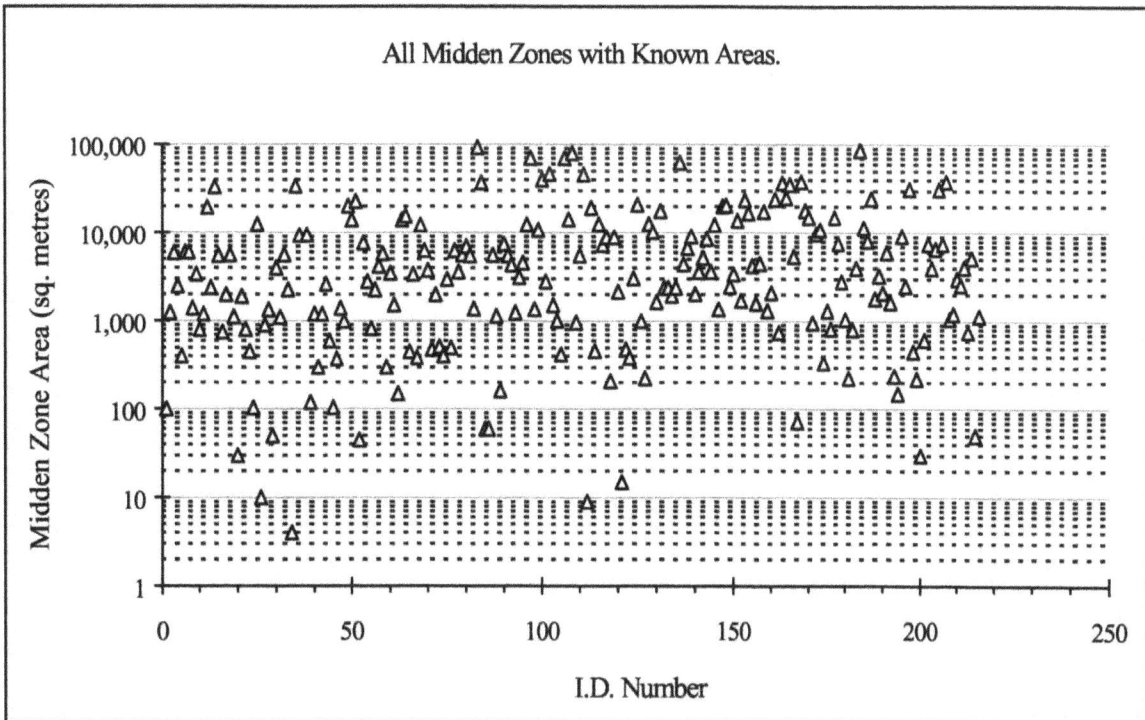

All Midden Zones with Known Areas.

Fig. 7.9 Location-allocation set for a single centre (iteration #1).

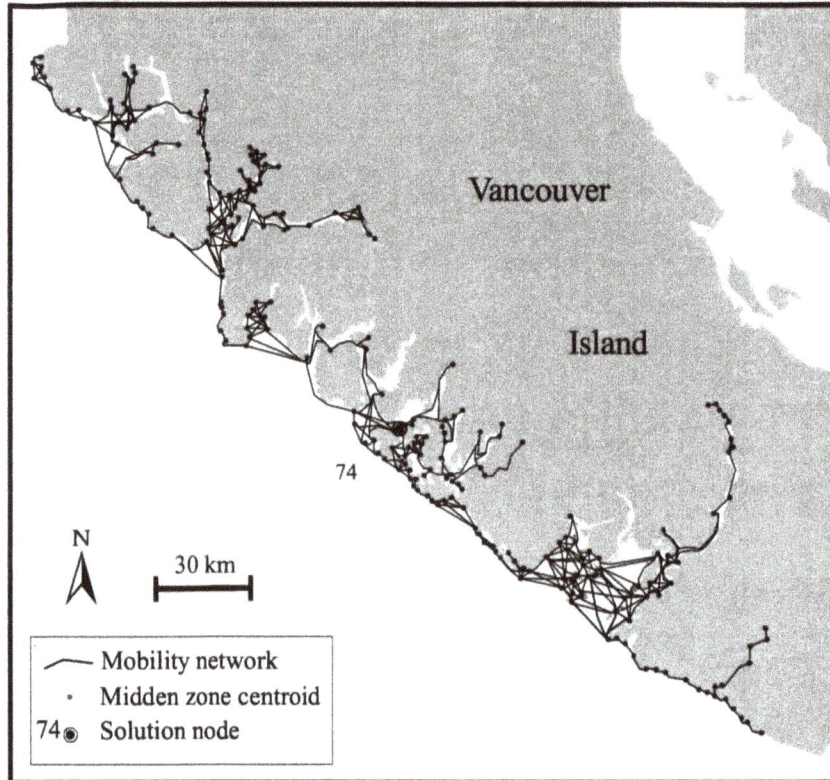

Fig. 7.10 Location-allocation set for three centres (iteration #3).

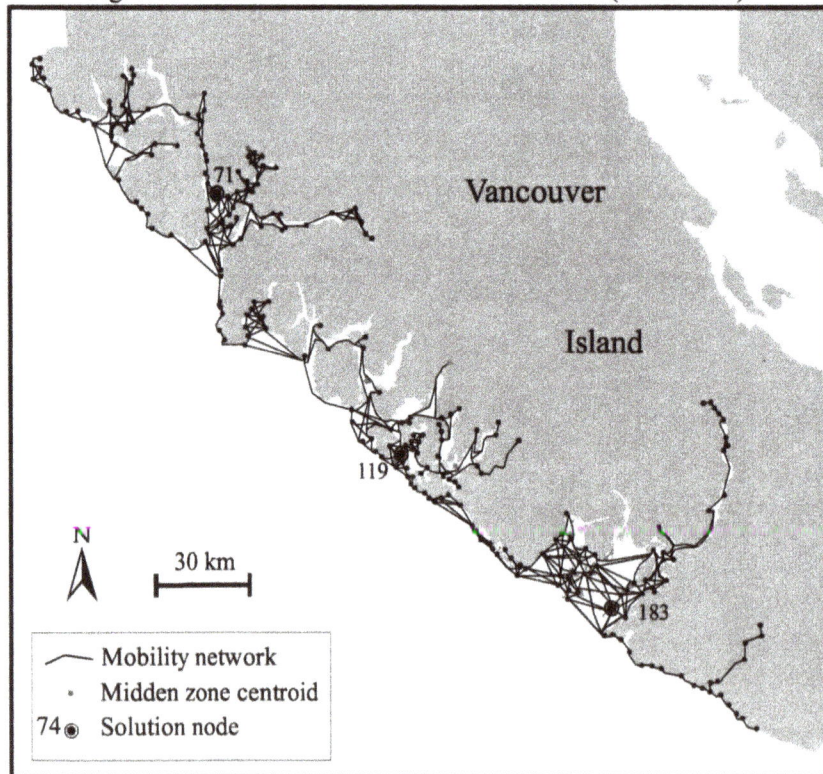

Fig. 7.11   Location-allocation solution set for five centres (iteration #5).

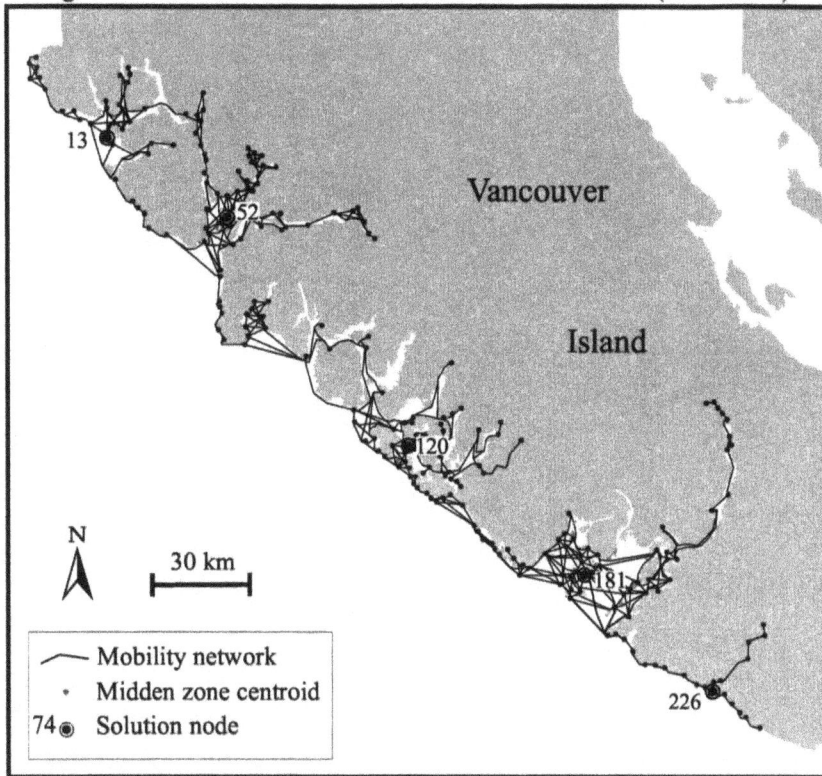

Fig. 7.12   Location-allocation solution set for six centres (iteration #6).

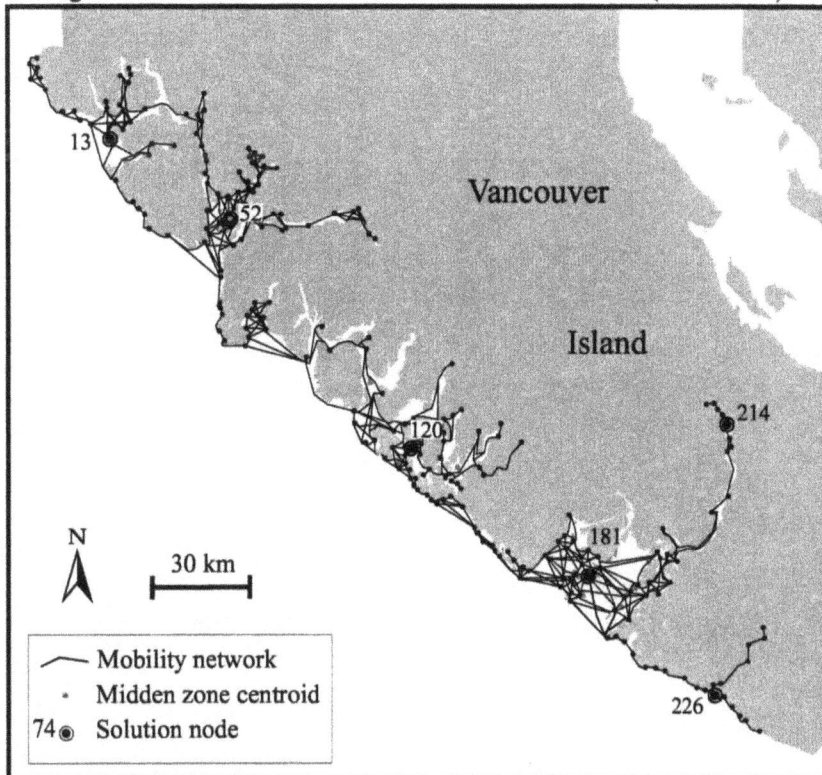

Fig. 7.13   Location-allocation solution set for seven centres (iteration #7).

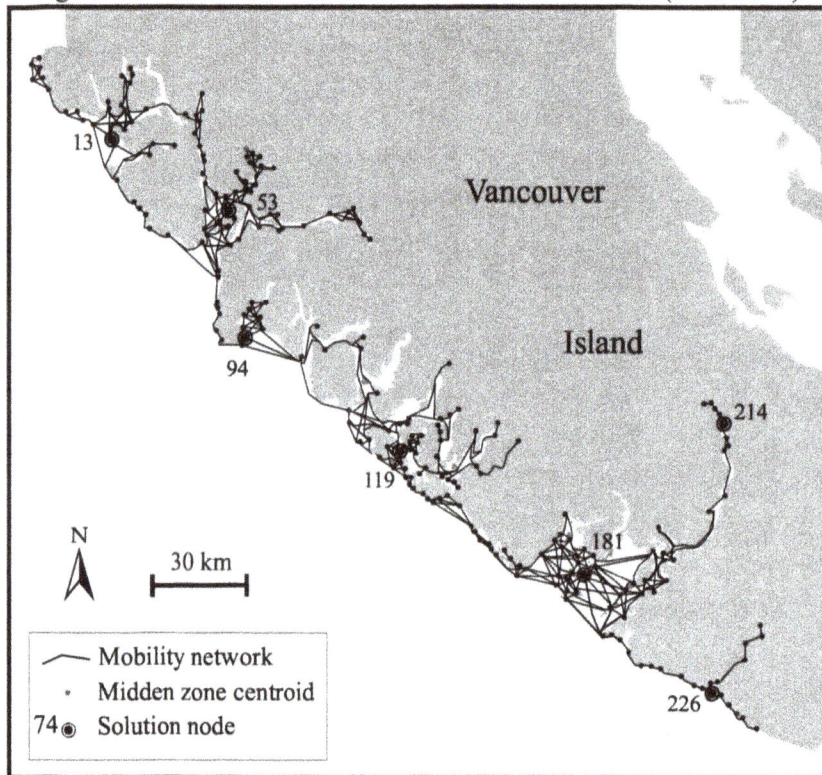

Fig. 7.14   Location-allocation solution set for eight centres (iteration #8).

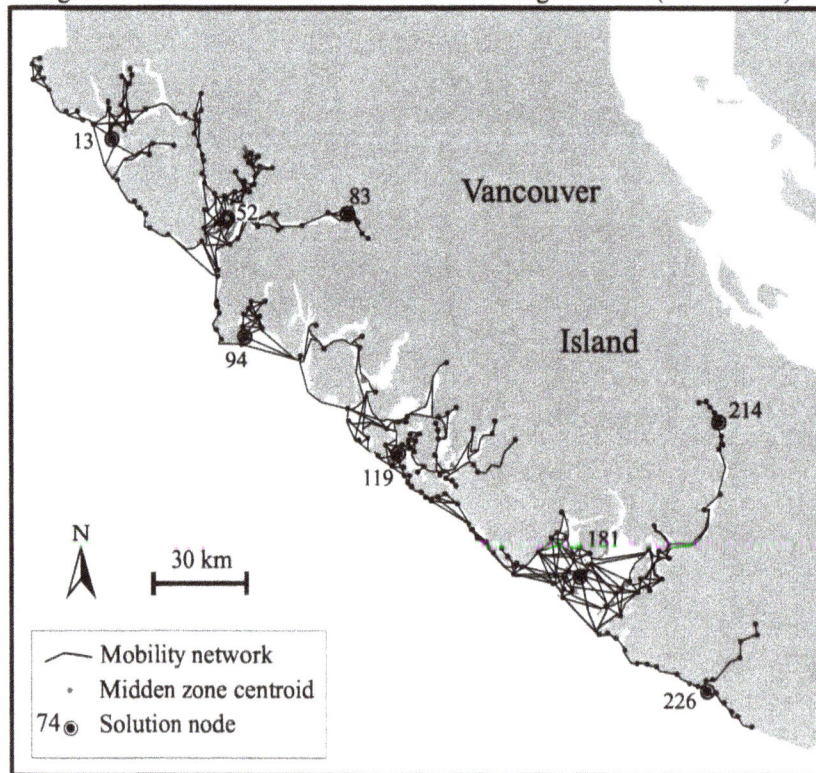

Fig. 7.15  Location-allocation solution set for nine centres (iteration #9).

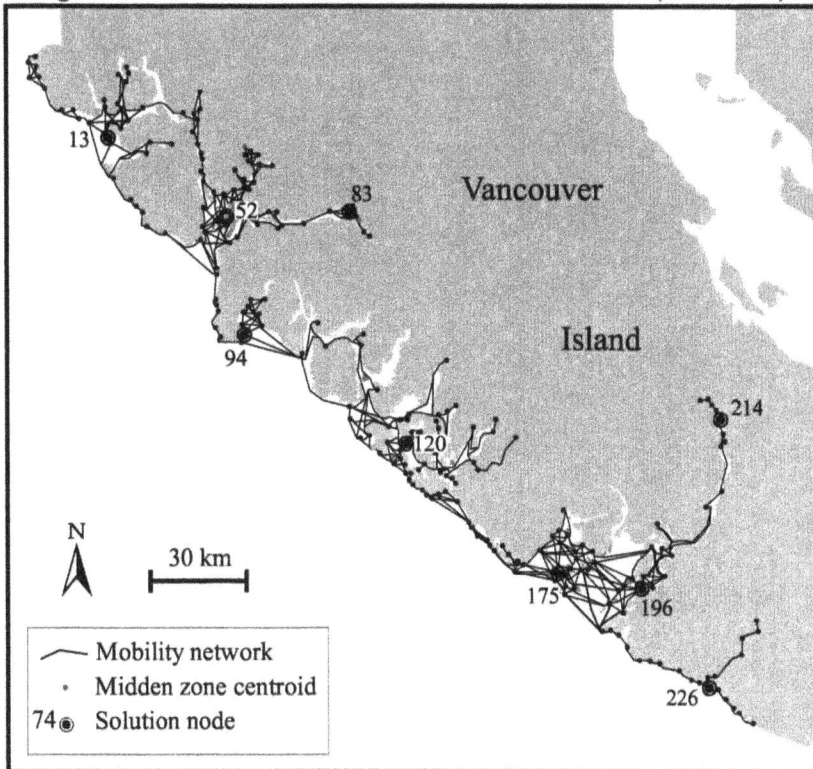

Fig. 7.16  Cumulative map of all midden zones selected at least once during 25 iterations of the location-allocation model.

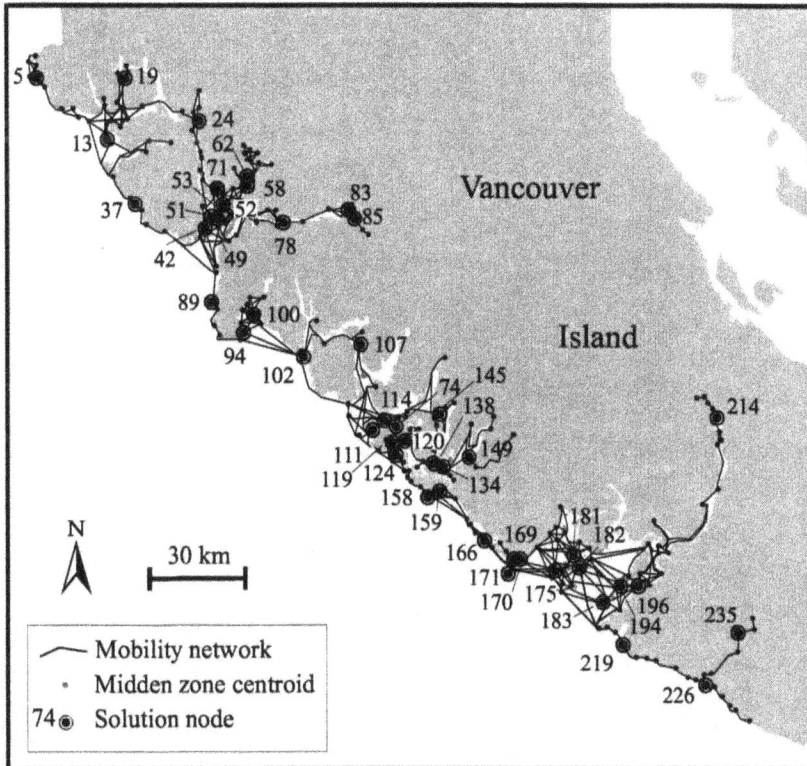

# CHAPTER 8—CONCLUSIONS

## 8.1 Summary of research program

The multiplex variable "social complexity" needs to be unpacked. One way to start this process is by looking at time-space constraints, because these are central to surplus, storage, sedentism, the division of labour, specialisation, and other traits of "complexity." Time geography can provide the inspiration for this unpacking by focusing attention on, and providing a notation for, the regularities which emerge from the collective routinized behaviour of individuals. In most archaeological applications, knowledge of the routes that connect sites and other places in the landscape is normally lacking, or severely incomplete. Only in the relatively rare cases of an extensive built transportation infrastructure could this be known, and even then the knowledge is probably incomplete. However, in the case of a fjordland archipelago with its highly directional topography, many of these time-space constraints *are* knowable, especially mobility. Mobility is centred on the human body, and, in accordance with time-geographic theory, must be considered in relationship to universal constraints on the body. A need therefore arises for theory which links the individual to the environment. Such a theory can be provided by amalgamating locational analysis (especially the recognition of the importance of linearity) with ecological psychology and Ingoldian monism: namely an appreciation of the individual centred taskscape, paths, routes, and the built environment.

These disparate analytical tools are situated at opposite ends of the theoretical spectrum, yet the *habitus*, by recognising the partially-determined contingency which the individual faces through their life-path, unites quantitative geography with humanistic social theory. Thus, a research program was needed which can deal with both ends of the behavioural scale (individual/short-term and regional/long-term) and cut culture out of the middle. In order to attain this, one must accept "social practice" as a contributing generator of the archaeological record, and avoid "totalisation" by ascribing regularities in the archaeological record to goal-directed planning behaviour. This is particularly apt because in the case of an archipelago, "the sea can create a greater sense of community in which the whole is quite different to the sum of its parts (Gosden and Pavlides 1994:163)."

This program has been achieved in this thesis using a GIS application of the network implementation of the location-allocation model. It is concerned with routes, places, and individuals, but operates on a schematic map that melds the built environment (the sites) and the natural environment (routes) External information (site size/ intensity of use) was withheld from the model to validate the results. As discussed in the previous chapter, a good result was obtained which demonstrates the "fallacy of the rule" when analysing large scale spatial patterning (cf. Shennan's (1993) "affirming the consequent"; Thomas (1993) on "totalisation"). It is argued that Gosden's concept of the Landscape of Habit is useful, especially if it can be *discovered* as a scalar property of the archaeological landscape.

This thesis does not argue that *all* spatial patterning is the result of habitual action. Rather, one can isolate a subset of the archaeological signature which is more likely to be the result of that kind of action, while leaving the rest (e.g., large sites that never enter a solution set) for some other sorts of analysis or explanations. While these alternatives were not able to be explored in this thesis, they are nonetheless worthy of examination.

## 8.2 Size thresholds and the identification of relevant spatial units of analysis

The research program achieved in this thesis is self-evidently useful in that using it can put a kilometre size and a behavioural context onto discovered spatial-analytic units. In comparison, Thiessen Polygons (e.g., Renfrew 1973) seem very static and rule-bound and Locational Analyses (e.g., Wobst 1976) seem very unrealistic and rule-driven. The sorts of spatial units possible through location-allocation network modelling are more comparable to "household archaeology" (emic units of analysis) than to block excavation quadrats (etic units of analysis). Each are useful, but must be directed towards different questions and offer different possibilities.

In reference to "magic number" analyses of social scale, (e.g., Kosse 1990; Gamble 1995) we can see that spatial "magic numbers" may be derivable on a case by case basis, and perhaps some cross-cultural generalisations might be derivable. In reference to social complexity, one can see that a regional "settlement hierarchy" of site sizes is not necessarily an indicator of social complexity. Rather it could be an example of habitual action harmonised with the shape of the environment. There is likely an instructive referral to the Tierra del Fuego case (see Chapter 3) of some quite large shell middens interspersed with small ones, in the context of presumed "social simplicity." Blake and Clark (1985:1) argued that "the shape of the environment, in the very broadest terms, is not usually a factor that anthropologists examine when studying the evolution of civiliztion [sic]," their point being,

> The potential for social development of a community is a function of its access to *social resources* .. such access depends upon relative topographic position within the region." (Clark and Blake 1994:19; emphasis in original).

Clark and Blake's focus on the *shape* of the environment is laudable, yet their underlying assumption that shape is defined by topographic position (and not to the built environment) and is a variable that in some way is apprehended and acted upon is not clearly supported.

Equally, this study cast question onto areal ecological concepts such as "population density." Persons per square kilometre is not a relevant measure for humans (such as hunters and gatherers) who tend not to appropriate the land two-dimensionally, as defined by Ingold (1986). It is welcome to see such seemingly odd theories as Ingold's analysis of zero- and one-dimensional land tenure turn out to have such direct utility to the solution of central archaeological problems.

### 8.3 Relevance of this study to Northwest Coast archaeology

As was noted in the Introduction, archaeology on the Northwest Coast is, in general, hampered by an overly normative view of culture, and a culture-historical approach dependent on the direct-historical method. In the latter, ethno-linguistic groups have their current territories taken as the spatial units of archaeological analysis. The present is thus imposed onto the past in a way that is not always justified, or justifiable. However, adoption of this method of discovering units of spatial analysis might point the way to a more sophisticated direct-historical or culture-historical method that was not so closely bound to artificial units of analysis yet was still sensitive to long term continuities of behaviour. In this way, one might work towards answering the call (Donald and Mitchell 1988:342) for more attention to be given to the direct-historic approach on the Northwest Coast.[69]

More generally, this thesis shows the advantages of introducing social theory in place of (or as prelude to) ethnography, thus breaking the culture-historical vicious circle. The intention of breaking from the ethnographic record was to re-arrive at the starting point, but with a gain in knowledge. From this new vantage point, it would be a natural extension of this project to examine the midden zones included in each significant solution set from an ethnographic and archaeological viewpoint. Do they share archaeological characteristics, such as trade goods or exotica which might reflect their interdependent centrality across the network as a whole? Do they feature in particular ways in oral tradition or family histories? Such investigation would require a considerable extension of this research into the realms of "dirt archaeology" and ethnology, in which the Solution Sets themselves become the topic of analysis.

---

[69]. Interestingly, Galloway (1992) calls for a consideration of *habitus* to inform direct-historical analogy in a Spanish-colonial case study.

### 8.4 Relevance of the study for predictive modelling

Adapting the current study model to incorporate the *shape* of the environment as an input variable (and hence to create a network in the absence of site locations) has exciting possibilities for predictive modelling. Apparently, there is not an intentional planning of the optimality of the locations, but a patterning arising from the relationship between the individual and the environment. This is shown by the fact that some of the solution set midden zones are not "villages "or even "big sites" but agglomerations of many small sites, which itself demonstrates the utility of a non-site landscape approach. Also, some of the sites chosen are very small. By starting with the site network itself, not with the landscape, the model as it stands cannot be generative, unlike the environmental variables that enter most predictive modelling. The way forward for predictive modelling will be the inclusion of regional landform structure, together with micro-environmental features and, as shown in this study, a consideration of the lessons of the effect of the built environment. In predictive modelling proper, since the aim is to find the sites rather than to explain their relationships, if network analysis is to be used one would need to develop a network that is not dependent on site location, perhaps one generated through an iterative cost-surface procedure.

Indeed, I see the present study as a preliminary step in this potentially worthwhile archaeological middle ground. There is clearly a need to explore the case study methodology in other fjordlands. The southern Queen Charlotte Islands (Gwaii Haanas) of the north British Columbian coast have excellent regional data and a similar ecological adaptation. It would be interesting to see whether similar patterns emerge there and if not, why not. Equally, southern New Zealand might afford some intensive study, with the added advantage of an even narrower time depth of human occupation and the ensuent possibility of close exploration of the colonisation or landscape-infilling process. In other words, it might be possible to explore some aspects of how the environment was "built" within a time period that is relatively shallow and reasonably well documented. In Tierra del Fuego and the Chono Archipelago, should sufficient site survey data become available, it would be interesting to explore in more detail environmental possibilism and thus examine the link between environment and the different archaeological signatures of "complexity."

Location-allocation analysis has been applied in some terrestrial situations where there is a built transportation network (Church and Bell 1988). It might be possible to apply in terrestrial situations lacking such built networks if some conditions were met, mainly a degree of "knowability" of the decision sets which led people to take certain routes between places. This is not necessarily impossible. First, the Location-Allocation model does not have to be implemented on a network, it is also possible to implement it in continuous space. In the latter, the paths between places would be defined as the shortest connecting paths, which is not readily defensible as it ignores topography. However, the use of cost-surfaces could introduce some simple parameters into such a model, which, within limits, could make it possible to explore some of the underlying assumptions of the principle of least effort. Second, through the use of cost-surfaces, it might be possible to build or iteratively grow a network that was an abstraction of the transportation space in a certain environment. By averaging out possible routes and settling on optimal ones, a network could be postulated which was itself the topic of investigation, rather than the means of investigation as it was in this study. Furthermore, more sophisticated Network Analytic tools, such as dynamic segmentation, could be applied to bring greater modelling subtlety to local differences in mobility potential and landscape directionality.

For example, if one started with Maschner and Stein's (1995) method for predicting the location of sites, one could then identify which places in the environment are likely to have sites, and then predict via Location-allocation network analysis which of these potential sites might be large. Then one could go out and field test it. If Maschner and Stein are correct in their assessment of their model's utility, then the *predicted* site location network should be almost as good at predicting site size as the *observed* site location network used in this thesis with all its attendant data imperfections. This would be useful in poorly accessible areas with reasonable terrain mapping. For example, with increasing interest in the coastal route of North American colonization, and with the fine-scale bathymetry available, one might model the submerged Pleistocene shorelines and predict where both sites and *large* sites might be. These predicted large site locations, which would be difficult to access via scuba diving and expensive to access via submersible, could be targeted for inexpensive sampling using "clamshell" buckets or some similar technology. By narrowing the sampling to predicted large site locations, a strategy which would otherwise have a very low success-probability might be viable.

## 8.5 Comments and future directions

This thesis re-affirms the importance of theory — especially interdisciplinary theory—to guide archaeological questions and to interpret anomalous results. Without the guidance from the ecological psychologist J.J. Gibson the questions would never have been asked and the model never constructed because it was self-evident from an ethnographic and archaeological viewpoint that there was no reason to treat the study area as a coherent unit of analysis. Thus the decision to abandon ethnographic information in pursuit of a "pure" archaeological approach was also essential. Without methodology from quantitative geography and inspiration from Martin Wobst's locational

analyses, there would be no spatial pattern to discuss. And, without the aid of social theory developed in archaeological and sociological contexts it would have been even more difficult to fit an explanation to the observed pattern. Thus, by simultaneously considering both the "knowability" of the archaeological record and the universality of certain aspects of human life, this thesis shows one way of moving beyond the rhetoric of post-processual archaeology. This middle ground in archaeology, here manifested as the alliance of social theory to quantitative geography — the production of demonstrable, testable results and their alliance to humanistic explanations — is what I would term a *humanistic human ecology*. In particular, the use of the *habitus* as a bridging argument, similar to "middle range" theory (although not as empirically grounded), offers one path out of the theoretical canyon between what Patty Jo Watson (1991:170) has termed the "methodless soul" of post-processualist archaeology and the "soul-less method" of processualist archaeologies.

# REFERENCES

Allen, K., Stanton Green and Ezra Zubrow, 1990. *Interpreting Space: GIS and archaeology*. London: Taylor and Francis.

Ames, Kenneth M., 1991a. Sedentism: a temporal shift or a transitional change in hunter-gatherer mobility patterns? Pp. 108-34 in S. Gregg (ed.) *Between Bands and States*. Carbondale Illinois: Center for Archaeological Investigations, Occasional Paper No. 9.

Ames, Kenneth M., 1991b. The archaeology of the *longue durée*: temporal and spatial scale in the evolution of social complexity on the southern Northwest Coast. *Antiquity* 65:935-45.

Ames, Kenneth M., 1994. The Northwest Coast: complex hunter-gatherers, ecology, and social evolution. *Annual Review of Anthropology* 23: 209-29.

Arcas Associates, 1989. *Patterns of Settlement of the Ahousaht (Kelsemaht) and Clayoquot Bands*. Unpublished report prepared for Ahousaht and Clayoquot Bands.

Arima, Eugene, 1983. *The West Coast People: The Nootka of Vancouver Island and Cape Flattery*. Victoria, B.C.: British Columbia Provincial Museum Special Publication No. 6.

Arima, Eugene and John Dewhirst, 1990. Nootkans of Vancouver Island. Pp. 391-411 in W. Suttles (ed.) *Handbook of North American Indians Volume 7: Northwest Coast*. Washington, D.C.: Smithsonian Press.

Arnold, Jeanne, 1992. Complex hunter-gatherer-fishers of prehistoric California: chiefs, specialists, and maritime adaptations of the Channel Islands. *American Antiquity* 57(1):60-84.

Arnold, Jeanne, 1993. Labour and the rise of complex hunter-gatherers. *The Journal of Anthropological Archaeology* 12:75-119.

Arnold, Jeanne, 1995. Transportation innovation and social complexity among maritime hunter-gatherer societies. *American Anthropologist* 97(4):733-47.

Bailey, Geoffrey, 1983. Hunter-gatherer behaviour in prehistory: problems and prospectives. Pp. 1-22 in G. Bailey, *Hunter-Gatherer Economy in Prehistory*. Cambridge: Cambridge University Press.

Bailey, Geoffrey and John Parkington (eds.), 1988. *The Archaeology of Prehistoric Coastlines*. Cambridge: Cambridge University Press, New Directions in Archaeology.

Bailey, Trevor C., 1994. A review of statistical spatial analysis in geographical information systems. Pp. 13-44 in S. Fotheringham and P. Rogerson (eds.) *Spatial Analysis and GIS* London: Taylor and Francis.

Barnard, Alan, 1983. Contemporary hunter gatherers: current theoretical issues in ecology and social organization. *Annual Review of Anthropology* 12:193-214.

Barnard, Henry, 1990. Bourdieu and ethnography: reflexivity, politics and praxis. Pp. 58-85 in R. Harker, C. Mahar and C. Wilkes (eds.) *an Introduction to the Work of Pierre Bourdieu*. London: MacMillan.

Barrett, John, 1994. *Fragments from Antiquity: An archaeology of social life in Britain, 2,900-1,200 BC*. Oxford: Blackwell.

Bayliss-Smith, Timothy, 1977. Human ecology and island populations: the problems of change. In T. Bayliss-Smith and R. Feachem (eds.) *Subsistence and Survival: Rural ecology in the Pacific*. London: Academic Press.

Beattie, Grant, 1995. *Archaeological Landscapes of the Lower Mainland, British Columbia: a settlement study using a Geographic Information System*. M.A. Thesis, Anthropology and Sociology, UBC.

Becker, Gary S., 1965. A theory of the allocation of time. *The Economic Journal* 75:493-517.

Bell, James A., 1994. *Reconstructing Prehistory: Scientific method in archaeology*. Philadelphia: Temple University Press.

Bell, Thomas L. and Richard Church, 1985. Location-allocation modelling in archaeological settlement pattern research: some preliminary applications. *World Archaeology* 16(3):354-71.

Bell, Thomas L. and Richard Church, 1987. Location-allocation modeling in archaeology. Pp. 76-100 in A. Ghosh and G. Rushton (eds.) *Spatial Analysis and Location-Allocation Models*. New York: Van Nostrand Reinhold.

Bell, Thomas L., Richard Church and Larry Gorenflo, 1988. Late horizon regional efficiency in the Northeastern Basin of Mexico: a location-allocation perspective. *Journal of Anthropological Archaeology* 7: 163-202.

Bender, Barbara, 1985. Prehistoric developments in the American midcontinent and in Brittany, Northwest France. Pp. 21-57 in T. Douglas Price and James A. Brown (eds.) *Prehistoric Hunter-Gatherers: the emergence of cultural complexity*. New York: Academic Press.

Bender, Barbara, 1989. The roots of inequality. Pp. 83-95 in D. Miller *et al* (eds.) *Domination and Resistance*. London: Unwin Hyman.

Bender, Barbara, 1990. The dynamics of nonhierarchical societies. Pp. 247-63 in S. Upham (ed.) *The Evolution of Political Systems: sociopolitics in small-scale sedentary societies*. Cambridge: Cambridge University Press.

Bettinger, R., 1980. Explanatory/Predictive models of hunter-gatherer adaptation. Pp. 189-255 in M. Schiffer (ed.) *Advances in Archaeological Method and Theory, Volume 3*. Academic Press, New York

Bhaskar, Roy, 1989. *Reclaiming Reality: a critical introduction to contemporary philosophy*. London: Verso.

Binford, Lewis R., 1978. *Nunamiut Ethnoarchaeology*. New York: Academic Press.

Binford, Lewis R., 1990. Mobility, housing, and environment: a comparative study. *The Journal of Anthropological Research:* 119-52.

Binford, Lewis R., 1992. Seeing the present and interpreting the past—and keeping things straight. Pp. 43-59 in J. Rossignol and L. Wandsnider (eds.) *Space, Time and Archaeological Landscapes*. London: Plenum.

Bloch, M., 1989. The past and the present in the present. Pp. 1-18 in M. Bloch: *Ritual, History and Power: selected papers in anthropology*. London School of Economics, Monographs on Social Anthropology No. 58. London: Athlone.

Boaz, J.S. and E. Uleberg, 1995. The potential of GIS-based studies of Iron Age cultural landscapes in eastern Norway. Pp. 249-59 in G. Lock and Z. Stancic (eds.) 1995: *Archaeology and Geographical Information Systems: a European perspective*. London: Taylor & Francis.

Borgatti, Everett and Freeman [sic], 1992. *UCINET IV Version 1.0 Reference Manual*. Columbia: Analytic Technologies.

Borrero, Luis Alberto, 1994. The extermination of the Selk'nam. Pp. 247-61 in Burch E. and L. Ellanna (eds.) *Key Issues in Hunter-Gatherer Research*. Oxford: Berg.

Bourdieu, Pierre, 1977. *Outline of a Theory of Practice*. Cambridge: Cambridge University Press

Bourdieu, Pierre, 1990. *The Logic of Practice*. Cambridge: Polity Press.

Boyd, Robert T., 1990. Demographic History, 1774-1874. In Wayne Suttles (ed.): *Handbook of North American Indians, vol. 7: Northwest Coast*. Smithsonian Institution, Washington, 1990.

Brothwell, Don and Geoffrey Dimbleby (eds.), 1981. *Environmental Aspects of Coasts and Islands*. British Archaeological Reports International Series 94. Oxford: BAR

Brown, James A., 1985. Long-term trends to sedentism and the emergence of complexity in the American Midwest. Pp. 201-35 in T. Douglas Price and James A. Brown (eds.) *Prehistoric Hunter-Gatherers: the emergence of cultural complexity*. New York: Academic.

Brown, James A. and T.D. Price, 1985. Complex hunter-gatherers: retrospect and prospect. Pp. 435-42 in T. Douglas Price and James A. Brown (eds.) *Prehistoric Hunter-Gatherers: the emergence of cultural complexity*. New York: Academic.

Brumfiel, Elizabeth M., 1989. Factional competition in complex society. Pp. 127-39 in D. Miller *et al* (eds.) *Domination and Resistance*. London: Unwin Hyman.

Brumfiel, Elizabeth M. and John Fox (eds.), 1994. *Factional Competition and Political Development in the New World*. Cambridge: Cambridge University Press.

Brumfiel, Elizabeth M. and Timothy Earle, 1987. Specialization, exchange, and complex societies: an introduction. Pp. 1-9 in E. Brumfiel and T. Earle (eds.) *Specialization, Exchange, and Complex Societies*. Cambridge: Cambridge University Press, New Directions in Archaeology Series.

Bura, Stephane, F. Guerin-Pace, H. Mathian, D. Pumain, and L. Sanders, 1996. Multiagent systems and the dynamics of a settlement system. *Geographical Analysis* 28(2): 161-78.

Burrough, P.A., 1986. *Principles of Geographical Information Systems for Land Resources Assessment*. Oxford: Clarendon Press.

Carlstein, Tommy, 1981. The sociology of structuration in time and space: a time-geographic assessment of Giddens' theory. In *Svensk Geografisk Arsbok* 57:41-57.

Carlstein, Tommy, 1982. *Time Resources, Society and Ecology. Volume 1: Preindustrial Societies*. London: Allen and Unwin.

Carver, M.O.H., 1990. Pre-Viking traffic in the North Sea. In S. McGrail (ed.) *Maritime Celts, Frisians and Saxons*. Council for British Archaeology: CBA Research Report 71.

Cherry, John F., 1981. Pattern and process in the earliest colonization of Mediterranean islands. *Proceedings of the Prehistoric Society* 47:41-68.

Church, Richard L. and Thomas L. Bell, 1988. An analysis of ancient Egyptian settlement patterns using Location-allocation covering models. *Annals of the Association of American Geographers* (78(4):701-14.

Claassen, Cheryl, 1991. Normative thinking and shell-bearing sites. Pp. 249-98 in M. Schiffer (ed.) *Archaeological Method and Theory 3*. Tucson: University of Arizona Press.

Claessen, H.J.M., 1981. Reaching for the moon? Some problems and prospects of cultural evolutionism. Pp. 15-40 in S.E. van der Leeuw (ed.) *Archaeological Approaches to the Study of Complexity*. Amsterdam: Universiteit van Amsterdam.

Clark, John E. and Michael Blake, 1994. The power of prestige: competitive generosity and the emergence of rank societies in lowland Mesoamerica. Pp. 17-30 in E. Brumfiel and J. Fox (eds.) *Factional Competition and Political Development in the New World*. Cambridge: Cambridge University Press.

Claxton, J.B., 1995. Future enhancements to GIS: implications for archaeological theory. Pp. 335-48 in G. Lock and Z. Stancic (eds.) 1995: *Archaeology and Geographical Information Systems: a European perspective*. London: Taylor & Francis.

Cohen, Mark N., 1985. Prehistoric hunter-gatherers: the meaning of social complexity. Pp. 99-119 in T. Douglas Price and James A. Brown (eds.) *Prehistoric Hunter-Gatherers: The Emergence of Cultural Complexity*. New York: Academic Press.

Colten, Roger H. and Andrew Stewart, 1996. An adaptionist model of emergent complexity among hunter-gatherers in the Santa Barbara, California region. *Research in Economic Anthropology* 17: 227-50.

Conkey, Margaret, 1984. To find ourselves: art and social geography of prehistoric hunter gatherers. Pp. 253-76 in Schrire, Carmel (ed.) *Past and Present in Hunter Gatherer Studies*. London: Academic Press.

Conkey, Margaret, 1985. Ritual communication, social elaboration, and the variable trajectories of Palaeolithic material culture. Pp. 201-235 in T.Douglas Price and James A. Brown (eds.) *Prehistoric Hunter-Gatherers: the emergence of cultural complexity*. New York: Academic.

Conkey, Margaret, 1987. Interpretive problems in hunter-gatherer regional studies: some thoughts on the European Upper Palaeolithic. In Soffer, Olga (ed.) *The Pleistocene Old World: Regional Perspectives*. London: Plenum.

Cooper, John M., 1946. The Yahgan. In Julian Steward (ed.) *Handbook of South American Indians*. Washington: Bureau of American Ethnology, Bulletin 143(1).

Cosgrove, Denis, 1989. Geography is everywhere: culture and symbolism in human landscapes. Pp. 118-35 in D. Gregory and R. Walford (eds.) *Horizons in Human Geography*. Basingstoke, U.K.: MacMillan.

Coupland, Gary, 1988. Prehistoric social and economic change in the Tsimshian area. Pp. 211-43 in B. Isaac (ed.): *Research in Economic Anthropology, Supplement 3: Prehistoric Economies of the Northwest Coast*. Greenwich CT: JAI Press.

Croes, Dale and Steven Hackenberger, 1988. Hoko river archaeological complex: modeling prehistoric northwest coast economic evolution. Pp. 19-86 in B. Isaac (ed.): *Research in Economic Anthropology, Supplement 3: Prehistoric Economies of the Northwest Coast*. Greenwich CT: JAI Press.

Davis, Stanley D., 1990. Prehistory of Southeastern Alaska. Pp. 197-202 in Wayne Suttles (ed.): *Handbook of North American Indians, vol. 7: Northwest Coast*. Smithsonian Institution, Washington, 1990.

De Laguna, Frederica, 1990. Tlingit. Pp. 203-28 in Wayne Suttles (ed.): *Handbook of North American Indians, vol. 7: Northwest Coast*. Smithsonian Institution, Washington, 1990.

Donald, Leland and Donald H. Mitchell, 1994. Nature and culture on the Northwest Coast of North America: The case of Wakashan salmon resources. Pp. 95-117 in E. Burche and J. Ellanna (eds.): *Key Issues in Hunter-Gatherer Research*. Oxford: Berg.

Drennan, R. and C. Uribe (eds.), 1987. *Chiefdoms in the Americas*. Lanham MD: University Press of the Americas.

Drucker, Philip, 1951. *The Northern and Central Nootkan Tribes*. Washington, D.C.: Bureau of American Ethnology, Bulletin 144.

Dunnell, Robert C., 1992. The notion site. Pp. 21-42 in J. Rossignol and L. Wandsnider (eds.) *Space, Time and Archaeological Landscapes*. London: Plenum.

Earle, Timothy K., 1987a. Specialization and the production of wealth: Hawaiian chiefdoms and the Inka empire. Pp. 64-75 in E. Brumfiel and T. Earle (eds.) *Specialization, Exchange, and Complex Societies*. Cambridge: Cambridge University Press, New Directions in Archaeology.

Earle, Timothy K., 1987b. Chiefdoms in archaeological and ethnohistorical perspective. *Annual Review of Anthropology* 16:279-308.

Earle, Timothy K. (ed.), 1991. *Chiefdoms: Power, Economy, and Ideology*. Cambridge: Cambridge University Press

Easton, N. Alexander, 1985. *The Underwater Archaeology of Coast Salish Reef Netting*. Unpublished M.A. thesis in Anthropology, University of Victoria, British Columbia.

Eldridge, Morley and Alexander Mackie, 1993. *Predictive Modelling and the Existing Archaeological Inventory in British Columbia*. Unpublished non-permit report prepared for the Archaeology Task Group of the Geology, Soils, and Archaeology Task Force of the Resource Inventory Committee, Province of British Columbia. On file at the Archaeology Branch, Province of British Columbia, Victoria.

Eldridge, Morley and Heather Moon, 1992. *Archaeological Inventory in British Columbia*. Unpublished non-permit report prepared for the Archaeology Task Group of the Geology, Soils, and Archaeology Task Force of the Resource Inventory Committee, Province of British Columbia. On file at the Archaeology Branch, Province of British Columbia, Victoria.

Ellen, Roy, 1996. The cognitive geometry of nature: a contextual approach. Pp. 103-23 in P. Descola and G. Palsson (eds.) *Nature and Society: Anthropological Perspectives*. London: Routledge.

77

Emmons, George Thornton, 1991. *The Tlingit Indians.* Frederica de Laguna (ed.). Anthropological Papers of the American Museum of Natural History no. 70. Washington, D.C.: Smithsonian.

ESRI, 1995. *ArcDoc 7.0* (Relational database manual for Arc/Info). Redlands, California: Environmental Systems Research Institute.

Firth, Raymond, 1953. *Elements of Social Organization.* London: Watts.

Fladmark, Knut, 1982. An introduction to the prehistory of British Columbia. *Canadian Journal of Archaeology* 6:95-156.

Flanagan, James G., 1989. Hierarchy in 'simple' and 'egalitarian' Societies. *Annual Review of Anthropology* 18:245-66.

Flanagan, James G. and Steve Rayner, 1988. Introduction. Pp. 1-19 in James G. Flanagan and Steve Rayner (eds.) *Rules, Decisions, and Inequality in Egalitarian Societies.* Aldershot U.K.: Gower.

Fletcher, Roland, 1995. *The Limits of Settlement Growth: a theoretical outline.* Cambridge: Cambridge University Press, New Studies in Archaeology.

Foley, Robert, 1981. A model of regional archaeological structure. *Proceedings of the Prehistoric Society* 47: 1-17.

Fox, John, 1994. Conclusions: moietal opposition, segmentation, and factionalism in New World political arenas. Pp. 199-206 in E. Brumfiel and J. Fox (eds.) *Factional Competition and Political Development in the New World.* Cambridge: Cambridge University Press.

Gaffney V. and M. van Leusen, 1995. Postscript—GIS, environmental determinism and archaeology: a parallel text. Pp. 366-382 in G. Lock and Z. Stancic (eds.) 1995: *Archaeology and Geographical Information Systems: A European Perspective.* London: Taylor & Francis.

Gaffney, Vincent, Zoran Stancic and Helen Watson, 1995. Moving from catchments to cognition: tentative steps towards a larger archaeological context for GIS. *Scottish Archaeological Review* 15:41-64.

Gaines, Sylvia (ed.), 1987. *Coasts, Plains and Deserts: essays in honor of Reynold J. Ruppe.* Anthropological Research Papers No. 38, Arizona State Unversity. Temple AZ.

Galloway, Patricia, 1992. The unexamined habitus: direct historic analogy and the archaeology of the text. Pp. 178-95 in J-C. Gardin and C. Peebles (eds.) *Representations in Archaeology.* Bloomington: Indiana University Press.

Gamble, Clive S., 1986. Hunter-gatherers and the origin of states. Pp. 23-47 in J.A. Hall (ed.) *States in History.* Oxford: Basil Blackwell.

Gamble, Clive S., 1987. Archaeology, geography and time. *Progress in Human Geography* 11(2):227-46.

Gamble, Clive S., 1992. Archaeology, history, and the uttermost ends of the earth — Tasmania, Tierra del Fuego and the Cape. *Antiquity* 66:712-20.

Gamble, Clive S., 1993. The centre at the edge. Pp. 313-21 in Olga Soffer and N.D. Praslov (eds.) *From Kostenki to Clovis: Upper Palaeolithic — Palaeo-Indian Adaptations.* New York: Plenum.

Gamble, Clive S., 1995. Making Tracks: Hominid networks and the evolution of the social landscape. Pp. 253-77 in J. Steele and S. Shennan (eds.) *The Archaeology of Human Ancestry: Power, Sex and Tradition.* London: Routledge.

Gamble, Clive S., 1998. Palaeolithic society and the release from proximity: a network approach to intimate relations. *World Archaeology* 29(3):426-49.

Gell, Alfred, 1985. How to read a map: remarks on the practical logic of navigation. *Man* (n.s.) 20: 271-86.

Gell, Alfred, 1992. *The Anthropology of Time: cultural constructions of temporal maps and images.* Oxford: Berg.

Gibson, J.J., 1979. *The Ecological Approach to Visual Perception.* Hillsdale, New Jersey: Lawrence Erlbaum Assoc.

Giddens, Anthony, 1984. *The Constitution of Society.* Cambridge: Polity Press.

Gilman, Antonio, 1991. Trajectories towards social complexity in the later prehistory of the Mediterranean. Pp. 146-69 in T. Earle (ed.) *Chiefdoms: power, economy, and ideology.* Cambridge: Cambridge University Press.

Gorenflo, L. and N. Gale, 1990. Mapping regional settlement in information space. *The Journal of Anthropological Archaeology* 9:240-74

Gorenflo, L. and T. Bell, 1992. Network analysis and the study of past regional organization. Pp. 80-98 in C. Trumbold (ed.) *Ancient Road Networks and Settlement Hierarchies in the New World.* Cambridge: Cambridge University Press.

Gorenstein, Shirley and Helen P. Pollard, 1992. *Xanhari*: protohistoric Tarascan routes. Pp. 169-85 in C. Trumbold (ed.) *Ancient Road Networks and Settlement Hierarchies in the New World.* Cambridge: Cambridge University Press.

Gosden, Christopher and Christina Pavlides, 1994. Are islands insular? landscape vs. seascape in the case of the Arawe Islands, Papua New Guinea. *Archaeology in Oceania* 29:162-71.

Gosden, Christopher and Lesley Head, 1994. Landscape: a usefully ambiguous concept. *Archaeology in Oceania* 29:113-16.

Gosden, Christopher, 1994. *Social Being and Time.* Oxford: Blackwell.

Gosden, Christopher, 1995. Arboriculture and agriculture in coastal Papua New Guinea. *Antiquity* 69: 807-17.

Gould, Richard A., 1985. 'Now Let's Invent Agriculture' . . . : a critical review of concepts of complexity among hunter-gatherers. Pp. 427-35 in T. Douglas Price and James A. Brown (eds.) *Prehistoric Hunter-Gatherers: the emergence of cultural complexity.* New York: Academic Press.

Graves, Paul M., 1990. *The Biological and the Social in Human Evolution.* Unpublished Ph.D. thesis, Department of Archaeology, University of Southampton.

Green, S.W., 1990. Introduction. Pp. 3-8 in Allen, K.M.S., S.W. Green and E.B.W. Zubrow (eds.) *Interpreting Space: GIS and Archaeology.* London: Taylor & Francis.

Gregg, Susan, 1991. Introduction. to S. Gregg (ed.) *Between Bands and States.* Carbondale Illinois: Center for Archaeological Investigations, Occasional Paper No. 9.

Gregg, Susan (ed.), 1991. *Between Bands and States.* Carbondale Illinois: Center for Archaeological Investigations, Occasional Paper No. 9.

Gruber, Jacob W., 1986. Archaeology, history and culture. Pp. 163-186 in D. Meltzer, D. Fowler and J. Sabloff (eds.) *American Archaeology Past and Future.* Washington, D.C.: Smithsonian Press.

Gusinde, Martin, 1961 [1931]. *The Yamana: the Life and Thought of the Water Nomads of Cape Horn.* Human Relations Area Files, New Haven, Connecticut. Bound in three volumes.

Hage, Per and Frank Harary, 1983. *Structural Models in Anthropology.* Cambridge: Cambridge University Press.

Haggarty, James, 1982. *The Archaeology of Hesquiat Harbour: The Archaeological Utility of an Ethnographically Defined Social Unit.* Unpublished Ph.D. thesis, Department of Anthropology, Washington State University.

Haggarty, James and Richard Inglis, 1983. Westcoast Sites: an archaeological and macro-environmental synthesis. Pp. 11-33 in R. greengo (ed.) *Prehistoric Places on the Southern Northwest Coast.* Seattle: University of Washington, Burke Museum.

Hames, Raymond, 1992. Time allocation. Pp. 203-235 in Smith, E.A. and B. Winterhalder (eds.) *Evolutionary Ecology and Human Behavior.* Hawthorn, New York: Aldine de Gruyter.

Hannerz, Ulf, 1992. The global ecumene as a network of networks. Pp. 34-56 in A. Kuper (ed.) *Conceptualizing Society* London: Routledge.

Hannerz, Ulf, 1994. *Cultural Complexity: Studies in the Social Organization of Meaning,* New York: Columbia University Press.

Harris, Albert, 1987. Cell motility and the problem of anatomical homeostasis. *Journal of Cell Science,* Supplement 8: 121-40.

Harris, T.M. and G.R. Lock, 1995. Toward an evaluation of GIS in European archaeology: the past, present and future of theory and applications. Pp. 349-365 in G. Lock and Z. Stancic (eds.) 1995: *Archaeology and Geographical Information Systems: A European Perspective.* London: Taylor & Francis.

Hastings, C., 1987. Implications of Andean verticality in the evolution of political complexity: a view from the margins. Pp. 145-157 in J. Haas, S. Pozorski and T. Pozorski (eds.) *The Origins and Development of the Andean State.* Cambridge: Cambridge University Press.

Hayden, Brian, 1990. Nimrods, piscators, pluckers and planters: the emergence of food production. *The Journal of Anthropological Archaeology:* 9: 31-69.

Hayden, Brian, 1992. Conclusions: ecology and complex hunter/gatherers. Pp. 524-563 in B. Hayden (ed.) *A Complex Culture of the British Columbia Plateau.* Vancouver: U.B.C. Press.

Hayden, Brian, 1994. Competition, labour, and complex hunter-gatherers. Pp. 223-242 in Burch E. and L. Ellanna (eds.) *Key Issues in Hunter-Gatherer Research.* Oxford: Berg.

Haynes, Kingsley and A.S. Fotheringham, 1984. *Gravity and Spatial Interaction Models.* Scientific Geography Series vol. 2. London: Sage.

Headland, Thomas N., 1997. Revisionism in Ecological Anthropology. *Current Anthropology* 38(4):605-30.

Hebda, Richard J. and Rolf W. Mathewes, 1984. Holocene history of cedar and Native Indian cultures of the North American Pacific Coast. *Science* 225:711-13.

Hillsman, E.L., 1984. The $p$-median structure as a unified linear model for location-allocation analysis. *Environment and Planning A* 16:305-18.

Hodder, Ian, 1992. Towards a coherent archaeology. Chapter 12 in I. Hodder (ed.) *Theory and Practice in Archaeology.* London: Routledge.

Hoffmeyer, Jesper, 1997. The swarming body. Paper presented at the 5th IASS congress in Berkeley, June 1995, Pp. 937-940 in Irmengard Rauch and Gerald F. Carr (eds.) *Semiotics Around the World. Proceedings of the Fifth Congress of the International Association for Semiotic Studies. Berkeley 1994.* New York: Mouton de Gruyter 1997. Also web published at: http://www.molbio.ku.dk/MolBioPages/abk/Persona lPages/Jesper/Swarm.html

Ingold, Tim, 1986a. Territoriality and tenure: the appropriation of space in hunting and gathering societies. Pp. 130-64 in T. Ingold (ed.) *The Appropriation of Nature.* Manchester: Manchester University Press.

Ingold, Tim, 1986b. The principle of individual autonomy and the collective appropriation of nature. Pp. 222-42 in T. Ingold (ed.) *The Appropriation of Nature.* Manchester: Manchester University Press.

Ingold, Tim, 1992. Culture and the perception of the environment. Pp. 39-56 in E. Croll and D. Parkin (eds.) *Bush Base: Forest Farm. Culture, Environment and Development.* London: Routledge.

Ingold, Tim, 1993. The temporality of the landscape. *World Archaeology* 25(2):152-74.

Ingold, Tim, 1994. From trust to domination: an alternative history of human-animal relations. Pp. 1-22 in A. Manning and J. Serpell (eds.) *Animals and Human Society: Changing Perspectives*. London: Routledge.

Ingold, Tim, 1995. Work, time and industry. *Time & Society* 49(1):5-28.

Ingold, Tim, 1996. The optimal forager and economic man. Pp. 25-44 in P. Descola and G. Palsson (eds.) *Nature and Society: Anthropological Perspectives*. London: Routledge.

Ingold, Tim (ed.), 1996. *Key Debates in Anthropology*. London: Routledge.

Ingold, Tim, 1997. The picture is not the terrain. Maps, paintings and the dwelt-in world. *Archaeological Dialogues* 4(1):29-31.

Irwin, Geoffrey, 1974. The emergence of a central place in coastal Papuan prehistory: a theoretical approach. *Mankind* 9: 268-72.

Irwin, Geoffrey, 1985. *The Emergence of Mailu: as a central place in coastal Papuan prehistory*. Canberra: Terra Australis no. 10, Department of Prehistory, Research School of Pacific Studies, The Australian National University.

Irwin, Geoffrey, 1992. *The Prehistoric Exploration and Colonisation of the Pacific*. Cambridge: Cambridge University Press.

Jackson, H. Edwin and Virginia Popper, 1980. Coastal hunter-gatherers: the Yahgan of Tierra del Fuego. In *Michigan Discussions in Anthropology* 5(1-2):40-61.

Johnson, Gregory A., 1982. Organizational structure and scalar stress. Pp. 389-421 in C. Renfrew, M. Rowlands and B. Abbot-Seagraves *Theory and Explanation in Archaeology*. London: Academic Press.

Keeley, Lawrence H., 1988. Hunter-gatherer economic complexity and 'population pressure': a cross cultural analysis. *The Journal of Anthropological Archaeology:* 7:373:411.

Kelly, Robert L., 1983. Hunter-gatherer mobility strategies. *Journal of Anthropological Research* 39:277-306.

Kelly, Robert L., 1991. Sedentism, socio-political inequality, and resource fluctuations. Pp. 135-158 in S. Gregg (ed.) *Between Bands and States*. Carbondale Illinois: Center for Archaeological Investigations, Occasional Paper No. 9.

Kirch, Patrick V. (ed.), 1986. *Island Societies: archaeological approaches to evolution and transformation*. Cambridge: Cambridge University Press.

Kosse, Krisztina, 1990. Group size and societal complexity: thresholds in the long-term memory. *The Journal of Anthropological Archaeology:* 9: 275-303.

Koyama, S and D. Thomas (eds.), 1981. *Affluent Foragers*. Osaka: National Museum of Ethnology, Senri Ethnological Series No. 9.

Krause, Aurel, 1956 [1885]. *The Tlingit Indians*. American Ethnological Society Monograph no. 26. University of Washington Press, Seattle.

Kuper, Adam, 1993. Post-modernism, Cambridge, and the Great Kalahari Debate. *Social Anthropology* 1:57-71.

Kvamme, Kenneth L., 1989. Geographic Information Systems in regional archaeological research and data management. Pp. 139-203 in M. Schiffer (ed.) *Archaeological Method and Theory, Volume 1*. Tucson: University of Arizona Press.

Kvamme, Kenneth L., 1995. A view from across the water: the North American experience in archaeological GIS. Pp. 1-14 in G. Lock and Z. Stancic (eds.) 1995: *Archaeology and Geographical Information Systems: a European perspective*. London: Taylor & Francis.

Langran, Gail, 1993. *Time in Geographic Information Systems*. London: Taylor & Francis.

Lee, Richard, 1990. Primitive communism and the origin of social inequality. Pp. 225-246 in S. Upham (ed.) *The Evolution of Political Systems: Sociopolitics in Small-Scale Sedentary Societies*. Cambridge: Cambridge University Press

Lee, Richard and I. DeVore (eds.), 1968. *Man the Hunter*. Chicago: Aldine.

Lee, Richard and Mathias Guenther, 1993. Problems in Kalahari historical ethnography and the tolerance of errors. *History in Africa* 20:185-235.

Leroi-Goruhan, Andre, 1993. *Gesture and Speech*. Cambridge, MA: MIT Press.

Lesser, Alexander, 1961. Social fields and the evolution of society. In *Southwestern Journal of Anthropology* 17: 40-48.

Lewontin, R.C., 1982. Organism and environment. Pp. 151-170 in H. Plotkin (ed.) *Learning, Development, and Culture*. New York: John Wiley & Sons.

Lightfoot, Kent G., 1984. *Prehistoric Political Dynamics: a case study from the American Southwest*. DeKalb, Illinois: NIU Press.

Llobera, Marcus, 1996. Exploring the topography of mind: GIS, social space and archaeology. *Antiquity* 70: 612-22.

Lowe, John C. and S. Moryadas, 1977. *The Geography of Movement*. Boston: Houghton Mifflin.

MacArthur, Robert and Edward O. Wilson, 1967. *The Theory of Island Biogeography*. Princeton, NJ: Princeton University Press.

Mackie, Alexander, 1983. *The 1982 Meares Island Archaeological Survey: An inventory and evaluation of heritage resources*. Non-permit report on file at the Archaeology Branch, Victoria, British Columbia.

Mackie, Alexander, 1986. A closer look at coastal survey results. *The Midden*: vol. xviii: 3-5.

Madden, Marcie, 1983. Social network systems amongst hunter-gatherers considered within southern Norway. Pp. 191-200 in G. Bailey, *Hunter-Gatherer Economy in Prehistory*. Cambridge: Cambridge University Press.

Mandryk, Carole A. Stein, 1993. Hunter-gatherer social costs and the nonviability of submarginal environments. *Journal of Anthropological Research* 49:39-71.

Marble, Duane F., 1990. The potential methodological impact of geographic information systems on the social sciences. In Allen, Kathleen M.S., Stanton Green and Ezra Zubrow (eds.): *Interpreting Space: GIS and archaeology*. London: Taylor and Francis.

Marquardt, William H., 1985. Complexity and scale in the study of fisher-gatherer-hunters: an example from the Eastern United States. Pp. 59-98 in T. Douglas Price and James A. Brown (eds.) *Prehistoric Hunter-Gatherers: The Emergence of Cultural Complexity*. New York: Academic Press.

Marshall, Yvonne M., 1993. *A Political History of the Nuu-Chah-Nulth People: A Case Study of the Mowachaht and Muchalaht Tribes*. Unpublished PhD thesis, Department of Archaeology, Simon Fraser University, Burnaby, British Columbia.

Martin, David, 1991. *Geographic Information Systems and their Socioeconomic Applications*. London: Routledge.

Maschner, H., 1991. The emergence of cultural complexity on the Northwest Coast. *Antiquity* 65:924-34.

Maschner, H., 1997. Settlement and subsistence in the later prehistory of Tebenkof Bay, Kuiu Island, Southeast Alaska. *Arctic Anthropology* 34(2):74-99.

Maschner, H. and Brian Fagan, 1991. Hunter-gatherer complexity on the west coast of North America. *Antiquity* 65:921-3.

Maschner H. and J. Stein, 1995. Multivariate approaches to site location on the Northwest Coast of North America. *Antiquity*: 69: 61-73.

Mathien, Frances Joan, 1992. Political, economic, and demographic implications of the Chaco road network. Pp. 99-110 in C. Trumbold (ed.) *Ancient Road Networks and Settlement Hierarchies in the New World*. Cambridge: Cambridge University Press.

Matson, R.G., 1983. Intensification and the Development of Cultural Complexity: The Northwest Versus the Northeast Coast. Pp. 125-48 in Ronald. Nash (ed.) *The Evolution of Maritime Cultures on the Northeast and Northwest Coasts of America*. Burnaby, B.C.: Simon Fraser University Department of Archaeology Publication No. 11.

Matson, R.G. and G. Coupland, 1995. *The Prehistory of the Northwest Coast*. New York: Academic Press.

McCarthy, F. and M. McArthur, 1961. The food quest and the time factor in aboriginal economic life. Pp. 145-94 in C. Mountford (ed.) *Records of the American-Australian Scientific Expedition to Arnhem Land Volume II: Anthropology and Nutrition*. Melbourne, Melbourne University Press.

McCartney, A.P., 1975. Maritime adaptations in cold archipelagoes: an analysis of environment and culture in the aleutian and other island chains. Pp. 281-338 in W. Fitzhugh (ed.) *Prehistoric Maritime Adaptations of the Circumpolar Zone*. The Hague: Mouton.

McGuire, Randall H., 1983. Breaking down cultural complexity: inequality and heterogeneity. Pp. 91-142 in M. Schiffer (ed.) *Advances in Archaeological Method and Theory, Volume 6*. London: Academic Press.

McMillan, Alan D., 1996. *Since Kwatyat Lived on Earth: An Examination of Nuu-Chah-Nulth Culture History*. Unpublished Ph.D thesis, Department of Archaeology, Simon Fraser University, Burnaby, British Columbia.

McMillan, Allan and Denis St. Claire, 1982. *Alberni Prehistory: Archaeological and ethnographic investigations on western Vancouver Island*. Port Alberni: Theytus Books and Alberni Valley Museum.

Meacham, William, 1984. Coastal landforms and archaeology in the Hong Kong archipelago. *World Archaeology* 16(1):128-135.

Milicic, Bojka, 1993. Exchange and social stratification in the eastern Adriatic: a graph-theoretic model. *Ethnology* 32(4):375-395.

Miller, Bruce G., 1989. Centrality and measures of regional structure in aboriginal western Washington. *Ethnology* 28:265-76.

Miracle, Preston, L. Fisher and J. Brown, 1991. *Foragers in Context: Long Term, Regional, and Historical Perspectives in Hunter Gatherer Societies*. Ann Arbor: University of Michigan, Michigan Discussions in Anthropology Volume 10.

Mitchell, Donald H., 1990. Prehistory of the Coasts of Southern British Columbia and Northern Washington. Pp. 340-58 in W. Suttles (ed.) *Handbook of North American Indians Volume 7: Northwest Coast*. Washington, D.C.: Smithsonian Press.

Mitchell, Donald H. and Leland Donald, 1988. Archaeology and the study of Northwest Coast economies. Pp. 293-351 in Isaac, B (ed.) *Research in Economic Anthropology, Supplement 3*. Greenwich, CT: JAI Press.

Molyneaux, B.L., 1991. *Perception and Situation in the Analysis of Representations*. Unpublished Ph.D. thesis, Department of Archaeology, University of Southampton, U.K..

Monks, Greg, 1987. Prey as bait. *Canadian Journal of Archaeology* 11:119-42.

Moss, Madonna, J. Erlandson and R. Stuckenrath, 1989. Wood stake weirs and salmon fishing on the Northwest Coast: Evidence from southeast Alaska. *Canadian Journal of Archaeology*. 14:143-58.

Moss, Madonna and Jon Erlandson, 1992. Fort and refugexx

Moss, Madonna and Jon Erlandson, 1995. Reflections on North American Pacific coast prehistory. *Journal of World Prehistory* 9(1) 1-45.

Mueller, John H., Karl Schuessler and Herbert Costner, 1977. *Statistical Reasoning in Sociology 3rd Edition*. Boston: Houghton-Mifflin.

Murra, John V., 1985. 'El arcipelago vertical' revisited. Pp. 3-13 in S. Masuda (ed.) *Andean Ecology and Civilizations*. Tokyo: University of Tokyo.

Murray, Tim, 1997. Dynamic modelling and new social theory of the mid- to long term. Pp. 449-63 in J. McGlade and S. van der Leeuw (eds.) *Time, Process and Structured Transformation in Archaeology*. London: Routledge.

Nash, Ronald J., 1983. Preface. Pp. vi-viii in R. Nash (ed.) *The Evolution of Maritime Cultures on the Northeast and the Northwest Coasts of America*. Burnaby, B.C.: Simon Fraser University, Archaeology Press, Publication No. 11.

Netting, Robert McC., 1990. Population, permanent agriculture, and polities: unpacking the evolutionary portmanteau. Pp. 21-61 in S. Upham (ed.) *The Evolution of Political Systems: socioploitics in small-scale sedentary societies*. Cambridge: Cambridge University Press

O'Kelly, Morton E., 1994. Spatial Analysis and GIS. Pp. 65-79 in S. Fotheringham and P. Rogerson (eds.) *Spatial Analysis and GIS*. London: Taylor and Francis.

Oberg, Kalervo, 1973 [1937]. *The Social Economy of the Tlingit Indians*. American Ethnological Society Monograph no. 55., University of Washington Press, Seattle.

Orton, C., 1980. *Mathematics in Archaeology*. London: Collins.

Oswalt, Wendell H., 1976. *An Anthropological Analysis of Food-Getting Technology*. New York: Wiley.

Paynter, Robert, 1989. The Archaeology of Equality and Inequality. *Annual Review of Anthropology* 18:369-99.

Perusek, Glenn, 1994. Factional competition and historical materialism. Pp. 191-198 in E. Brumfiel and J. Fox (eds.) *Factional Competition and Political Development in the New World*. Cambridge: Cambridge University Press.

Peuquet, Donna J. and Duane F. Marble (eds.), 1990. *Introductory readings in Geographic Information Systems*. London: Taylor and Francis.

Pinxten, Rik, Ingrid van Dooren and Frank Harvey, 1983. *The Anthropology of Space: explorations into the natural philosophy and semantics of the Navaho*. Philadelphia: University of Pennsylvania Press.

Price, T. Douglas, 1981. Complexity in 'Non-Complex' Societies. Pp. 55-99 in S.E. van der Leeuw (ed.) *Archaeological Approaches to the Study of Complexity*. Amsterdam: Universiteit van Amsterdam.

Price, T. Douglas and James A. Brown, 1985. Aspects of Hunter-Gatherer Complexity. Pp. 3-20 in T. Douglas Price and James A. Brown (eds.) *Prehistoric Hunter-Gatherers: the emergence of cultural complexity*. New York: Academic Press.

Price, T. Douglas and James A. Brown (eds.), 1985. *Prehistoric Hunter-Gatherers: the emergence of cultural complexity*. New York: Academic Press.

Rautman, Alison E., 1993. Resource variability, risk, and the structure of social networks: an example from the prehistoric Southwest. *American Antiquity* 58(3):403-424.

Rayner, Steve, 1988. The Rules that Keep Us Equal: complexity and costs of social organization. Pp. 20-42 in James G. Flanagan and Steve Rayner (eds.) *Rules, Decisions, and Inequality in Egalitarian Societies*. Aldershot U.K.: Gower.

Reed, Edward S., 1988. The affordances of the animate environment: social science from the ecological point of view. In Ingold, T. (ed.) *What is an Animal?* London: Unwin Hyman.

Renfrew, Colin, 1973. Monuments, mobilization and social organization in Neolithic Wessex. Pp. 539-58 in C. Renfrew (ed.) *The Explanation of Culture Change: Models in prehistory*. London: Duckworth.

Renfrew, Colin, 1994. Towards a cognitive archaeology. Pp. 3-12 in C. Renfrew and E. Zubrow *The Ancient Mind* Cambridge: Cambridge University Press..

Renouf, M.A.P., 1991. Sedentary Hunter-Gatherers: a case for northern coasts. Pp. 89-107 in S. Gregg (ed.) *Between Bands and States*. Carbondale Illinois: Center for Archaeological Investigations, Occasional Paper No. 9.

Richardson, Allan S., 1982. The control of productive resources on the Northwest Coast of North America. Pp. 93-112 in N. Williams and E. Hunn (eds.) *Resource Managers: North American and Australian Hunter-Gatherers*. Boulder, Colorado: Westview Press.

Rival, Laura, 1996. Blowpipes and Spears: The social significance of Huaorani technological choices. Pp. 145-64 in P. Descola and G. Palsson (eds.) *Nature and Society: Anthropological Perspectives*. London: Routledge.

Rocha, Jorge M., 1996. Rationality, culture, and decision making. *Research in Economic Anthropology* 17:13-41.

Rossignol, Jacqueline and LuAnn Wandsnider (eds.), 1992. *Space, Time and Archaeological Landscapes*. London: Plenum.

Rowlands, Michael, 1989. A Question of Complexity. Pp. 29-40 in D. Miller *et al* (eds.) *Domination and Resistance*. London: Unwin Hyman.

Rowley-Conwy, Peter, 1983. Sedentary Hunters: the Ertebolle example. Pp. 111-126 in G. Bailey (ed.) *Hunter-Gatherer Economy in Prehistory*, Cambridge:Cambridge University Press.

Rowntree, Lester, 1986. Cultural/humanistic geography. *Progress in Human Geography* 10(4):581-86.

Sahlins, Marshall, 1968. Notes on the Original Affluent Society. Pp. 85-89 in R. Lee and I. DeVore (eds.) *Man the Hunter*. Chicago: Aldine.

Saitta, Dean J., 1983. On the evolution of 'tribal' social networks. *American Antiquity* 48(4):820-824.

Santley, Robert S., 1992. The structure of the Aztec transport network. Pp. 198-210 in C. Trumbold (ed.) *Ancient Road Networks and Settlement Hierarchies in the New World*. Cambridge: Cambridge University Press.

Savage, Stephen H., 1990a. GIS in archaeological research. Pp 22-32 in Allen, Kathleen M.S., Stanton Green and Ezra Zubrow (eds.): *Interpreting Space: GIS and archaeology*. London: Taylor and Francis.

Savage, Stephen H., 1990b. Modelling the late archaic social landscape. Pp. 330-55 in Allen, Kathleen M.S., Stanton Green and Ezra Zubrow (eds.): *Interpreting Space: GIS and archaeology*. London: Taylor and Francis.

Schalk, Randall, 1977. The structure of an anadramous fish resource. Pp. 207-49 in Binford, L.R., *For Theory Building in Archaeology*. New York: Academic Press.

Schalk, Randall, 1981. Land use and organisational complexity among foragers of Northwestern North America. Pp. 53-75 in S. Koyama and D. Thomas (eds.): *Affluent Foragers*. Senri Ethnological Series, No. 9. Osaka: National Museum of Ethnology.

Schlanger, Sarah, 1992. Recognizing persistent places in Anasazi settlement systems. Pp. 91-112 in J. Rossignol and L. Wandsnider (eds.) *Space, Time and Archaeological Landscapes*. London: Plenum.

Schlee, Gunther, 1992. Ritual topography and ecological use. Pp. 110-128 in E. Croll and D. Parkin (eds.) *Bush Base: Forest Farm. Culture, Environment and Development*. London: Routledge.

Schwartz, Theodore, 1978. The size and shape of a culture. Pp. 215-52 in F. Barth (ed.) *Scale and Social Organization*. Oslo: Universitetsforlagets.

Scott, John, 1991. *Social Network Analysis: a handbook*. London:Sage.

Service, Elman, 1962. *Primitive Social Organization: an evolutionary perspective*. New York: Random House.

Shennan, Stephen, 1988. *Quantifying Archaeology*. Edinburgh: Edinburgh University Press.

Shennan, Stephen, 1993. After social evolution: a new archaeological agenda? Pp. 53-59 in N. Yoffee and A. Sherratt (eds.) *Archaeological Theory: who sets the agenda?* Cambridge: Cambridge University Press.

Sherratt, Andrew, 1996. 'Settlement patterns' or 'landscape studies?' Reconciling reason and romance. *Archaeological Dialogues* 3(2):140-59.

Smith, Eric Alden and Bruce Winterhalder (eds.), 1992. *Evolutionary Ecology and Human Behavior*. Hawthorn, New York: Aldine de Gruyter

Smith, Michael E., 1993. New World complex societies: recent economic, social, and political studies. *Journal of Archaeological Research* 1(1): 5-42.

Stahl, Ann Brewer, 1993. Concepts of time and approaches to analogical reasoning in historical perspective. *American Antiquity* 58(2) 235-60.

Stark, Barbara and Barbara Voorhies (eds.), 1978. *Prehistoric Coastal Adaptations: the economy and ecology of maritime middle America*. London: Academic Press.

Stead, Stephen, 1993. GIS in archaeology: a research summary. *Mapping Awareness & GIS in Europe* 7(3):41-43.

Stead, Stephen, 1995. Humans and PETS in space. Pp. 313-17 in G. Lock and Z. Stancic (eds.) 1995: *Archaeology and Geographical Information Systems: a European perspctive*. London: Taylor & Francis.

Stein, Julie K. (ed.), 1991. *Deciphering a Shell Midden*. New York: Academic.

Steponaitis, Vincas P., 1978. Location Theory and Complex Chiefdoms: A Mississippian Example. Pp. 417-53 in B. Smith (ed.) *Mississippian Settlement Patterns*. London: Academic.

Stocking, George, 1966. Franz Boas and the culture concept in historical perspective. *American Anthropologist* 68(3):867-82.

Stopak, David and Albert Harris, 1982. Connective tissue morphogenesis by fibroblast traction. *Developmental Biology* 90:383-98.

Suttles. Wayne, 1968. Coping with Abundance: Subsistence on the Northwest Coast. Pp. 56-68 in R. Lee and I. DeVore (eds.) *Man the Hunter*. Chicago: Aldine.

Testart, Alain, 1982. The significance of food storage among hunter-gatherers: residence patterns, population densities, and social inequalities. *Current Anthropology* 23(5):523-537.

Thomas, Julian, 1993. The Politics of Vision and the Archaeologies of Landscape. Pp. 19-48 in B. Bender (ed.) *Landscape: Politics and Perspectives*. Oxford: Berg.

Thrift, Nigel, 1977. *An Introduction to Time Geography*. Concepts and Techniques in Modern Geography No. 13. Norwich: GeoAbstracts.

Thrift, Nigel, 1985. Bear and mouse or bear and tree? Anthony Giddens' reconstitution of social theory. *Sociology* 19(4):609-23.

Tilley, Christopher, 1994. *A Phenomonology of Landscape. Paths, Places and Monuments*. Oxford: Berg.

Tobler, W. and S. Wineburg, 1971. A Cappadocian speculation. *Nature* 231:39-41.

Torrence, Robin, 1983. Time budgeting and hunter-gatherer technology. Pp. 11-22 in G. Bailey (ed.) *Hunter-Gatherer Economy in Prehistory*, Cambridge: Cambridge University Press.

Trigger, Bruce, 1995. Expanding middle-range theory. *Antiquity* 69:449-58.

Trumbold C. (ed.), 1992. *Ancient Road Networks and Settlement Hierarchies in the New World*. Cambridge: Cambridge University Press.

Upham, Steadman, 1987. A Theoretical Consideration of Middle Range Societies. Pp. 345-68 in R. Drennan and C. Uribe (eds.) *Chiefdoms in the Americas*. Lanham MD: University Press of the Americas.

Upham, Steadman, 1990a. Decoupling the Processes of Political Evolution. Pp. 1-17 in S. Upham (ed.) *The Evolution of Political Systems: Sociopolitics in Small-Scale Sedentary Societies*. Cambridge: Cambridge University Press

Upham, Steadman, 1990b. Analog or Digital: Toward a Generic Framework for Explaining the Development of Emergent Political Systems. Pp. 87-115 in S. Upham (ed.) *The Evolution of Political Systems: Sociopolitics in Small-Scale Sedentary Societies*. Cambridge: Cambridge University Press

Upham, Steadman, 1992. Interaction and Isolation: The Empty Spaces in Panregional Political and Economic Systems. In E. Schortman and P. Urban (eds.) *Resources, Power, and Inter-regional Interaction*. NY: Plenum.

Veth, Peter, 1989. Islands in the Interior: a model for the colonization of Australia's arid zone. *Archaeology in Oceania* 24:81-92.

Wallace, Dwight T., 1992. The Chincha roads: economics and symbolism. Pp. 251-63 in C. Trumbold (ed.) *Ancient Road Networks and Settlement Hierarchies in the New World*. Cambridge: Cambridge University Press.

Wansleeben, Milco and Leo Verhart, 1997. Geographical Information Systems: Methodological progress and theoretical decline. *Archaeological Dialogues* 4(1):53-64.

Ward, Mark, 1998. There's an ant in my phone. *New Scientist* 2118:32-5.

Wason, Paul K., 1994. *The Archaeology of Rank*. Cambridge: Cambridge University Press, New Studies in Archaeology.

Watanabe, Hiroshi, 1968. Subsistence and Ecology of Northern Food gatherers with Special Reference to the Ainu. Pp. 69-77 in R. Lee and I. DeVore (eds.) *Man the Hunter*. Chicago: Aldine.

Watson, Patty Jo, 1991. A Parochial Primer: The New Dissonance As Seen from the Midcontinental United States. Pp. 265-274 in R. Preucel (ed.) *Processual and Postprocessual Archaeologies: Multiple Ways of Knowing the Past*. Carbondale: Southern Illionis University Press, Center for Archaeological Investigations Occasional Paper #10

Wheatley, D., 199. Going over old ground: GIS, archaeological theory and the act of perception....Pp. 133-8 in J. Andresen, J. Madsen and I. Scollar (eds.) *Computing the Past: Computer Applications and Quantitative Methods in Archaeology 1992*. Aarhus: Aarhus University Press.

Wheatley, D., 1995. Cumulative Viewshed Analysis: A GIS-based method for investigating intervisibility, and its archaeological application. Pp. 171-85 in G. Lock and Z. Stancic (eds.) *Archaeology and Geographical Information Systems: A European perspective*. London: Taylor and Francis.

White, Leslie A., 1949. Energy and the Evolution of Culture. Pp. 363-96 in Leslie White *The Science of Culture: a study of man and civilization*. New York: Grove.

Wickwire, Wendy, 1992. Ethnography and archaeology as ideology: the case of the Stein River Valley. *BC Studies* 91-92: 51-78.

Williams, Elizabeth, 1987. Complex Hunter-Gatherers: a view from Australia. *Antiquity* 61: 310-21.

Wilmsen, Edwin, 1989. *Land Filled with Flies: A Political Economy of the Kalahari*. Chicago: University of Chicago Press.

Wilson, Edward O., 1975. *Sociobiology: The New Synthesis*. Cambridge, MA: Harvard University Press.

Wilson, Robin J., 1984. *Introduction to Graph Theory (3rd edition)*. New York: Longman.

Wobst, Martin, 1974. Boundary conditions for palaeolithic social systems: a simulation approach. *American Antiquity*:39(2):147-78.

Wobst, Martin, 1976. Locational relationships in Palaeolithic society. *Journal of Human Evolution* 5:49-58.

Wobst, Martin, 1978. The archaeo-ethnology of hunter-gatherers or the tyranny of the ethnographic record in archaeology *American Antiquity* 43(2):303-309.

Wobst, Martin, 1981. Palaeolithic Archaeology-some problems with form, space and time. Pp. 220-25 in G. Bailey (ed.) *Hunter-Gatherer Economy in Prehistory*. Cambridge: Cambridge University Press.

Wobst, Martin, 1990. Afterword: minitime and megaspace in the Palaeolithic at 18K and otherwise. Pp. 322-34 in O. Soffer and C. Gamble (eds.) *The World at 18,000 B.P.* London: Unwin-Hyman.

Wolf, Eric R., 1981. The mills of inequality: a Marxian approach. Pp. 41-57 in G. Berreman (ed.) *Social Inequality: comparative and developmental approaches*. London: Avademic Press.

Wylie, Alison, 1993 A proliferation of New
    Archaeologies: Beyond objectivism and relativism.
    Pp. 20-26 in N. Yoffee and A. Sherratt (eds.),
    *Archaeological Theory: who sets the agenda?*
    Cambridge: Cambridge University Press, New
    Directions in Archaeology.

Yesner, David R., 1984. Population pressure in coastal
    environments: an archaeological test. *World
    Archaeology* 16(1):108-127.

Yesner, David R., 1990. Fuegians and other hunter-
    gatherers of the subantarctic region: 'cultural
    devolution' reconsidered. In Meehan, B. and N.
    White (eds.) *Hunter-Gatherer Demography: past
    and present.* Oceania Monograph number 39,
    Sydney.

Yesner, David R., 1994. Seasonality and resource 'stress'
    among hunter-gatherers: archaeological signatures.
    Pp. 151-67 in Burch E. and L. Ellanna (eds.) *Key
    Issues in Hunter-Gatherer Research.* Oxford: Berg.

Yoffee, Norman, 1993. Too many chiefs? (or, Safe texts
    for the '90s). Pp. 60-78 in N. Yoffee and A. Sherratt
    (eds.) *Archaeological Theory: who sets the agenda?*
    Cambridge: Cambridge University Press.

Zeidler, James A., 1987. The Evolution of Prehistoric
    'Tribal' Systems as Historical Process:
    Archaeological Indicators of Social Reproduction.
    Pp. 325-44 in R. Drennan and C. Uribe (eds.)
    *Chiefdoms in the Americas.* Lanham MD:
    University Press of the Americas.

# APPENDIX A: TABLES AND FIGURES OF MIDDEN ZONE AREAS

Table A1: Areas and accessibilities of all midden zones.

| Zone ID# | Descriptor | MZ Area (m2) | Rank of MZ Area | Network Accessibility | # of Sites in Zone |
|---|---|---|---|---|---|
| 1 | KY-Rugged Pt. N | 100 | 204 | 0.00316 | 1 |
| 2 | KY-Rugged Pt. | 1,250 | 148 | 0.00359 | 1 |
| 3 | KY-Rugged Pt. S | 5,900 | 75 | 0.00370 | 4 |
| 4 | KY-Grassy Islets | 2,500 | 116 | 0.00370 | 2 |
| 5 | KY-Kapoose Ck. S | unknown | unknown | 0.00386 | 1 |
| 6 | KY-Tatchu Ck. N | 400 | 186 | 0.00352 | 1 |
| 7 | NN-Tatchu Pt. | 6,000 | 72 | 0.00369 | 1 |
| 8 | NN-Tatchu Pt. E | 6,000 | 72 | 0.00390 | 1 |
| 9 | NN-Catala Is. W | 1,405 | 140 | 0.00421 | 3 |
| 10 | NN-Catala Is. E | 3,400 | 104 | 0.00435 | 1 |
| 11 | NN-Port Eliza 1 | 19,500 | 29 | 0.00454 | 2 |
| 12 | NN-Port Eliza 2 | 2,400 | 119 | 0.00428 | 1 |
| 13 | NN-Greater Nutchatlitz | 33,105 | 17 | 0.00449 | 16 |
| 14 | NN-Nutchatlitz Jct S | 5,500 | 82 | 0.00421 | 2 |
| 15 | NN-Esperanza SW | 750 | 171 | 0.00448 | 4 |
| 16 | NN-Espinosa SW | 2,000 | 129 | 0.00424 | 1 |
| 17 | NN-Esperanza S | unknown | unknown | 0.00449 | 1 |
| 18 | NN-Ehatisaht | 5,600 | 77 | 0.00406 | 1 |
| 19 | NN-Little Espinosa S | 1,120 | 156 | 0.00429 | 2 |
| 20 | NN-Little Espinosa C | 30 | 211 | 0.00437 | 1 |
| 21 | NN-Little Espinosa N | 1,893 | 132 | 0.00404 | 2 |
| 22 | NN-Espinosa NW | unknown | unknown | 0.00373 | 1 |
| 23 | NN-Ceepeecee S | unknown | unknown | 0.00437 | 1 |
| 24 | NN-Tahsis/Esperanza 1 | 800 | 168 | 0.00526 | 1 |
| 25 | NN Tahsis/Esperanza 2 | 450 | 181 | 0.00521 | 1 |
| 26 | NN-Tahsis/Esperanza 3 | 104 | 203 | 0.00481 | 1 |
| 27 | NN-Tahsis North End | 12,500 | 43 | 0.00384 | 1 |
| 28 | NN-Tahsis Central 1 | 10 | 214 | 0.00485 | 1 |
| 29 | NN-Tahsis Central 2 | 900 | 165 | 0.00522 | 1 |
| 30 | NN-Tahsis Central 2 | 1,200 | 151 | 0.00550 | 1 |
| 31 | NN-Tahsis Central 3 | 800 | 168 | 0.00545 | 1 |
| 32 | NN-Nutchatlitz C | 1,350 | 145 | 0.00361 | 3 |
| 33 | NN-Nutchatlitz SC | 50 | 208 | 0.00360 | 2 |
| 34 | NN-Nutchatlitz E | 4,000 | 95 | 0.00294 | 1 |
| 35 | NN-Nutchatlitz SW | 1,100 | 157 | 0.00372 | 1 |
| 36 | NK-W Nootka Is. 1 | 5,600 | 78 | 0.00413 | 1 |
| 37 | NK-W. Nootka Is. 2 | 2,250 | 123 | 0.00446 | 1 |
| 38 | NK-W Nootka Is. 3 | 4 | 216 | 0.00441 | 1 |
| 39 | NK-W. Nootka Is. Bajo | 33,750 | 16 | 0.00419 | 2 |
| 40 | NK-SW Nootka Is. | 9,300 | 54 | 0.00428 | 1 |
| 41 | NK-Greater Yuquot | 108,254 | 1 | 0.00545 | 1 |
| 42 | NK-Yuquot N 1 | 9,400 | 53 | 0.00661 | 1 |
| 43 | NK-Yuquot N 2 | unknown | unknown | 0.00652 | 1 |
| 44 | NK-Zuciarte Ch. SW | 120 | 201 | 0.00582 | 1 |
| 45 | NK-Escalante Pt. S | 1,200 | 151 | 0.00536 | 1 |

| Zone ID# | Descriptor | MZ Area (m2) | Rank of MZ Area | Network Accessibility | # of Sites in Zone |
|---|---|---|---|---|---|
| 46 | NK-Zuciarte Ch. C | 300 | 191 | 0.00550 | 1 |
| 47 | NK-Bligh Is. SW | 1,200 | 151 | 0.00622 | 1 |
| 48 | NK-Bligh Is Ewin Inlet | 2,625 | 114 | 0.00473 | 1 |
| 49 | NK-Bligh Is. W 3 | 600 | 175 | 0.00786 | 1 |
| 50 | NK-Bligh Is. W 2 | 105 | 202 | 0.00770 | 1 |
| 51 | NK-Bligh Is. W 1 | 375 | 189 | 0.00773 | 1 |
| 52 | NK-Bligh Is. NC | 1,400 | 141 | 0.00697 | 2 |
| 53 | NK-Bligh Is. NE | 1,000 | 161 | 0.00680 | 1 |
| 54 | NK-Hoiss Ck. | 20,050 | 27 | 0.00643 | 2 |
| 55 | NK-Argonaut Pt W | 14,100 | 39 | 0.00641 | 1 |
| 56 | NK-Hanna Channel | 22,582 | 24 | 0.00602 | 5 |
| 57 | NK-Escalante Pt. N | unknown | unknown | 0.00542 | 1 |
| 58 | NK-Tlupana C 3 | 45 | 210 | 0.00698 | 1 |
| 59 | NK-Tlupana Hisnit S | 7,650 | 61 | 0.00590 | 2 |
| 60 | NK-Tlupana Hisnit N | 2,800 | 111 | 0.00492 | 1 |
| 61 | NK-Tlupana C 2 | 825 | 166 | 0.00641 | 2 |
| 62 | NK-Tlupana C 1 | 2,250 | 123 | 0.00616 | 1 |
| 63 | NK-Tlupana E | 4,200 | 93 | 0.00535 | 1 |
| 64 | NK-Tlupana-Tlupana R. | 5,825 | 76 | 0.00453 | 2 |
| 65 | NK-Tlupana NE 1 | 300 | 191 | 0.00559 | 1 |
| 66 | NK-Tlupana Moutcha 1 | 3,500 | 102 | 0.00496 | 1 |
| 67 | NK-Tlupana Moutcha 2 | 1,525 | 138 | 0.00553 | 1 |
| 68 | NK-Tlupana NE 2 | 150 | 199 | 0.00561 | 1 |
| 69 | NK-Tlupana Head Bay | unknown | unknown | 0.00486 | 1 |
| 70 | NK-Cook Ch. N | unknown | unknown | 0.00563 | 1 |
| 71 | NK-Tahsis S End | 14,000 | 40 | 0.00609 | 1 |
| 72 | NK-Bodega Is S | 15,600 | 35 | 0.00560 | 1 |
| 73 | NK-Bodega Is N | 450 | 181 | 0.00536 | 1 |
| 74 | CL-Meares Cloothpitch | 46,376 | 8 | 0.00690 | 1 |
| 75 | NK-Muchalat Mooyah | 3,400 | 104 | 0.00532 | 1 |
| 76 | NK-Muchalat NW | 385 | 187 | 0.00535 | 1 |
| 77 | NK-Muchalat Kleeptee | 12,300 | 47 | 0.00505 | 1 |
| 78 | NK-Muchalat SW 1 | 6,300 | 70 | 0.00530 | 1 |
| 79 | NK-Muchalat SW 2 | 3,750 | 98 | 0.00526 | 1 |
| 80 | NK-Muchalat Houston | 480 | 178 | 0.00410 | 1 |
| 81 | NK-Muchalat C E | 2,000 | 129 | 0.00392 | 1 |
| 82 | NK-Muchalat Jacklah | unknown | unknown | 0.00405 | 1 |
| 83 | NK-Muchalat Gold R. W | 510 | 176 | 0.00452 | 1 |
| 84 | NK-Muchalat Gold R. E | 405 | 185 | 0.00433 | 2 |
| 85 | NK-Muchalat Matchlee N | 2,985 | 110 | 0.00387 | 2 |
| 86 | NK-Muchalat Matchlee C | 500 | 177 | 0.00369 | 1 |
| 87 | NK-Muchalat Burman R. | 6,250 | 71 | 0.00340 | 1 |
| 88 | NK-Barcester Bay N | 3,600 | 99 | 0.00501 | 1 |
| 89 | NK-Barcester Bay C | unknown | unknown | 0.00538 | 1 |
| 90 | NK-Barcester Bay S | 5,600 | 79 | 0.00521 | 1 |
| 91 | NK-Estevan Pt. N | 6,991 | 67 | 0.00460 | 1 |
| 92 | NK-Estevan Pt. | 5,500 | 82 | 0.00450 | 1 |
| 93 | HQ-Matlahaw Pt. | 1,380 | 142 | 0.00463 | 1 |

| Zone ID# | Descriptor | MZ Area (m2) | Rank of MZ Area | Network Accessibility | # of Sites in Zone |
|---|---|---|---|---|---|
| 94 | HQ-Hesquiat | 92,964 | 2 | 0.00489 | 1 |
| 95 | HQ-Hesquiat Hbr SW | 37,000 | 13 | 0.00481 | 1 |
| 96 | HQ-Hesquiat Hbr NW | 60 | 206 | 0.00483 | 1 |
| 97 | HQ-Boat Basin SW | 60 | 206 | 0.00499 | 1 |
| 98 | HQ-Boat Basin NW | 5,551 | 80 | 0.00455 | 1 |
| 99 | HQ-Boat Basin NE | 1,140 | 154 | 0.00405 | 2 |
| 100 | HQ-Hesquiat Hbr NE | 162 | 198 | 0.00488 | 1 |
| 101 | HQ-Hesquiat Hbr SE | 7,442 | 64 | 0.00470 | 1 |
| 102 | HQ-Hot Springs Cove | 5,500 | 82 | 0.00397 | 3 |
| 103 | FL-Sydney Inlet | unknown | unknown | 0.00323 | 1 |
| 104 | FL-Flores Is. N | unknown | unknown | 0.00352 | 1 |
| 105 | CL-Flores Is S | 4,325 | 91 | 0.00491 | 1 |
| 106 | FL-Obstruction Is | 1,250 | 148 | 0.00352 | 1 |
| 107 | FL-Millar Ch | 3,125 | 107 | 0.00377 | 1 |
| 108 | FL-Clifford Pt. | 4,550 | 88 | 0.00426 | 1 |
| 109 | CL-Bartlett Is. | 12,375 | 45 | 0.00501 | 1 |
| 110 | CL-Blunden Is | 70,705 | 5 | 0.00501 | 6 |
| 111 | CL-Vargas Ahous Bay | 1,360 | 143 | 0.00530 | 1 |
| 112 | CL-Vargas Ahous Pt. | 10,750 | 50 | 0.00565 | 2 |
| 113 | CL-Vargas SW | 40,016 | 10 | 0.00602 | 3 |
| 114 | CL-Vargas NE | 2,800 | 111 | 0.00636 | 1 |
| 115 | CL-Meares NW 1 | 1,519 | 139 | 0.00650 | 5 |
| 116 | CL-Meares NW 2 | 1,004 | 160 | 0.00621 | 2 |
| 117 | CL-Meares NW 3 | 420 | 184 | 0.00594 | 1 |
| 118 | CL-Vargas Yarksis | 70,000 | 6 | 0.00663 | 1 |
| 119 | CL-Tofino Stubbs Is. | 14,200 | 38 | 0.00810 | 3 |
| 120 | CL- Opitsit | 79,872 | 4 | 0.00811 | 2 |
| 121 | CL- Lemmens S | 966 | 163 | 0.00844 | 1 |
| 122 | CL- Lemmens C W | 5,510 | 81 | 0.00785 | 2 |
| 123 | CL-Echachis Is | 45,800 | 9 | 0.00734 | 4 |
| 124 | CL-Esowista NW | 9 | 215 | 0.00795 | 1 |
| 125 | CL-McKenzie Bch | 19,099 | 30 | 0.00732 | 4 |
| 126 | CL-Chesterman 1 | 460 | 180 | 0.00784 | 2 |
| 127 | CL-Chesterman 2 | 12,500 | 43 | 0.00743 | 2 |
| 128 | CL-Lemmens NW | 7,250 | 66 | 0.00710 | 5 |
| 129 | CL-Lemmens C E | 8,894 | 57 | 0.00740 | 8 |
| 130 | CL-Lemmens NE | 208 | 197 | 0.00605 | 1 |
| 131 | CL-Lemmens SE | 8,879 | 58 | 0.00776 | 11 |
| 132 | CL-Tsapee N | 2,152 | 125 | 0.00645 | 3 |
| 133 | CL-Tsapee S | unknown | unknown | 0.00564 | 1 |
| 134 | CL-Meares SE | 15 | 213 | 0.00702 | 1 |
| 135 | CL-Indian Is SW | 480 | 178 | 0.00697 | 1 |
| 136 | CL-Indian Is NW | 384 | 188 | 0.00662 | 1 |
| 137 | CL-Heelboom Bay | 3,062 | 108 | 0.00549 | 8 |
| 138 | CL-Indian Is SE | 20,756 | 25 | 0.00649 | 1 |
| 139 | CL-Grice Bay N | 1,000 | 161 | 0.00597 | 1 |
| 140 | CL_Grice Bay E | 224 | 195 | 0.00528 | 1 |
| 141 | CL-Mosquito Inlet S | 12,615 | 42 | 0.00538 | 16 |
| 142 | CL-Mosquito Inlet C | 10,200 | 51 | 0.00526 | 2 |

| Zone ID# | Descriptor | MZ Area (m2) | Rank of MZ Area | Network Accessibility | # of Sites in Zone |
|---|---|---|---|---|---|
| 143 | CL-Mosquito Inlet N | 1,638 | 135 | 0.00478 | 5 |
| 144 | CL-Warn Bay | 17,540 | 32 | 0.00475 | 6 |
| 145 | CL-Matleset Narrows | 2,375 | 121 | 0.00489 | 1 |
| 146 | CL-Warn Bay N | 2,375 | 121 | 0.00421 | 1 |
| 147 | CL-Bedwell Sound C | 1,950 | 131 | 0.00387 | 1 |
| 148 | CL-Bedwell Sound N | 2,400 | 119 | 0.00343 | 1 |
| 149 | CL-Kennedy Cove | 62,900 | 7 | 0.00454 | 1 |
| 150 | CL-Tranquil Inlet | 4,400 | 90 | 0.00364 | 1 |
| 151 | CL-Tofino Inlet E | unknown | unknown | 0.00333 | 1 |
| 152 | CL-Tofino Inlet NE | 6,750 | 68 | 0.00311 | 1 |
| 153 | CL-Kennedy Lake Foot | 9,100 | 56 | 0.00428 | 1 |
| 154 | CL-Chesterman Cox Pt | 2,030 | 128 | 0.00733 | 2 |
| 155 | CL-Cox Pt S | 3,600 | 99 | 0.00647 | 1 |
| 156 | LB-Schooner Cove N | 5,200 | 86 | 0.00636 | 1 |
| 157 | LB-Schooner Cove C | 8,490 | 59 | 0.00655 | 2 |
| 158 | LB-Schooner Cove S | 3,600 | 99 | 0.00637 | 1 |
| 159 | LB-Wickaninnish N | 12,332 | 46 | 0.00611 | 7 |
| 160 | LB-Wickaninnish NE | 1,360 | 143 | 0.00550 | 3 |
| 161 | LB-Wickaninnish C | 20,000 | 28 | 0.00514 | 1 |
| 162 | LB-Wickaninnish S | 20,500 | 26 | 0.00521 | 2 |
| 163 | LB- Florencia N | 2,452 | 118 | 0.00542 | 5 |
| 164 | LB-Florencia C | 3,404 | 103 | 0.00547 | 3 |
| 165 | LB-Florencia S | 13,800 | 41 | 0.00559 | 1 |
| 166 | LB-Ucluth NW | 1,700 | 134 | 0.00561 | 2 |
| 167 | LB-Ucluth C | unknown | unknown | 0.00518 | 1 |
| 168 | BK-Macoah Pass SW | 2,100 | 126 | 0.00554 | 1 |
| 169 | BK-Tukwaa | 23,500 | 23 | 0.00576 | 1 |
| 170 | BK-Chuumata | 16,800 | 34 | 0.00587 | 1 |
| 171 | BK-George Fraser Is | 4,232 | 92 | 0.00559 | 2 |
| 172 | BK-Ucluelet C | 1,575 | 137 | 0.00490 | 1 |
| 173 | BK-Ucluelet N | 4,490 | 89 | 0.00440 | 3 |
| 174 | BK-Broken Gp W C | 17,485 | 33 | 0.00617 | 9 |
| 175 | BK-Broken Gp NW C | 1,312 | 146 | 0.00649 | 3 |
| 176 | BK-Broken Gp C | 24,006 | 22 | 0.00652 | 6 |
| 177 | BK-Broken Gp S C | 735 | 173 | 0.00650 | 2 |
| 178 | BK-Broken Gp S | 36,829 | 14 | 0.00602 | 12 |
| 179 | BK-Broken Gp SE | 25,048 | 20 | 0.00603 | 10 |
| 180 | BK-Broken Gp NC | 35,241 | 15 | 0.00669 | 14 |
| 181 | BK-Broken Gp NE C | 5,392 | 85 | 0.00685 | 2 |
| 182 | BK-Broken Gp N 1 | 72 | 205 | 0.00694 | 1 |
| 183 | BK-Deer Gp SW | 37,842 | 12 | 0.00519 | 14 |
| 184 | BK-Broken Gp NE 1 | 17,915 | 31 | 0.00642 | 17 |
| 185 | BK-Broken Gp NE 2 | 15,049 | 36 | 0.00601 | 3 |
| 186 | BK-Sechart E | 960 | 164 | 0.00574 | 2 |
| 187 | BK-Broken Gp N 2 | 9,716 | 52 | 0.00668 | 4 |
| 188 | BK-Sechart W | 10,850 | 49 | 0.00584 | 2 |
| 189 | BK-Stopper Is | 336 | 190 | 0.00578 | 1 |
| 190 | BK-St. Ines Is | 1,310 | 147 | 0.00617 | 1 |
| 191 | BK-Maggie River | 816 | 167 | 0.00573 | 1 |

| Zone ID# | Descriptor | MZ Area (m2) | Rank of MZ Area | Network Accessibility | # of Sites in Zone |
|---|---|---|---|---|---|
| 192 | BK-Macoah | 15,000 | 37 | 0.00554 | 1 |
| 193 | BK-Toquart | 7,580 | 62 | 0.00414 | 2 |
| 194 | BK-Deer Gp C | 2,800 | 111 | 0.00544 | 1 |
| 195 | BK-Deer Gp N | 1,050 | 159 | 0.00546 | 1 |
| 196 | BK-Trevor Ch | 225 | 194 | 0.00520 | 1 |
| 197 | BK-Tzartus Is S | 800 | 168 | 0.00478 | 2 |
| 198 | BK-Tzartus Is SW | 4,000 | 95 | 0.00511 | 2 |
| 199 | BK-Greater Bamfield | 86,291 | 3 | 0.00478 | 46 |
| 200 | BK-Cape Beale N | 11,386 | 48 | 0.00475 | 6 |
| 201 | BK-Cape Beale S | 8,130 | 60 | 0.00474 | 4 |
| 202 | SC-Pachena Bay N | 24,460 | 21 | 0.00455 | 2 |
| 203 | BK-Sarita W | 1,800 | 133 | 0.00449 | 1 |
| 204 | BK-Sarita E | 3,250 | 106 | 0.00413 | 1 |
| 205 | AB-Alberni/Barkley Jct N | 2,100 | 126 | 0.00410 | 1 |
| 206 | AB-Alberni/Barkley Jct S | 6,000 | 72 | 0.00387 | 1 |
| 207 | BK-Seddall Is | 1,625 | 136 | 0.00414 | 1 |
| 208 | AB-Uchucklesit | unknown | unknown | 0.00306 | 1 |
| 209 | AB-Nahmint Bay | 240 | 193 | 0.00275 | 1 |
| 210 | AB-Franklin River | unknown | unknown | 0.00268 | 1 |
| 211 | AB-Stamp Narrows W | unknown | unknown | 0.00341 | 1 |
| 212 | AB-Stamp Narrows E | 150 | 199 | 0.00356 | 1 |
| 213 | AB-Pt Alberni Polly Pt. | unknown | unknown | 0.00323 | 1 |
| 214 | AB-Pt Alberni Somass S | 9,200 | 55 | 0.00353 | 3 |
| 215 | AB-Somass C S | 2,500 | 116 | 0.00379 | 1 |
| 216 | AB-Somass C N | unknown | unknown | 0.00363 | 1 |
| 217 | AB-Somass | 31,300 | 18 | 0.00337 | 8 |
| 218 | AB-Sproat Lk | unknown | unknown | 0.00288 | 1 |
| 219 | SC-Pachena Bay S | 450 | 181 | 0.00420 | 1 |
| 220 | SC-Pachena Pt | 220 | 196 | 0.00412 | 1 |
| 221 | SC-Darling River | 30 | 211 | 0.00418 | 1 |
| 222 | SC-Darling River E | 616 | 174 | 0.00396 | 2 |
| 223 | SC-Klanawa River | 7,431 | 65 | 0.00379 | 3 |
| 224 | SC-Tsusiat | 3,975 | 97 | 0.00401 | 3 |
| 225 | SC-Tsuquanah | 6,600 | 69 | 0.00420 | 1 |
| 226 | SC-Whyac | 31,100 | 19 | 0.00454 | 4 |
| 227 | SC-Clo-oose | 7,472 | 63 | 0.00388 | 3 |
| 228 | SC-Nitinat Lk Foot | 38,025 | 11 | 0.00436 | 3 |
| 229 | SC-Nitinat Lk S | 1,064 | 158 | 0.00386 | 1 |
| 230 | SC-Dare Pt | 1,211 | 150 | 0.00367 | 4 |
| 231 | SC-Carmanah Pt N | 3,000 | 109 | 0.00353 | 1 |
| 232 | SC-Carmanah Pt S | 2,565 | 115 | 0.00321 | 1 |
| 233 | SC-Bonilla Pt | 4,050 | 94 | 0.00262 | 1 |
| 234 | SC-Nitinat Lk E C | 750 | 171 | 0.00292 | 1 |
| 235 | SC-Nitinat Lk W C | 5,175 | 87 | 0.00285 | 1 |

| Zone ID# | Descriptor | MZ Area (m2) | Rank of MZ Area | Network Accessibility | # of Sites in Zone |
|---|---|---|---|---|---|
| 236 | SC-Nitinat Lk NE | 50 | 208 | 0.00275 | 1 |
| 237 | SC-Nitinat Lk NW | 1,125 | 155 | 0.00255 | 1 |
| 238 | CL-Kennedy R. Inland | unknown | unknown | 0.00280 | 1 |

**KEY (see Fig. 6.2, p. 45 ):**
KY = Kyuquot Channel South
NN = North Nootka Island
NK = Nootka Sound
HQ = Hesquiat
FL = Flores Island
CL = Clayoquot Sound
LB = Long Beach
AB = Alberni Inlet
BK = Barkley Sound
SC = South Coast & Nitinaht

Figure A1: Histogram of individual site areas within study area, n = 526.

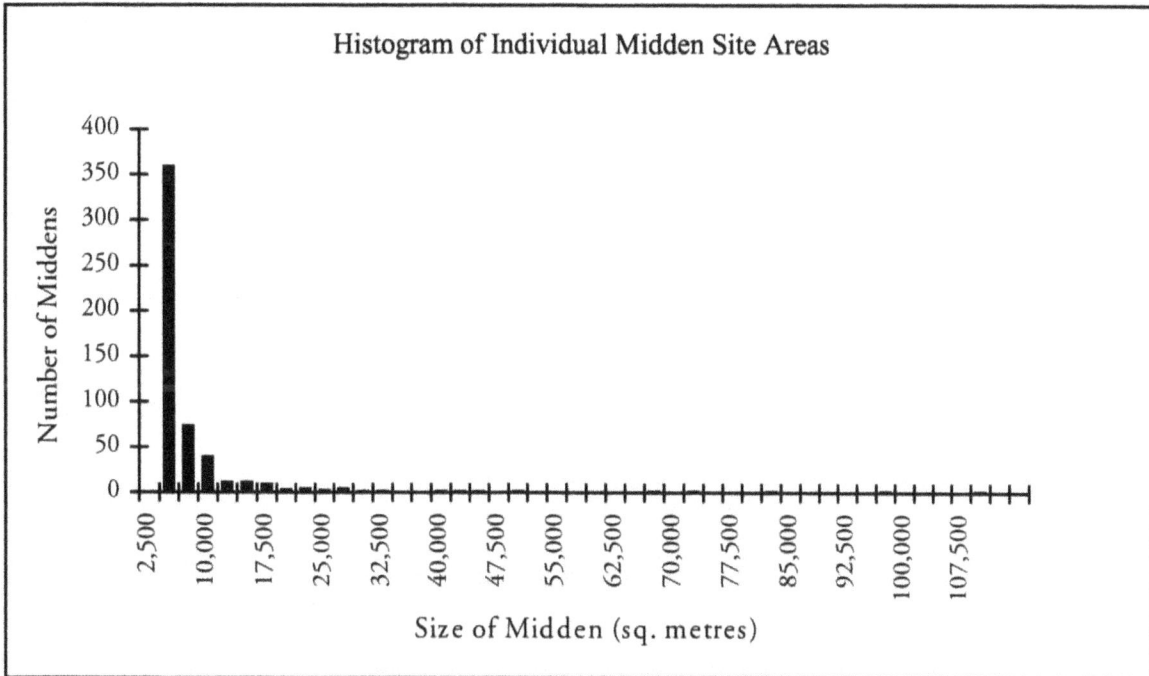

Figure A2: Histogram of midden zone areas within study area, n = 238.

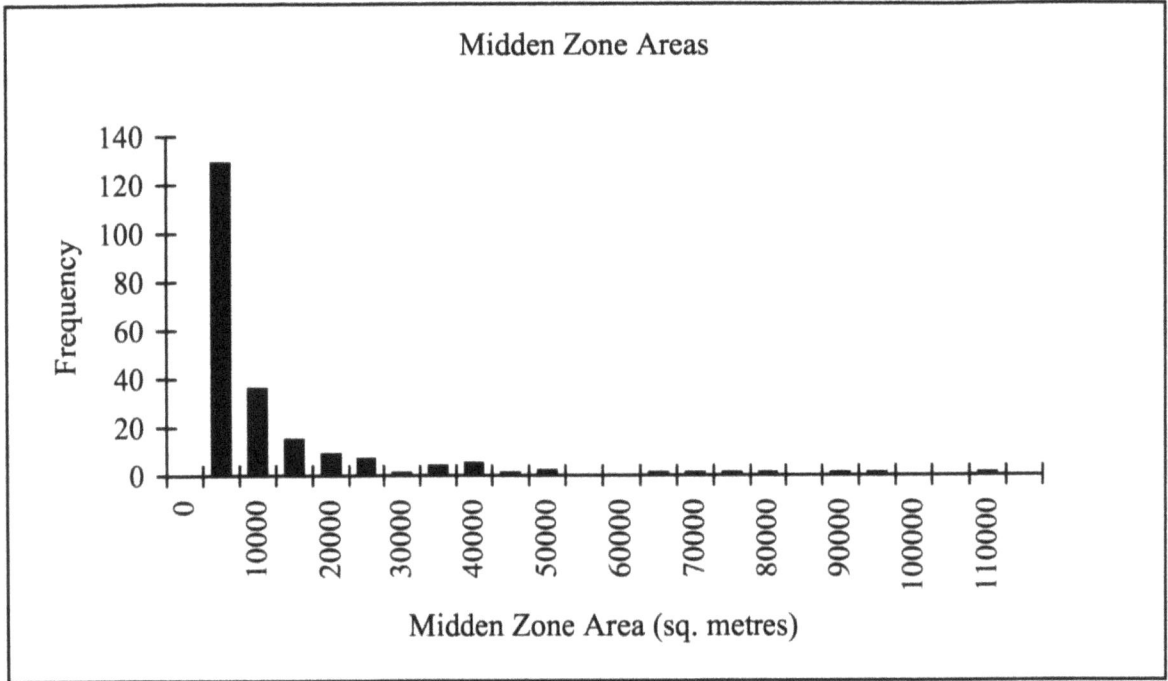
Midden Zone Areas

Figure A3: Histogram of base-10 Logarithm of midden zone areas.

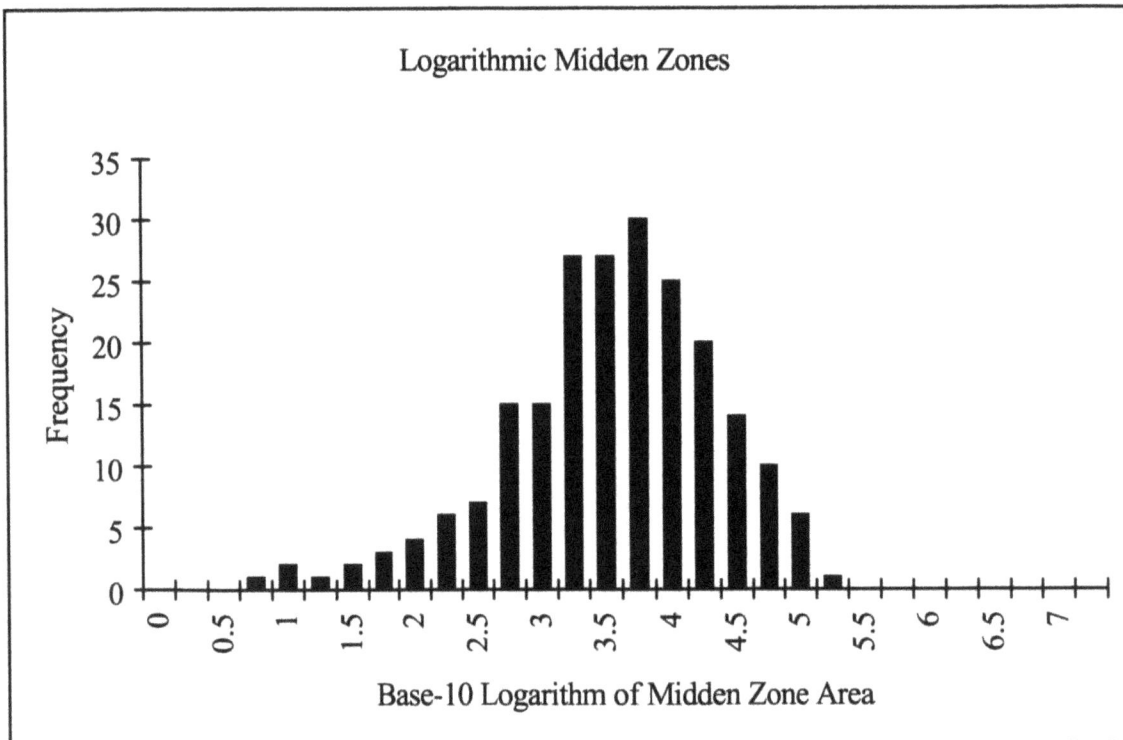
Logarithmic Midden Zones

Table B1: Location-allocation solution sets for 25
iterations of the $p = median$ model.

| Solution Set | ID | # of Sites in MZ | MZ Area (sq. metres) |
|---|---|---|---|
| 1 | 74 | 1 | 46,376 |
| 2 | 42 | 1 | 9,400 |
| 2 | 171 | 2 | 4,232 |
| 3 | 71 | 1 | 14,000 |
| 3 | 119 | 3 | 14,200 |
| 3 | 183 | 14 | 37,842 |
| 4 | 13 | 16 | 33,105 |
| 4 | 52 | 2 | 1,400 |
| 4 | 119 | 3 | 14,200 |
| 4 | 183 | 14 | 37,842 |
| 5 | 13 | 16 | 33,105 |
| 5 | 52 | 2 | 1,400 |
| 5 | 120 | 2 | 79,872 |
| 5 | 181 | 2 | 5,392 |
| 5 | 226 | 4 | 31,100 |
| 6 | 13 | 16 | 33,105 |
| 6 | 52 | 2 | 1,400 |
| 6 | 120 | 2 | 79,872 |
| 6 | 181 | 2 | 5,392 |
| 6 | 214 | 3 | 9,200 |
| 6 | 226 | 4 | 31,100 |
| 7 | 13 | 16 | 33,105 |
| 7 | 53 | 1 | 1,000 |
| 7 | 94 | 1 | 92,964 |
| 7 | 119 | 3 | 14,200 |
| 7 | 181 | 2 | 5,392 |
| 7 | 214 | 3 | 9,200 |
| 7 | 226 | 4 | 31,100 |
| 8 | 13 | 16 | 33,105 |
| 8 | 52 | 2 | 1,400 |
| 8 | 83 | 1 | 510 |
| 8 | 94 | 1 | 92,964 |
| 8 | 119 | 3 | 14,200 |
| 8 | 181 | 2 | 5,392 |
| 8 | 214 | 3 | 9,200 |

Table B1, *continued*

| Solution Set | ID | # of Sites in MZ | MZ Area (sq. metres) |
|---|---|---|---|
| 8 | 226 | 4 | 31,100 |
| 9 | 13 | 16 | 33,105 |
| 9 | 52 | 2 | 1,400 |
| 9 | 83 | 1 | 510 |
| 9 | 94 | 1 | 92,964 |
| 9 | 120 | 2 | 79,872 |
| 9 | 175 | 3 | 1,312 |
| 9 | 196 | 1 | 225 |
| 9 | 214 | 3 | 9,200 |
| 9 | 226 | 4 | 31,100 |
| 10 | 13 | 16 | 33,105 |
| 10 | 52 | 2 | 1,400 |
| 10 | 83 | 1 | 510 |
| 10 | 94 | 1 | 92,964 |
| 10 | 119 | 3 | 14,200 |
| 10 | 134 | 1 | 15 |
| 10 | 175 | 3 | 1,312 |
| 10 | 196 | 1 | 225 |
| 10 | 214 | 3 | 9,200 |
| 10 | 226 | 4 | 31,100 |
| 11 | 13 | 16 | 33,105 |
| 11 | 24 | 1 | 800 |
| 11 | 53 | 1 | 1,000 |
| 11 | 83 | 1 | 510 |
| 11 | 94 | 1 | 92,964 |
| 11 | 119 | 3 | 14,200 |
| 11 | 134 | 1 | 15 |
| 11 | 175 | 3 | 1,312 |
| 11 | 196 | 1 | 225 |
| 11 | 214 | 3 | 9,200 |
| 11 | 226 | 4 | 31,100 |
| 12 | 13 | 16 | 33,105 |
| 12 | 24 | 1 | 800 |
| 12 | 53 | 1 | 1,000 |
| 12 | 83 | 1 | 510 |
| 12 | 94 | 1 | 92,964 |
| 12 | 119 | 3 | 14,200 |
| 12 | 134 | 1 | 15 |

| Solution Set | ID | # of Sites in MZ | MZ Area (sq. metres) |
|---|---|---|---|
| 12 | 166 | 2 | 1,700 |
| 12 | 182 | 1 | 72 |
| 12 | 196 | 1 | 225 |
| 12 | 214 | 3 | 9,200 |
| 12 | 226 | 4 | 31,100 |
| 13 | 13 | 16 | 33,105 |
| 13 | 24 | 1 | 800 |
| 13 | 42 | 1 | 9,400 |
| 13 | 58 | 1 | 45 |
| 13 | 83 | 1 | 510 |
| 13 | 94 | 1 | 92,964 |
| 13 | 119 | 3 | 14,200 |
| 13 | 134 | 1 | 15 |
| 13 | 166 | 2 | 1,700 |
| 13 | 182 | 1 | 72 |
| 13 | 196 | 1 | 225 |
| 13 | 214 | 3 | 9,200 |
| 13 | 226 | 4 | 31,100 |
| 14 | 5 | 1 | unknown |
| 14 | 13 | 16 | 33,105 |
| 14 | 24 | 1 | 800 |
| 14 | 42 | 1 | 9,400 |
| 14 | 58 | 1 | 45 |
| 14 | 83 | 1 | 510 |
| 14 | 94 | 1 | 92,964 |
| 14 | 119 | 3 | 14,200 |
| 14 | 134 | 1 | 15 |
| 14 | 166 | 2 | 1,700 |
| 14 | 182 | 1 | 72 |
| 14 | 196 | 1 | 225 |
| 14 | 214 | 3 | 9,200 |
| 14 | 226 | 4 | 31,100 |
| 15 | 5 | 1 | unknown |
| 15 | 13 | 16 | 33,105 |
| 15 | 24 | 1 | 800 |
| 15 | 42 | 1 | 9,400 |
| 15 | 58 | 1 | 45 |
| 15 | 83 | 1 | 510 |

| Solution Set | ID | # of Sites in MZ | MZ Area (sq. metres) |
|---|---|---|---|
| 15 | 94 | 1 | 92,964 |
| 15 | 107 | 1 | 3,125 |
| 15 | 119 | 3 | 14,200 |
| 15 | 134 | 1 | 15 |
| 15 | 166 | 2 | 1,700 |
| 15 | 182 | 1 | 72 |
| 15 | 196 | 1 | 225 |
| 15 | 214 | 3 | 9,200 |
| 15 | 226 | 4 | 31,100 |
| 16 | 5 | 1 | unknown |
| 16 | 13 | 16 | 33,105 |
| 16 | 24 | 1 | 800 |
| 16 | 37 | 1 | 2,250 |
| 16 | 51 | 1 | 375 |
| 16 | 58 | 1 | 45 |
| 16 | 83 | 1 | 510 |
| 16 | 94 | 1 | 92,964 |
| 16 | 107 | 1 | 3,125 |
| 16 | 119 | 3 | 14,200 |
| 16 | 134 | 1 | 15 |
| 16 | 166 | 2 | 1,700 |
| 16 | 182 | 1 | 72 |
| 16 | 196 | 1 | 225 |
| 16 | 214 | 3 | 9,200 |
| 16 | 226 | 4 | 31,100 |
| 17 | 5 | 1 | unknown |
| 17 | 13 | 16 | 33,105 |
| 17 | 24 | 1 | 800 |
| 17 | 37 | 1 | 2,250 |
| 17 | 49 | 1 | 600 |
| 17 | 58 | 1 | 45 |
| 17 | 83 | 1 | 510 |
| 17 | 89 | 1 | unknown |
| 17 | 100 | 1 | 162 |
| 17 | 107 | 1 | 3,125 |
| 17 | 119 | 3 | 14,200 |
| 17 | 134 | 1 | 15 |
| 17 | 166 | 2 | 1,700 |

Table B1, *continued*

| Solution Set | ID | # of Sites in MZ | MZ Area (sq. metres) |
|---|---|---|---|
| 17 | 182 | 1 | 72 |
| 17 | 196 | 1 | 225 |
| 17 | 214 | 3 | 9,200 |
| 17 | 226 | 4 | 31,100 |
| 18 | 5 | 1 | unknown |
| 18 | 13 | 16 | 33,105 |
| 18 | 24 | 1 | 800 |
| 18 | 37 | 1 | 2,250 |
| 18 | 49 | 1 | 600 |
| 18 | 58 | 1 | 45 |
| 18 | 83 | 1 | 510 |
| 18 | 89 | 1 | unknown |
| 18 | 100 | 1 | 162 |
| 18 | 107 | 1 | 3,125 |
| 18 | 119 | 3 | 14,200 |
| 18 | 134 | 1 | 15 |
| 18 | 166 | 2 | 1,700 |
| 18 | 182 | 1 | 72 |
| 18 | 196 | 1 | 225 |
| 18 | 214 | 3 | 9,200 |
| 18 | 219 | 1 | 450 |
| 18 | 226 | 4 | 31,100 |
| 19 | 5 | 1 | unknown |
| 19 | 13 | 16 | 33,105 |
| 19 | 24 | 1 | 800 |
| 19 | 37 | 1 | 2,250 |
| 19 | 49 | 1 | 600 |
| 19 | 58 | 1 | 45 |
| 19 | 83 | 1 | 510 |
| 19 | 89 | 1 | unknown |
| 19 | 100 | 1 | 162 |
| 19 | 107 | 1 | 3,125 |
| 19 | 124 | 1 | 9 |
| 19 | 138 | 1 | 20,756 |
| 19 | 145 | 1 | 2,375 |
| 19 | 166 | 2 | 1,700 |
| 19 | 182 | 1 | 72 |
| 19 | 196 | 1 | 225 |

| Solution Set | ID | # of Sites in MZ | MZ Area (sq. metres) |
|---|---|---|---|
| 19 | 214 | 3 | 9,200 |
| 19 | 219 | 1 | 450 |
| 19 | 226 | 4 | 31,100 |
| 20 | 5 | 1 | unknown |
| 20 | 13 | 16 | 33,105 |
| 20 | 24 | 1 | 800 |
| 20 | 37 | 1 | 2,250 |
| 20 | 49 | 1 | 600 |
| 20 | 58 | 1 | 45 |
| 20 | 83 | 1 | 510 |
| 20 | 89 | 1 | unknown |
| 20 | 100 | 1 | 162 |
| 20 | 107 | 1 | 3,125 |
| 20 | 124 | 1 | 9 |
| 20 | 138 | 1 | 20,756 |
| 20 | 145 | 1 | 2,375 |
| 20 | 158 | 1 | 3,600 |
| 20 | 166 | 2 | 1,700 |
| 20 | 182 | 1 | 72 |
| 20 | 196 | 1 | 225 |
| 20 | 214 | 3 | 9,200 |
| 20 | 219 | 1 | 450 |
| 20 | 226 | 4 | 31,100 |
| 21 | 5 | 1 | unknown |
| 21 | 13 | 16 | 33,105 |
| 21 | 19 | 2 | 1,120 |
| 21 | 24 | 1 | 800 |
| 21 | 37 | 1 | 2,250 |
| 21 | 49 | 1 | 600 |
| 21 | 58 | 1 | 45 |
| 21 | 83 | 1 | 510 |
| 21 | 89 | 1 | unknown |
| 21 | 100 | 1 | 162 |
| 21 | 107 | 1 | 3,125 |
| 21 | 119 | 3 | 14,200 |
| 21 | 138 | 1 | 20,756 |
| 21 | 145 | 1 | 2,375 |
| 21 | 159 | 7 | 12,332 |
| 21 | 171 | 2 | 4,232 |

Table B1, *continued*

| Solution Set | ID | # of Sites in MZ | MZ Area (sq. metres) |
|---|---|---|---|
| 21 | 182 | 1 | 72 |
| 21 | 196 | 1 | 225 |
| 21 | 214 | 3 | 9,200 |
| 21 | 219 | 1 | 450 |
| 21 | 226 | 4 | 31,100 |
| 22 | 5 | 1 | unknown |
| 22 | 13 | 16 | 33,105 |
| 22 | 19 | 2 | 1,120 |
| 22 | 24 | 1 | 800 |
| 22 | 37 | 1 | 2,250 |
| 22 | 49 | 1 | 600 |
| 22 | 62 | 1 | 2,250 |
| 22 | 78 | 1 | 6,300 |
| 22 | 85 | 2 | 2,985 |
| 22 | 89 | 1 | unknown |
| 22 | 100 | 1 | 162 |
| 22 | 107 | 1 | 3,125 |
| 22 | 119 | 3 | 14,200 |
| 22 | 138 | 1 | 20,756 |
| 22 | 145 | 1 | 2,375 |
| 22 | 159 | 7 | 12,332 |
| 22 | 171 | 2 | 4,232 |
| 22 | 182 | 1 | 72 |
| 22 | 196 | 1 | 225 |
| 22 | 214 | 3 | 9,200 |
| 22 | 219 | 1 | 450 |
| 22 | 226 | 4 | 31,100 |
| 23 | 5 | 1 | unknown |
| 23 | 13 | 16 | 33,105 |
| 23 | 19 | 2 | 1,120 |
| 23 | 24 | 1 | 800 |
| 23 | 37 | 1 | 2,250 |
| 23 | 49 | 1 | 600 |
| 23 | 62 | 1 | 2,250 |
| 23 | 78 | 1 | 6,300 |
| 23 | 85 | 2 | 2,985 |
| 23 | 89 | 1 | unknown |
| 23 | 100 | 1 | 162 |
| 23 | 107 | 1 | 3,125 |

| Solution Set | ID | # of Sites in MZ | MZ Area (sq. metres) |
|---|---|---|---|
| 23 | 119 | 3 | 14,200 |
| 23 | 134 | 1 | 15 |
| 23 | 145 | 1 | 2,375 |
| 23 | 149 | 1 | 62,900 |
| 23 | 159 | 7 | 12,332 |
| 23 | 171 | 2 | 4,232 |
| 23 | 182 | 1 | 72 |
| 23 | 196 | 1 | 225 |
| 23 | 214 | 3 | 9,200 |
| 23 | 219 | 1 | 450 |
| 23 | 226 | 4 | 31,100 |
| 24 | 5 | 1 | unknown |
| 24 | 13 | 16 | 33,105 |
| 24 | 19 | 2 | 1,120 |
| 24 | 24 | 1 | 800 |
| 24 | 37 | 1 | 2,250 |
| 24 | 49 | 1 | 600 |
| 24 | 62 | 1 | 2,250 |
| 24 | 78 | 1 | 6,300 |
| 24 | 85 | 2 | 2,985 |
| 24 | 89 | 1 | unknown |
| 24 | 100 | 1 | 162 |
| 24 | 107 | 1 | 3,125 |
| 24 | 119 | 3 | 14,200 |
| 24 | 134 | 1 | 15 |
| 24 | 145 | 1 | 2,375 |
| 24 | 149 | 1 | 62,900 |
| 24 | 158 | 1 | 3,600 |
| 24 | 169 | 1 | 23,500 |
| 24 | 182 | 1 | 72 |
| 24 | 196 | 1 | 225 |
| 24 | 214 | 3 | 9,200 |
| 24 | 219 | 1 | 450 |
| 24 | 226 | 4 | 31,100 |
| 24 | 235 | 1 | 5,175 |
| 25 | 5 | 1 | unknown |
| 25 | 13 | 16 | 33,105 |
| 25 | 19 | 2 | 1,120 |
| 25 | 24 | 1 | 800 |

| Solution Set | ID | # of Sites in MZ | MZ Area (sq. metres) |
|---|---|---|---|
| 25 | 37 | 1 | 2,250 |
| 25 | 49 | 1 | 600 |
| 25 | 62 | 1 | 2,250 |
| 25 | 78 | 1 | 6,300 |
| 25 | 85 | 2 | 2,985 |
| 25 | 89 | 1 | unknown |
| 25 | 100 | 1 | 162 |
| 25 | 107 | 1 | 3,125 |
| 25 | 111 | 1 | 1,360 |
| 25 | 119 | 3 | 14,200 |
| 25 | 134 | 1 | 15 |
| 25 | 145 | 1 | 2,375 |
| 25 | 149 | 1 | 62,900 |
| 25 | 158 | 1 | 3,600 |
| 25 | 169 | 1 | 23,500 |
| 25 | 182 | 1 | 72 |
| 25 | 196 | 1 | 225 |
| 25 | 214 | 3 | 9,200 |
| 25 | 219 | 1 | 450 |
| 25 | 226 | 4 | 31,100 |
| 25 | 235 | 1 | 5,175 |

www.ingramcontent.com/pod-product-compliance
Lightning Source LLC
Chambersburg PA
CBHW051303270326
41926CB00030B/4706